Contemporary Philosophies and Theories in Education

Volume 13

Scope of the Series

Contemporary Philosophies and Theories in Education signifies new directions and possibilities out of a traditional field of philosophy and education. Around the globe, exciting scholarship that breaks down and reformulates traditions in the humanities and social sciences is being created in the field of education scholarship. This series provides a venue for publication by education scholars whose work reflect the dynamic and experimental qualities that characterize today's academy.

The series associates philosophy and theory not exclusively with a cognitive interest (to know, to define, to order) or an evaluative interest (to judge, to impose criteria of validity) but also with an experimental and attentive attitude which is characteristic for exercises in thought that try to find out how to move in the present and how to deal with the actual spaces and times, the different languages and practices of education and its transformations around the globe. It addresses the need to draw on thought across all sorts of borders and counts amongst its elements the following: the valuing of diverse processes of inquiry; an openness to various forms of communication, knowledge, and understanding; a willingness to always continue experimentation that incorporates debate and critique; and an application of this spirit, as implied above, to the institutions and issues of education.

Authors for the series come not only from philosophy of education but also from curriculum studies and critical theory, social sciences theory, and humanities theory in education. The series incorporates volumes that are trans- and inner-disciplinary.

The audience for the series includes academics, professionals and students in the fields of educational thought and theory, philosophy and social theory, and critical scholarship.

More information about this series at http://www.springer.com/series/8638

Michalinos Zembylas • André Keet

Critical Human Rights Education

Advancing Social-Justice-Oriented Educational Praxes

Springer

Michalinos Zembylas
Open University of Cyprus
Latsia, Cyprus

André Keet
Nelson Mandela University
Port Elizabeth, South Africa

ISSN 2214-9759 ISSN 2214-9767 (electronic)
Contemporary Philosophies and Theories in Education
ISBN 978-3-030-27197-8 ISBN 978-3-030-27198-5 (eBook)
https://doi.org/10.1007/978-3-030-27198-5

This Springer imprint is published by the registered company Springer Nature Switzerland AG.
The registered company address is: Gewerbestrasse 11, 6330 Cham, Switzerland

Acknowledgments

We have written this book while the two of us live and work in two different continents—Europe and Africa—something that could not be more symbolic of our longtime struggle to define a critical decolonial knowledge project in human rights education that extends beyond the epistemological form of European imperialism. Each of these continents has contributed something unique to our experiences of thinking, feeling, being, and writing. Each of these continents and beyond has given us the gift of many colleagues, friends, and students, who have helped us formulate our ideas and pushed us to be more bold and critical of our own taken-for-granted ideas. We are especially grateful for the support and intellectual stimulation we received from Shirley Anne Tate, Felisa Tibbitts, Monisha Bajaj, Willy Nel, Ronelle Carolissen, J.C de Merwe, Jonathan Jansen, Lis Lange, Vivienne Bozalek, and Tammy Shefer. We also thank Marisa Botha and Jenny du Preez for their enormous investment of time in offering editorial help. Finally, our deep appreciation goes to our families whose encouragement and love enable us to do what we do.

Permissions

Keet, A. (2012). Discourse, betrayal, critique. In C. Roux (Ed.), *Safe Spaces: Human rights education in diverse contexts* (pp. 7–28). Rotterdam, The Netherlands: Sense Publishers.

Keet, A. (2014). Plasticity, hope and the regeneration of human rights education. In V. Bozalek, B. Leibowitz, B. Carolissen, & M. Boler (Eds.), *Discerning critical hope in educational practices* (pp. 69–81). London/New York: Routledge.

Keet, A. (2015). It is time: Critical human rights education in an age of counter-Hegemonic Distrust. *Education as Change*, *19*(3), 46–64.

Keet, A. (2017). Does human rights education exist? *International Journal of Human Rights Education, 1*(1), 1–18.

Keet, A., & Zembylas, M. (2018). Introduction. In M. Zembylas & A. Keet (Eds.), *Critical human rights, citizenship, and democracy education: Entanglements and regenerations* (pp. 1–16). London: Bloomsbury.

Zembylas, M. (2016). Foucault's engagement with human rights: Seeking the renewal of human rights education. *Journal of Philosophy of Education, 50*(3), 384–397.

Zembylas, M. (2017). Re-contextualising human rights education: Some decolonial strategies and pedagogical/curricular possibilities. *Pedagogy, Culture & Society, 25*(4), 487–499.

Zembylas, M. (2017). Re-envisioning human rights in the light of Arendt and Rancière: Towards an agonistic account of human rights education. *Journal of Philosophy of Education, 51*(4), 709–724.

Zembylas, M. (2018). Affect and counter-conduct: Cultivating action for social change in human rights education. *Discourse: Studies in the Cultural Politics of Education, 39*(4), 629–641.

Zembylas, M. (2018). Political depression, cruel optimism and pedagogies of reparation: Questions of criticality and affect in human rights education. *Critical Studies in Education, 59*(1), 1–17.

Contents

Chapter 1
Introduction: Does Human Rights Education Exist?

Prelude

'Does human rights education exist?' is not an ill-judged or frivolous question. Neither is it a question that strikes through the vast body of work that goes by the name of *Human Rights Education* (henceforth HRE)—that is, education which aims to develop an awareness *about*, *through*, and *for* human rights (United Nations General Assembly, 2011). Rather, the question is purposefully exaggerated and provocative. Not to make a 'yes' answer the obvious outcome, but to consider the very possibility of a 'no' rejoinder. One can have a cluster of associated questions. Did HRE exist before? If it did, how did it 'disappear?' If it did not, what is it that goes by the appellation of HRE? Does HRE exist now? To engage with these questions is to work through the appearances of HRE in order to pierce through the surfaces and scenarios of the truths it produces. Such engagement is deeply concerned by what is clustered under its banner, and how its discursive authority is constructed and mobilised to thwart the global project of emancipation.

In this introductory chapter, we see it fit to revisit our research and engagement with HRE, trying to make sense of the shifts in our own theorisation to disclose radical-alternative possibilities for thinking and doing HRE. Through telling the story of how we entered the field and started writing about our concerns with HRE, we show the evolution of our thinking that has eventually become the present book. Most of the chapters in this book were originally published as articles or book chapters but are reworked here in an effort to gain a deeper understanding of our ongoing struggles and concerns with theorising and enacting *critical* formulations of HRE.

André entered the HRE field in the mid-1990s, as South Africa emerged as the international human rights poster child after the 1994 democratic elections that ushered in the 'post-Apartheid era.' During this time, he started engaging the processes of the United Nations agencies associated with HRE as the Decade for HRE (1995–2004) was proclaimed; and later on, was taken further by the World Programme of

M. Zembylas, A. Keet, *Critical Human Rights Education*, Contemporary Philosophies and Theories in Education 13,
https://doi.org/10.1007/978-3-030-27198-5_1

Human Rights Education (WPHRE) (2005–present). Responsible for HRE within the newly established South African Human Rights Commission, he subsequently directed the establishment of its National Centre for Human Rights Education and Training. Like any good HRE zealot, André modelled most of his entire praxes within the parameters established by the Decade of HRE and the WPHRE and the work of international and national non-governmental organisations (NGOs) and civil society organisations (CSOs) in the field. When he started with his doctoral studies in 2003, it was fitting and convenient for him to focus on HRE. During this time, he facilitated a series of human rights workshops across the country. It was in Qunu, the small rural village in South Africa's Eastern Cape where Nelson Mandela grew up, whilst putting these workshops into practice, that his uneasiness with a kind of HRE that takes its starting point to be authorised by human rights universals started and became the central catalyst for the arguments advanced in his doctoral work.

On his part, Michalinos began doing work related to HRE during his ethnographic studies in early 2000s on the role of education in conflict-affected societies such as Cyprus, Israel and N. Ireland. The issue of 'human rights'—*who* was a victim and *who* was a perpetrator of human rights violations—was often at the centre of his research investigations on public and education discourses, school practices and teacher professional development. More often than not, human rights were treated as universal ideals emphasising the entitlements of the victim's side as those have been violated by the perpetrator's side. Focusing on the violations of human rights by the perpetrator's side, but being largely indifferent to the abuse of rights *within* one's own ethnic or religious community, was a predominant view among many participants (teachers, students, parents) in these ethnographic studies. Michalinos started wondering how the 'universal' philosophical framework of human rights was prone to appropriation by different adversarial groups and in which ways this framework was complicit in attempts that perpetuated monolithic perspectives on peace and conflict. He began questioning whether HRE as an educational intervention could really enrich education efforts to invent practices of peace and reconciliation in schools, without purporting to stand for one-sided perspectives while claiming to speak for 'global justice' as a universal framework.

[Incessant] Critique as Fidelity

Experiencing first-hand how HRE can generate forms of actions for social justice as a democratic South African society struggled to emerge from a colonial-apartheid past post-1994, André more or less took it for granted that HRE would be configured to follow the trajectory of the people's education of the 1980s that functioned as the pedagogical arms of the struggle against apartheid, and social injustice in general. With an unmistaken Freirean and critical pedagogical orientation, people's education was "defined variously as an educational movement, a vehicle for political mobilisation, an alternative philosophy of education, or as a combination of all three" (Motala & Vally, 2003, pp. 182–183). Key for this enterprise, as Keet and

Carrim (2006) explored peoples' education and critical pedagogy in 'Human Rights Education and Curricular Reform in South Africa,' was the assumption that a South African HRE was in fact located within the tradition of critical pedagogy. On this score, HRE, at that time, existed; at least to André's mind. That is, in the true sense of the definition and purpose of education: the development of critical thinking and competencies.

Similarly, Michalinos took for granted that HRE, as an educational program that promoted the rights of all individuals, could become a vehicle for cultivating critical thinking, multiperspectivity and empathy, especially in the context of conflict-affected societies. The official adoption by the Greek-Cypriot educational system of UNESCO and the Council of Europe's guidelines and principles on the teaching of human rights, citizenship and democracy that was pushed in the late 1990s and early 2000s, did not always seem to 'translate' into teachers' pedagogical practices. Michalinos (e.g. see Zembylas, 2008) began to gradually realize the extent to which social, historical and political elements shaped teachers' understandings of human rights and HRE, and the degree to which meanings of human rights became 'nationalized', namely less universal and more rooted to nation-state ideologies. These one-sided pedagogical approaches that 'nationalized' human rights entailed the danger of a highly conservative framework of human rights defined primarily in relation to the negative experiences suffered as a result of the 'enemy's' violations of human rights rather than any positive alternatives (Gourevitch, 2009; Souter, 2009). Therefore, it became obvious that HRE was not necessarily synonymous with critical thinking, multiperspectivity and empathy, but rather it could be prone to political appropriation by national(ist) regimes and their victims.

We both later on came to realise, as we participated in the complex processes of the United Nations and other transnational agencies and their programs on HRE or state and NGO attempts to implement some of these programs, that the global 'wave' of democratisation of the 1980s and 1990s and the affirmation of human rights as a world-wide moral language, were closely knitted into the fabric of neo-liberal and capitalist expansion within which HRE was and is located. We can distinctly recall the Geneva encounters of the 1990s and 2000s, the debates on HRE as a critical endeavour, and the slow, painful, realisation of the inevitable conscription of HRE into a conservative, 'declarationist' frame. There are exceptions, of course. Nevertheless, the pragmatics demanded by every day and real-life work on the HRE front reveal that the HRE landscape is a complex one with pedagogical formulations of all varieties on the spectrum of conscription and resistance. To complicate matters further, the configuration of HRE into its own industry and economy generated additional contestations. Thus, critique became the inevitable orientation which our relationship with HRE took; critique as fidelity, as a 'higher' commitment.

Mapping exercises on the approaches to HRE surfaced as very useful schemes for making sense of the field and reflecting on praxes. The work of Tarrow (1987, 1992) and Reardon (1997) were instructive. However, it was Tibbitts' (2002) seminal work on 'Understanding What We Do: Emerging Models for Human Rights Education' that provided the basis for further critical reflections (see also Tibbitts [2017] for updated reflections). Almost a decade later, Bajaj (2011) published an influential piece, 'Human rights education: Ideology, locations, and approaches,' which followed André's own reflections on a 'Conceptual Typology of Human Rights Education' (Keet, 2010a). Recently, Coysh (2017) did us all a great favour by bringing together various musings on *Human Rights Education and the Politics of Knowledge*. Coysh not only treated the HRE field with critical sophistication, but she also charts HRE through the maze of work done by the United Nations and its agencies, and social actors across the globe to conclude that the

> institutionalisation and centralisation of the HRE discourse has gradually eroded diverse ways of knowing and interpreting human rights by regulating the production, distribution and consumption of the HRE discourse as a means of social control; something that has been perpetuated by a lack of questioning and critique. (2017, p. 174)

Coysh (2017) captures much better the arguments André had in mind since 2003, which he sought to formulate in his doctoral work. We always had a sort of respect, despite its declarationist orientation, for the 1997 compilation edited by Andreopoulos and Claude, *Human Rights Education for the Twenty-First Century*, and regarded our lack of a sustained engagement with the pointers, cautions and options relating to HRE within this book as a missed opportunity. In particular, it was Baxi's (1994) remarkable insights in the collection 'Human Rights Education: The Promise of the Third Millennium?' that influenced much of our work, and especially André's doctoral thesis as well as our subsequent engagements with HRE.

By the time André completed his doctoral study in 2007, he remained convinced about its critical intellectual direction, but soon afterwards started to dislike some of his own work given the haphazard nature of the arguments he tried to convey. The study concluded

> that the dominant conceptual structure of HRE has grown into a declarationist, conservative, positivistic, uncritical, compliance-driven framework that is in the main informed by a political literacy approach. Consequently, this study develops alternative conceptual principles buttressed by a non-declarationist conception of HRE that stands in a critical and anti-deterministic relationship with human rights universals. (Keet, 2007, p. i)

The alternative conceptual principles that Keet (2007) proposed were aimed at countering what he called an "epistemology of diplomatic consensus" (pp. 219–233), where knowledge claims and truths are nothing more than trade-offs between the interests of the nation-states that constitute the United Nations. These principles are: HRE as a political activity; anti-declarationism and mutual vulnerability; human rights decolonisation; perspectivism, particularism and universalism; human needs, human suffering and solidarity; human agency; and problematising 'social justice.' Later, when André joined the academy, he had the flexibility to experiment with these principles in the university setting and built his scholarly citizenship around them. While not perfect at all, they have yet to fail us. These principles also touched on a decolonised HRE and Michalinos (Zembylas, 2018; see Chap. 11) has now taken it further in ways we could not have imagined a decade ago. A key interpretive mistake André made was to 'label' what he saw as an alternative HRE as a "critical postmodern pedagogy" (Keet, 2007, p. 230) to make provision for the key criticisms levelled at human rights in general which were derived from 'postmodernism' and 'poststructuralism.' In this, he followed Giroux (1997, pp. 218–225) who suggested that through a convergence of "various tendencies within modernism, postmodernism, and postmodern feminism," a Critical Postmodern Pedagogy can retain modernism's commitment to critical reason, agency and the power of human beings to overcome human suffering' as well as engage with postmodernism's "powerful challenge to all totalising discourses" (Giroux, 1997, p. 218). It was less about Giroux's framing, and more around the apolitical 'notions' that were unfairly tagged under the rubric of postmodernism, that petitioned us to rethink our trajectory and simply designate that which we envisioned as *Critical Human Rights Education* (CHRE).

Since 2008, André started rethinking his career track after spending 12 years in the human rights field. He joined the university sector and began exploring social justice issues in higher education in general. He also found the time to translate his dissertation into a book which was published in 2010 (Keet, 2010b). Not being so firmly rooted in HRE anymore, he was, from time to time, simply re-interpellated into the field but generally experienced the HRE 'emancipatory' project as moribund. HRE does not exist, he concluded, neither in South Africa nor elsewhere in the world.

Around the same period, Michalinos' ethnographic studies on teachers' practices of teaching about peace and human rights in Cyprus (e.g. Zembylas, 2015; Zembylas, Charalambous, & Charalambous, 2016) highlighted the resources available to teachers to make sense and deal with local educational and political demands concerning the teaching of/about human rights. In their efforts to respond to these demands in relation to human rights, teachers seemed to use these resources along different trajectories. On the one hand, teachers reframed and re-inscribed human rights as part of national memory; existing educational policies imposed or reinforced this 'limited' understanding of human rights restricted by the framework of victims perpetrators. On the other hand, there were also examples of teacher practices that acknowledged the different complexities in HRE and managed to create productive spaces of engaging with human rights teaching and learning in transformative ways. The potential for inventing 'critical' spaces of HRE was not completely lost.

Critical Human Rights Studies and Human Rights Critiques

Given our location in higher education and work parameters of social justice, we further explored human rights critiques from the social sciences, law, and humanities perspectives and encountered some fascinating work in the field, including the growth on critical human rights studies, which re-awakened our interest in human rights education. These have profoundly influenced our views on our university work, which began to take shape around the theme of change in higher education and knowledge and pedagogical transformations. This new 'energy' first found expression in 'Human Rights, Juridical Forms and the Crisis of Values in Education'

(Keet, 2010c) and 'Peace and Human Rights Education: Dilemmas of Compatibility and Prospects for Moving Forward' (Zembylas, 2011), and then later on in position papers on socially just pedagogies and higher education transformation. Realising that the resources for a CHRE were already being crafted in the disciplines, we found new avenues to approach HRE from 'unfamiliar' directions. In addition, we came to know about the work of those we regard as a new generation of CHRE praxes-practitioners together with productive engagements with our established collaborators. These affirm the critical and transformative turn at the margins of HRE. It was and is the margin, unfortunately.

On the back of our experiences in the higher education sector, the possibilities for a critical HRE through human rights critiques took tentative form in efforts to develop a critical anthropology of human rights (Goodale, 2006) and a sociology of human rights (Dunn, 2012) and citizenship (Somers, 2008). A key shift in our thinking was to merge the ideas of a critical HRE rooted in critical pedagogy with human rights critiques as the essential content of HRE. This kind of formulation will have, as its logical consequence, the confirmation that HRE does not exist. That is, except for a few university programs, the idea of a CHRE with critical content is much further away from what we are seeing at present.

When a pedestrian United Nation Declaration on Human Rights Education and Training was adopted in 2011, André was already working on rethinking HRE from the angle of a paired critical: critical pedagogy and human rights critiques. Thus, at the time that Cornelia Roux invited him to contribute a chapter for the book *Safe Spaces: Human Rights Education in Diverse Contexts* (2012), he took the opportunity to present, in a different format, the human rights critiques that he engaged with in his doctoral study. André argued in 'Discourse, Betrayal, Critique: The Renewal of HRE' that it is possible to make human rights critiques pedagogically intelligible within a critical HRE. That is, HRE has to be subversive, even in relation to its own content claims, and its renewal can only proceed on the basis of incessant human rights critiques. This chapter was followed by a contribution in *Discerning Critical Hope in Educational Practices* (Bozalek et al., 2014) on 'Plasticity, Critical Hope and the Regeneration of Human Rights Education' (Keet, 2014a). He offered a plastic reading of 'critical hope' as a 'left over' form of a radical and transformative human rights education that has not yet materialised (see Chap. 7). Suggesting that these 'left overs' cannot be accommodated within mainstream HRE because it (HRE) works against 'the critical,' we suggest that a radical HRE will probably develop, not within HRE, but as its challenge (Baxi, 1994).

Michalinos started writing about the 'critical' in HRE, while engaging with André's works and reflecting on what different ideas from critical social theories could offer to renew theorisation towards a CHRE. Responding to human rights critiques, Michalinos drew on some of the literature in the affective turn and posthumanism to critique the liberal framework as well as the moral superiority of humanism on which the human rights regime has been built (Zembylas & Bozalek, 2014). Both the affective turn and posthumanism—although not monolithic—are based on two important premises that favor an *agonistic* account of rights (an idea that eventually led to Chap. 4): the first is that human beings are regarded in social and relational rather than in atomistic terms or as individuals without connections. Secondly, a reading of human rights through perspectives of the affective turn and posthumanism highlights a critical post-humanist engagement with human rights, conducted in the name of an unfinished and ambiguous humanity connected to other sentient beings and the environment, rather than a singular or absolute political identity of humanity. This reading recognizes the social, economic and political consequences of human rights and thus their potential to upset the dominant social, economic and political order, rather than accepting human rights as universal norms of social life while ignoring the ideological frame in which they are exercised.

The human rights critiques that we have presented up until 2014 as key to the renewal of HRE, grew in depth, width, and sophistication, neatly summarised by Gündoğdu (2015):

> Some critics see the discourse of human rights, especially as it is utilised in the new practice of international humanitarian intervention, as a distinct type of neo-imperialism. Some others highlight more subtle forms of political power at work in this discourse and suggest that human rights subject us to the very state power from which they promise to protect us. What is more troubling, they contend, is that this hegemonic discourse has such a strong hold on our political imagination that it has become almost impossible to invent alternative forms of politics that can bring to light different understandings of equality, freedom, justice, and emancipation. (p. 12)

In addition, Schippers (2019) has critiqued human rights' regulatory, disciplinary and exclusionary effects; the anthropocentric assumptions underpinning rights discourse; and human rights' predilection for 'jurocratic rule' at the expense of democratic practices. These scholars maintain that human rights facilitate the expansion and legitimisation of neoliberal logics; contribute to the reproduction of inequalities and unequal geopolitical arrangements; and facilitate the exercise of bio-power and the overregulation of bodies (Keet, 2015).

An Order of Simulation

The disquiet that emerged for us from 2015 onwards was the growing evidence of the development of a global mistrust in human rights, human rights institutions and the international democratic project. The global protests that have spread across the world express a pervasive distrust of democratic institutions, and human rights, as Krastev (2014) has argued in *Democracy Disrupted: The Politics of Global Protest*. In relation to the massive increase in student protests, Shay (2016) also notes that though

> each [protest] has its national character, scholars of protest have identified a number of common themes: this generation of students is profoundly disillusioned with current democratic processes. They are angry with neo-liberalism's capture of higher education and the consequences for fees and increasing inequality. They are also critical of the ways in which Eurocentric, white, middle class culture is unquestionably the norm – hence the calls for 'decolonising the curriculum.'

Intensely aware that the HRE field contributed to this distrust by not investing rights with its radical potential, Keet (2015) argued for a greater urgency in renewing HRE into a CHRE in 'It Is Time: Critical Human Rights Education in an Age of Counter-Hegemonic Distrust' (see Chap. 3). As HRE has opted to become the uncritical legitimating arm of human rights universals, it has added to a counter-hegemonic distrust. Its dominant forms also lack the conceptual and practical resources to be transformative, let alone emancipatory. Apart from restating his arguments, the 'It Is Time' piece also allowed André to update his 'periodisation' of HRE, critique some of his previous formulations, engage with new typologies of HRE, and bring himself up-to-date with ever evolving human rights critiques.

HRE has dislodged itself from its own human rights principles. If HRE ever existed, it has disappeared. For example, there are countless courses, programmes, seminars, and educational materials produced, advertising to do so in the name of HRE. Drawing from the theories of Baudrillard (Clarke, Doel, Merrin, & Smith, 2008), we tried to make sense of the HRE phenomenon both as simulation and advertising whose images and signs have no reality equivalence. That is, its practices are so far removed from its promise that it has lost its original meaning, but it still operates as a spectacle that enforces its own charisma. It is thus possible to imagine the disappearance of HRE as its appropriation into a global spectacle (Keet, 2014b). This line of reasoning tries to make urgent the advancement of a CHRE. Still, it is logically plausible and empirically grounded. That is, one can mobilise an infinite number of evidentiary instances in support of the argument that HRE belongs to the orders of simulation and spectacle. Thus, what goes by its name, in large part, is not education (see Chaps. 2 and 3 for more details).

André located the 'It Is Time' piece as a cautionary note premised on a straightforward logic: the task of an education is first and foremost the critique of the receivable categories with which it works. In this way, it creates the conditions for the generatively 'new,' advances our knowledge base, examines acceptable truths, develops praxes, stimulates agency, builds itself and its subject matter, provides the interpretive schemes for understanding a world that is awash in human rights violations, and discloses the mechanisms of power at the roots of human rights discourse. This criticality, though embedded within the broader purposes of education, Keet (2015) suggested, is absent from HRE.

Michalinos continued reporting on his research project with colleagues in Cyprus on HRE practices in primary and secondary schools and the possibilities of inventing transformative pedagogies (Zembylas, Lesta, Charalambous, & Charalambous, 2016, Zembylas, Charalambous, Charalambous, & Lesta, 2017), while also sustaining a theorisation of various challenges in HRE and the prospects of formulating 'critical' responses (Zembylas, 2016b). A particular challenge that he tackled was the conceptualisation of a pedagogical orientation that avoided both the pitfalls of a purely juridical address of human rights and a 'cheap sentimental' approach. For example, 'mainstream' teacher practices tended to teach human rights as a list of articles from various declarations of human rights over the last few decades; the emphasis was on human rights violations around the world and locally, framed in voyeuristic and rather sentimental ways. However, a *critical* orientation of HRE goes beyond voyeuristic and sentimental approaches; such an orientation will not only encourage learners to become more sympathetic to the living realities of those who suffer, but it will also interrogate the conditions of hearing narratives of suffering so that possibilities for cheap sentimentality are minimized as much as possible. This sort of criticality was absent in 'mainstream' HRE policies and practices, yet Michalinos' ethnographic research and intervention showed that it was possible, under certain conditions, to create 'small pockets' of CHRE.

HRE, Inc.

Following the 'It Is Time' article, André started reporting on a research project with colleagues on human rights and citizenship framings amongst university students (Keet & Nel, 2016; Keet, Nel, & Sattarzadeh, 2017). Using the lens of human rights critiques, these studies disclose the paradoxical nature of the human rights project, and the less than potent capacities of human rights for social justice activism. That is, articulating with the increasing global disillusionment with the institutions of democracy and human rights, there is a marked debility in how the transformative potential of human rights and HRE is perceived. But, there are welcoming developments taking shape. The growth of human rights critiques in the general polity and critical human rights studies in the university space is one. The other relates to the enlargement of the pool of scholar-practitioners that tarry with the critical transformative promise of HRE (Bajaj, 2017; Keet & Zembylas, 2018; Zembylas, 2016a).

If there is an organising concept that brings CHRE and human rights critiques together it would be the perpetual (de/re)disciplining of HRE or of that which goes by its name. What is interchangeably referred to as the 'renewal' (Zembylas, 2016a) or 'regeneration' (Keet, 2014a) of HRE presupposes such cyclical processes. That is, the never-ending reorganisation of knowledges, values, skills and practices that are the constituents of HRE, and the disclosure of the mechanics of power undergirding it. The (de/re)disciplining of HRE will bring into view its incorporation into neoliberalism and multinational consumer capitalism (Slaughter, 2007). HRE, dedisciplined via human rights critiques, as Baxi (1994, p. 30) argued more than two decades ago, will be summoned to 'beyond [its] untruth' via a liberatory pedagogy in the Freirean mould.

> In this image, HRE will be a distinctly autonomous, decolonising, deglobalising, heretical project in which the very act of learning will be simultaneously an act of insurrection aiming at the dissipation of imposed knowledges. (Baxi, 1994, p. 21)

Yet, this idea of HRE was more or less aborted at the very inception of the UN Decade for HRE in the 1990s, hastening HRE into nonexistence in terms of education properly understood as education. Discounting human rights critiques, HRE opened itself up for appropriation into project capital, incorporated in every sense of the word. The logical consequence is reflected in Hopgood's (2013) treatise on *The Endtimes of Human Rights* in which he dismissed rights as "imperialism in the guise of moralism" (Hopgood, 2013, p. 2). Hopgood further suggests that human rights function as an "ideological alibi to a global system whose governance structures sustain persistent unfairness and blatant injustice," and "it reveals that human rights and liberal capitalism were allies, not enemies" (2013, p. 13).

Our interest in human rights critiques, as central to the program of HRE, was based on our calculation that such critiques will bulwark HRE against incorporation. Thus, André's recent work, especially 'Capital Rights' (Keet, 2017; see Chap. 5), a formulation borrowed from Brown (2015), tackles the question of the conversion of human rights into capital rights more pressingly, and engages with the decolonial and Africana critique of critical pedagogy (Keet, 2018). We have now settled on the idea that the (de/re)disciplining of HRE has to have, as its central focus, the dislocation of rights from capital. Such CHRE has to engage with the erosion of citizenship, democracy, and human rights under the annihilating influence of neoliberalism's stealth revolution (Brown, 2015). Moreover, since human rights are implicated in Eurocentric notions of progress and social evolution, a CHRE must be decolonising in nature as well (Zembylas, 2018). What is thus on offer is an HRE that is folded into both a radical decolonial critical theory (Grosfoguel, 2011, p. 2) and Africana Critical Theory (Keet, 2018). That is, the critical pedagogy that should steer HRE, must, of necessity, be informed by radical decolonial critical theory, and an African Critical Theory that situates critical theory within the interpretive schemes provided by Du Bois, James, Fanon, Cabral, etc. and the "developments in philosophy of race, sociology of race, psychology of race, anthropology of race, history of race, and critical race theory; pan-Africanism, anti-colonialism, decolonisation theory, and critical postcolonial theory; black Marxism, black nationalism," and so forth (Rabaka, 2009, p. ix).

The Purpose and Structure of the Book

Having sketched the trajectories that have led each of us and together to explore the potential of CHRE, the present book discusses various ideas that engage with human rights and HRE in ways that offer opportunities for criticality and renewal. In particular, the book takes up various ideas—from critical and decolonial theories to philosophers and intellectuals such as Michel Foucault, Hannah Arendt, Jacques Rancière, Boaventura de Sousa Santos, Ann Cvetkovich, Walter Mignolo, Lauren Berlant, Reiland Rabaka, to name a few—to theorize the renewal of HRE as *critical* HRE. That is, our point of departure is that the acceptable 'truths' of human rights are seldom critically examined, and productive interpretations for understanding and acting in a world that is soaked in the violations these rights try to address cannot emerge. Most HRE curriculum programs and pedagogical practices struggle to give expression to the 'critical' that must accompany any educational endeavour. They are incapable of critiquing the categories they work with and struggle to create the conditions to advance 'new' understandings of their own knowledge base.

In this sense, then, a double critique is at play in relation to our theorization of HRE in this book: critique of HRE as pedagogical formations, and critique of their subject matter and content. From this double critique a *critical* HRE will source its orientation. However, the *critical* praxes that should emerge must also challenge the "self- certainty of the critical attitude that confidently assumes that it is really in the know" (Hoy, 2004, p. 237). The *critical* is called upon to confront its own codes, dogmas, and doctrines. The praxes and transformative actions that emerge from the *critical* must, therefore, address their respective positionalities and reflexivities and discard their own self-certainty so as to be self-critical, "reflect on [their] own contingent circumstances and contextual limitations, and thus, remain open to moderation and other possibilities" (Hoy, 2004, pp. 238–239).

The purpose of this book is to develop various theoretical aspects of our notion of CHRE not only by rejecting the moral superiority of humanism—the grounding for the dominant liberal framework of international human rights—but also by making visible the complexities of human rights as illimitable and as strategic tools for new political and educational struggles. A principal concern of this book, therefore, is to challenge educators to use theory and concepts to rethink HRE and therefore act *differently* in order to accomplish a 'reading' of human rights violations that are both *within* and *against* normalized vocabulary. We argue that analysis and interpretation of HRE curricula and pedagogies in contemporary schools and other sites of education does not happen via using a vocabulary that perpetuates declarationalist, conservative and uncritical vocabulary and doing little to critique what is taken for granted in human rights and HRE. Thus we offer a different theoretical language which adopts Foucault's 'critical affirmation' of human rights (Golder, 2011)—that is, an approach which is neither a full embrace nor a total rejection (see Chap. 3)—or Hoover's (2013) 'agonistic' orientation providing a critique that can be disruptive to the 'conventional approach to HRE' (see Chap. 4) and creates openings that might renew HRE, both politically and pedagogically. Such renewal will entail a complex set of movements in the direction of critical and decolonial pedagogies and critical social theories in general.

Overall, the book is organized into 11 chapters. After this Introduction, Chap. 2 summarises the global dominance of human rights discourse and the well-established international consensus on its importance, focusing on how HRE has proliferated from the mid-1990s onwards. Instead of advancing criticality as a central purpose of education, however, HRE, as co-constructed within the agencies of the United Nations, became the uncritical legitimating arm of human rights universals. Thus, it has ultimately contributed to the counter-hegemonic distrust in human rights that we experience today. Popular and dominant formulations of HRE, we argue, lack the conceptual and practical resources to be transformative, let alone emancipatory. Steering our reasoning through the historical development of HRE, we conclude that the time for *Critical Human Rights Education* has arrived.

Chapter 3 takes up Foucault's politics of human rights and suggests that it may contribute to the renewal of HRE not only because it rejects the moral superiority of humanism—the grounding for the dominant liberal framework of international human rights—but also because it makes visible the complexities of human rights as illimitable and as strategic tools for new political struggles. Enriching human rights critiques has important implications for HRE, precisely because these critiques prevent the dominance of unreflexive and unproductive forms of HRE that lead toward a declarationalist, conservative and uncritical approach. It is argued that Foucault's critical affirmation of human rights—that is, an approach which is neither a full embrace nor a total rejection—provides a critique that can be disruptive to the conventional HRE approach and creates openings that might renew HRE, both politically and pedagogically.

Chapter 4 takes up Arendt's 'aporetic' framing of human rights as well as Rancière's critique and suggests that reading them together may offer another way to re-envision human rights and HRE along the lines discussed throughout this book—not only because they make visible the perplexities of human rights, but also in that they call for an *agonistic* understanding of rights; namely, the possibility to make new and plural political and ethical claims about human rights as practices that can be evaluated critically rather than taken on faith. This chapter contributes to discussions in other chapters about the need for a renewal of HRE by suggesting that the paradoxes of human rights—such as the disparity between the reality of the human condition and the abstract ideal of human rights—can be politically and pedagogically invigorating by rethinking human rights in agonistic terms and formulating more robust practices of HRE.

Chapter 5 explores how inequality and rights violations are legitimated and discursively organised by the prevailing discourses on Human Rights and Transformative Constitutionalism (HR&TC). Our case example is post-1994 South Africa, focusing on the notions of HR&TC as idolatry that generate a fictitious narrative of inclusive socio-economic and cultural-political progress in the 'aftermath' of apartheid, but we also extend our argument to the global human rights discourse. This narrative, into which HRE is hooked, produces a phantasmal 'reality'. It follows, so we argue, that mainstream HRE does not have the praxes-related resources to escape the logic of neoliberal pedagogies and thus does not work against the economisation of rights and its conversion into capital rights. Consistent with our overarching project on CHRE, we suggest critique as a strategy to work against idolatry for HRE to contribute to developing antidotes to the phantasmagoria.

Chapter 6 argues that there is an urgent need to engage with a deeper analysis of the contemporary culture of 'political depression' and its affective implications in HRE. In particular, this chapter focuses on the following questions: How might a theorisation of political depression be relevant to efforts that aim to renew criticality in HRE? In which ways can a 'critical' HRE turn our attention to important ethical, political and affective questions on human rights? Can the negativity of political depression become a site for HRE pedagogies that are 'reparative'? This chapter makes an attempt to articulate some of the content and strategies of pedagogies of reparation and their significance in formulating CHRE. Reparative pedagogies invite in the classroom the challenge of how students can learn from unimaginable traumatic histories, while acknowledging the affective politics of histories of violence, oppression, and social injustice, without falling into the trap of sentimentality, but rather engaging in social justice-oriented action and activism.

Chapter 7 offers a plastic reading of 'critical hope' and a 'left over' form of a radical and transformative HRE that has not yet materialised. The premise of our argument is that generally HRE has, despite its explosive reserves, developed into an unproductive and declarationist pedagogy that works against the 'critical'. Using Malabou's concept of 'plasticity', a case is made that the regenerating HRE can best be conceived of on the level of 'left over' forms within which 'critical hope' is viewed as constitutive of its radicalisation.

Chapter 8 explores the entanglement between two partially connected concerns that offer the potential to animate current discussions on human rights teaching and learning: 'affect' and 'counter-conduct'. Both terms are at the heart of HRE approaches that aim at cultivating resistance in children and youth so that they respond in critically affective and action-oriented ways to human rights violations and social injustices in 'the everyday'. These concepts are used to explore: first, how to encourage children and youth to enact forms of counter-conduct that are critical in human rights struggles, rather than responses which are sedimented through the governing technologies of declarational approaches of HRE; and second, how these counter-conduct practices may constitute ethical and political practices that critique liberal and sentimental forms of affect about human rights violations. It is argued that theoretical insights that pay attention to counter-conduct and affect offer possibilities for reconsidering normalised ideas in HRE.

Chapter 9 argues that the implications of reconsidering normalised ideas in HRE can become more intelligible by engaging, through critique, with the crises of our times. The interplay between crisis and critique, so this chapter argues, will open up new possibilities for emancipatory praxes within HRE that are better rooted within social reality. An enhancement of the social justice potential of HRE is also anticipated. Treating crisis and critique as analytically and historically central to the program of critical theory, this chapter further suggests that the major shifts in critical theory provide productive pathways for the renewal of HRE.

Chapter 10 argues that a *decolonising* approach in HRE needs to examine human rights issues through a critical lens that interrogates the Eurocentric grounding of human rights universals and advances the project of re-contextualising human rights in the historical horizon of modernity/coloniality. This alternative configuration of HRE as 'critical' and 'transformative' offers pedagogical and curricular possibilities that go beyond conventional forms of HRE and create openings for pedagogical praxis along social justice lines. The quest to create these openings and possibilities is a fundamental element for decolonising the theory and pedagogical practices of human rights. It is argued that the move to create spaces for decolonising pedagogy and curriculum in HRE can take HRE theory and practice to a less Eurocentric outlook and thus a more multiperspectival and pluriversal understanding of human rights—one that recognises the histories of coloniality, the entanglements with human rights and the consequences for social justice projects.

Finally, Chap. 11 revisits the theoretical contributions of this book in relation to the unfinished project of renewing and reimagining a critical and pluriversal HRE. We argue that engaging in this project is an unfinished and ongoing endeavour of highlighting that the struggle for global social justice is inseparable from the struggle for enriching HRE policies and practices around the world. Our theorisation in this book, then, makes a modest contribution to the efforts that view the pluriversalisation of HRE as inextricable parts of the wider task of decolonising knowledge and education and struggling for social justice.

If we follow Brown's (2015) argument that human rights have been collapsed into capital, then, as such, one cannot talk about 'Human Rights Education'; rather, it would be more appropriate to name that what we do 'Capital Rights Education'. HRE does not exist. But cynicism is not a creative option, "it is the abandonment of self–reflection, let alone self–critique" (McDermott, 2007, p. 270), as Dewey, whose insights permeate the endeavour of critical pedagogy, reminded us. We would certainly not want our arguments to be read as cynical, but as the opening up of possibilities as is the real function of critique. That is, HRE does not exist insofar as it is modelled on an uncritical relationship with human rights universals. But it would be downright erroneous to argue that all practices in the name of HRE have this orientation. So, in a sense, for the purposes of putting the question which the title of this chapter on the table is, we, as HRE practitioners, would do well to align our work with the real purposes of education. In doing so, a CHRE will, intuitively, be called into existence.

References

Andreopoulos, G. J., & Claude, R. P. (Eds.). (1997). *Human rights education for the twenty-first century*. Philadelphia: University of Pennsylvania Press.

Bajaj, M. (2011). Human rights education: Ideology, locations, and approaches. *Human Rights Quarterly, 33*(2), 481–508.

Bajaj, M. (2017). *Human rights education: Theory, research, praxis*. Philadelphia: University of Pennsylvania Press.

Baxi, U. (1994). *Human rights education: The promise of the third millennium?* Paper presented to U.N. Member States and Non-Governmental Organisations in the occasion of the launching of the U.N. Decade for Human Rights Education. Retrieved from http://eric.ed.gov/?id=ED409221

Bozalek, V. G., McMillan, W., Marshall, D. E., November, M., Daniels, A., & Sylvester, T. (2014). Analysing the professional development of teaching and learning from a political ethics of care perspective. *Teaching in Higher Education, 19*(5), 447–458.

Brown, W. (2015). *Undoing the demos: Neoliberalism's stealth revolution*. Cambridge, MA: Zone Books, MIT Press.

Clarke, D. B., Doel, M., Merrin, W., & Smith, R. G. (Eds.). (2008). *Jean Baudrillard: Fatal theories*. New York: Routledge.

Coysh, J. (2017). *Human rights education and the politics of knowledge*. Abingdon, UK: Taylor & Francis.

Dunn, T. (2012, August 18). *Emerging sociological theories of human rights: Social structure, human agency, and inequality (& immigration)*. Paper presented at the Annual Meeting of the American Sociological Association, Denver, CO.

Giroux, H. (1997). *Pedagogy and politics of hope: Theory, culture and schooling*. Oxford, UK: Westview Press.

Golder, B. (2011). Foucault's critical (yet ambivalent) affirmation: Three figures of rights. *Social & Legal Studies, 20*(3), 283–312.

Goodale, M. (2006). Toward a critical anthropology of human rights. *Current Anthropology, 47*(3), 485–511.

Gourevitch, A. (2009). Are human rights liberal? *Journal of Human Rights, 8*, 301–322.

Grosfoguel, R. (2011). Decolonising post-colonial studies and paradigms of political-economy: Transmodernity, decolonial thinking, and global coloniality. *Transmodernity: Journal of Peripheral Cultural Production of the Luso-Hispanic World, 1*(1), 1.

Gündoğdu, A. (2015). *Rightlessness in an age of rights: Hannah Arendt and the contemporary predicament*. Oxford, UK: Oxford University Press.

Hoover, J. (2013). Towards a politics of human rights: Ambiguous humanity and democratizing rights. *Philosophy & Social Criticism, 39*(9), 935–961.

Hopgood, S. (2013). *The endtimes of human rights*. Ithaca, NY: Cornell University Press.

Hoy, D. C. (2004). *Critical resistance: From poststructuralism to post-critique*. Cambridge, MA: MIT Press.

Keet, A. (2007). *Human rights education or human rights in education: A conceptual analysis*. Doctoral dissertation, Retrieved from? Dissertation Abstracts International Section A: Humanities and Social Sciences, 68(8-A), 32–64.

Keet, A. (2010a). A conceptual typology of human rights education and associated pedagogical forms. *Journal for Social Science Education, 1*, 30–41.

Keet, A. (2010b). *Human rights education: A conceptual analysis*. Saarbrücken, Germany: Lambert Academic Publishers.

Keet, A. (2010c). Human rights, juridical forms and the crisis of values in education. *Journal for Juridical Sciences, 35*, 24–44.

Keet, A. (2014a). Plasticity and human rights education. In V. Bozalek, B. Leibowitz, R. Carolissen, & M. Boler (Eds.), *Discerning critical hope in educational practices* (pp. 69–81). New York: Routledge.

Keet, A. (2014b). Spectacle and spectators: Higher education and the 'disappearance' of democracy. *South African Journal of Higher Education, 28*(3), 849–865.

Keet, A. (2015). It is time: Critical human rights education in an age of counter-hegemonic distrust. *Education as Change, 19*(3), 46–64.

Keet, A. (2017, April). Capital rights: Decolonial thought and 'rights-emancipations' in South Africa. In *Socio-cultural transformation and decolonial thought. Understanding local entanglement of global inequalities*. Seminar conducted from Justus-Liebig University, Giessen, Germany.

Keet, A. (2018). Crisis and critique: Critical theories and the renewal of citizenship, democracy and human rights education. In M. Zembylas & A. Keet (Eds.), *Entanglements and regenerations: Critical human rights, citizenship and democracy education* (pp. 17–34). London: Bloomsbury.

Keet, A., & Carrim, N. (2006). Human rights education and curricular reform in South Africa. *Journal of Social Science Education, 5*(1), 87–105.

Keet, A., & Nel, W. (2016). Rights, regulation and recognition: Making sense of student leaders' experiences of citizenship within a university. *International Journal for Educational Sciences, 13*(1), 129–144.

Keet, A., Nel, W., & Sattarzadeh, S. D. (2017). Retreating rights: Human rights, pre-theoretical praxes and student activism in South African universities. *South African Journal for Higher Education, 31*(6), 79–95.

Keet, A., & Zembylas, M. (2018). Introduction. In M. Zembylas & A. Keet (Eds.), *Entanglements and regenerations: Critical human rights, citizenship and democracy education* (pp. 1–16). London: Bloomsbury.

Krastev, I. (2014). *Democracy disrupted: The politics of global protest*. Philadelphia: University of Pennsylvania Press.

McDermott, J. (2007). *The drama of possibility: Experience as philosophy of culture*. New York: Fordham University Press.

Motala, S., & Vally, S. (2003). People's education: From people's power to Tirisano. In P. Kallaway (Ed.), *The history of education under apartheid, 1948–1994: The doors of learning and culture shall be opened* (pp. 174–194). Cape Town, SA: Pearson Education.
Rabaka, R. (2009). *Africana critical theory: Reconstructing the black radical tradition, from W. E. B. Du Bois and C. L. R. James to Frantz Fanon and Amilcar Cabral*. Lanham, MD: Lexington Books.
Reardon, B. (1997). Human rights education as education for peace. In G. J. Andreopoulous & R. P. Claude (Eds.), *Human rights education for the 21st century* (pp. 21–34). Philadelphia: University of Pennsylvania Press.
Schippers, B. (2019). Introduction. In B. Schippers (Ed.), *Critical perspectives on human rights* (pp. ix–xx). London: Rowman & Littlefield.
Shay, S. (2016, December 20). To survive, South Africa's universities must learn to engage with chaos. Retrieved from https://mg.co.za/article/201612-20-to-survive-south-africas-universities-must-learn-to-engagewith-chaos
Slaughter, J. (2007). *Human rights, inc.: The world novel, narrative form, and international law*. New York: Fordham University Press.
Somers, M. R. (2008). *Genealogies of citizenship: Markets, statelessness, and the right to have rights*. Cambridge, UK: Cambridge University Press.
Souter, J. (2009). Humanity, suffering and victimhood: A defence of human rights pragmatism. *Politics, 29*(1), 45–52.
Tarrow, N. (Ed.). (1987). *Human rights and education*. Oxford, UK: Pergamon Press.
Tarrow, N. (1992). Human rights education: Alternative conceptions. In J. Lynch et al. (Eds.), *Human rights, education and global responsibilities* (pp. 21–50). London: Falmer Press.
Tibbitts, F. (2002). Understanding what we do: Emerging models for human rights education. *International Review of Education, 48*(34), 159–171.
United Nations General Assembly. (2011). *United Nations declaration on human rights education and training, A/RES/66/137*. Retrieved from https://documents-ddsny.un.org/doc/UNDOC/GEN/N11/467/04/PDF/N1146704.pdf?OpenElement.
Zembylas, M. (2008). *The politics of trauma in education*. New York: Palgrave Macmillan.
Zembylas, M. (2011). Peace and human rights education: Dilemmas of compatibility and prospects for moving forward. *Prospects, 41*(4), 567–579.
Zembylas, M. (2015). *Emotion and traumatic conflict: Re-claiming healing in education*. Oxford, UK: Oxford University Press.
Zembylas, M. (2016a). Foucault's engagement with human rights: Seeking the renewal of human rights education. *Journal of Philosophy of Education, 50*(3), 384–397.
Zembylas, M. (2016b). Towards a critical-sentimental orientation in human rights education. *Educational Philosophy and Theory, 48*(11), 1151–1167.
Zembylas, M. (2018). Towards a decolonising approach in human rights education: Pedagogical openings and curricular possibilities. In M. Zembylas & A. Keet (Eds.), *Entanglements and regenerations: Critical human rights, citizenship and democracy education* (pp. 35–50). London: Bloomsbury.
Zembylas, M., & Bozalek, V. (2014). A critical engagement with the social and political consequences of human rights: The contribution of the affective turn and posthumanism. *Acta Academica, 46*(4), 30–48.
Zembylas, M., Charalambous, C., & Charalambous, P. (2016). Teachers' pedagogical perspectives and teaching practices on human rights in Cyprus: An empirical exploration and implications for human rights education. *Pedagogies, 11*(3), 197–217.
Zembylas, M., Lesta, S., Charalambous, C., & Charalambous, P. (2016). Toward a critical hermeneutical approach in human rights education: Transformative possibilities and the challenges of implementation. *European Education, 48*(2), 137–157.

Chapter 2
It Is Time: Critical Human Rights Education in an Age of Counter-Hegemonic Distrust

Introduction

In the introductory chapter, we have outlined the development of our own thinking regarding human rights and HRE, as we grew more sceptical and critical of the ways in which they became manifest. Our conclusion is not that this concept and form of education should be discarded, but rather renewed through critique, which could find expression in a *Critical* Human Rights Education (CHRE). This chapter, by tracing the history of the proliferation of HRE from the 1990s onwards, shows how HRE has been co-constructed with the UN, and why the contemporary moment – which might be characterised as one of counter-hegemonic distrust – is so resistant to the dominant form of human rights and HRE. This historical approach to HRE thus provides the basis for our argument that the time has arrived for a CHRE. The rest of this book is devoted to exploring various theoretical resources and what potential they might offer for to co-creation of a CHRE by educators in multiple locations.

As right articulations have come to drench the globe over the past six decades, human rights violations became the prevailing expressions of structurally anchored inequalities in social, economic, cultural, political and environmental spheres. These challenges range from poverty, hunger, discrimination of all sorts, wars and conflict, political instability, environmental degradation, social fragmentations on national and international levels, unequal global arrangements, authoritarian regimes, the decadence of wealth, and the survivalist struggles of poor communities on a daily basis.[1]

One of the defining features of our time is that the normative horizon set by a commitment to human rights has gradually grown at odds with the way in which the

---

[1] The United Nations Development Reports provide a good indication of the world's challenges, see, for example, http://hdr.undp.org/en/2014-report; World Report from Human Rights Watch, http://www.hrw.org/world-report/2015

M. Zembylas, A. Keet, *Critical Human Rights Education*, Contemporary Philosophies and Theories in Education 13,
https://doi.org/10.1007/978-3-030-27198-5_2

twinned narratives of constitutional democracy and human rights came to constitute the 'human' within the logic of techno-capitalist ontologies. Human rights, in general, align its bearers ontologically into conformity with predatory socio-economic and cultural-political arrangements (Malabou, 2008). It, thus, seems incapable of responding to how its own project of equality and of freedom is subverted because it is constitutive of the much-vaunted network society that functions as the capillary mechanisms for advancing self-regulation through individual rights and autonomy (Fraser, 2009, pp. 116–131). Human rights are in total alignment with these connexionist arrangements that serve neoliberal logics as an expression of the new spirit of capitalism, as Boltanksi and Chiapello (2007) argue. It is a spirit that drives the "transformation of everyday morality as regards money, work, assets and relations to the self … [and] the new form of normativity underlying it" (Boltanksi & Chiapello, 2007, p. 155). Functioning as its distributive ducts, human rights play a legitimising role in organising this normativity with its ontological implications. Khoja-Moolji (2014, p. 103), for instance, demonstrates how an HRE programme in Pakistan functions as a "technology of neo-liberalism in that it was productive of neoliberal rationalities." This is suggestive of a global trend, we argue.

Reports that reflect on mainstream HRE[2] projects in schools, universities, non-governmental organisations and communities seldom question this ontological function of human rights; it is accepted as 'things are what they are'. Thus, instead of challenging structurally anchored rights' violations, it renders the foundations of socio-economic and other inequalities more solid through human rights and their educations. Even the sporadic dissent, protests and agitation ensuing from HRE and activism are provided for in this pre-determined way, one may argue. The 'emancipation' and 'transformation' that result are imprisoned in the logic governing the relationship between human rights, constitutional democracy and the market; it has very limited disruptive capacities.

These patterns emerging from the HRE field itself signpost an unacknowledged crisis within HRE. Because HRE is historically attuned to uncritically advancing human rights universals as an uncontested social good, it has not yet, as a field, paused to consider how human rights are intrinsically tied onto the global, neoliberal stage on which massive human rights violations are performed. The collapse of human rights into law, as evidenced in contemporary developments, has imprisoned human rights in service of regulation (Douzinas, 2013). This was followed by the collapse of classical liberalism and social democracy into what has become known as neoliberalism (Douzinas, 2013, p. 25). The two collapses, that of human rights into law, and of classical liberalism and social democracy into neoliberalism, gave rise to two dominant movements of our time: 'rights' and 'late capitalism'. And with that came the emergence of human rights markets, that is, the development of a trade-related market-friendly human rights paradigm; or to put it differently, markets form and inform the practices of human rights activism (Baxi, 2002). An HRE

[2] See the reports available on human rights education as submitted to the Office of the High Commissioner for Human Rights: http://www.ohchr.org/EN/Issues/Education/Training/Pages/HREducationTrainingIndex.aspx

that does not engage with these functions of human rights is both unqualified and unable to critique the conditions that make possible the rights violations it aims to address.

If hegemony is taken to mean the manufacturing of consent, which is constructed around floating signifiers (Laclau & Mouffe, 1985, p. 112), human rights discourse can then certainly be regarded as hegemonic. We are in an 'age of rights', as Baxi (1994) and Gündoğdu (2015) would say. These rights have a "reified normativity" (Goodale, 2006, p. 498). Such normativity is, however, tied to 'regressive human rights' associated with "the chaos of contemporary human rights praxis" (Goodale, 2006, p. 498). These forms of human rights critiques culminated in Hopgood's (2013) dismissal of human rights as 'imperialism in the guise of moralism' and Douzinas's (2013) argument that connects human rights with surveillance, in order to create a machine of total regulation that is primarily located within the law. The global distrust in human rights is not countered by HRE because such distrust is directed at the very understandings of human rights on which HRE is based. HRE, inadvertently, thus contributes to this wariness and the crisis in human rights itself; a distrust in the hegemonic human rights discourse as counter- hegemonic movements. This is the era, we submit, we have been entering since the turn of the previous century and which has become more pronounced since the beginning of the present decade. This is an era in which CHRE has much more to offer than conventional, declarationist HRE. An education, such as HRE, is declarationist because it organises itself around the dogmatic belief that all human rights truths are generated and consummated within human rights instruments such as declarations, conventions and covenants (Keet, 2007). HRE, generally, is an education with an aversion towards human rights critiques.

HRE is problematic, as Coysh (2014) argues; and, it is ahistorical, apolitical and uncritical (Keet, 2007). In the praxes of most of its key proponents, HRE is presented not only as being inaugurated by the Universal Declaration of Human Rights (UDHR) of 1948 (Campbell, 2001, p. 17), but that the UDHR is also the blueprint for an HRE curriculum (Lohrenscheit, 2002, p. 175). It seems plausible to argue, then, that instead of bringing human rights together with its critique from where, dialectically, the field should be advanced, HRE, as co-constructed within the agencies of the United Nations, has opted to become the uncritical legitimating arm of human rights universals and has ultimately contributed to the counter-hegemonic distrust in human rights we experience today. If we accept that criticality in education includes critical thinking, critical self-reflection and the capacity to engage with the merits and demerits of what is being considered (Ford et al., 2004, pp. 185–186), we also have to acknowledge that the dominant formulations of HRE would lack the conceptual and practical resources to be transformative, let alone emancipatory.

This chapter, then, is cautionary. It is premised on a straightforward logic: the task of an education is first and foremost the critique of the receivable categories with which it works. In this way, it creates the conditions for the generatively 'new'; advances our knowledge base; examines acceptable truths; develops praxes; stimulates agency; builds itself and its subject matter; provides the interpretive schemes for understanding a world that is awash in human rights violations; and discloses the mechanisms of power at the roots of human rights discourse. This criticality, though embedded within the broader purposes of education, we suggest, is absent from HRE.

The Historical Development of HRE

Given that primers on "rights monotonously repeat a sycophantic, hardly accurate, and simplistic history" (Douzinas, 2006, p. 623), a treatment of the historical development of HRE faces the same risks. "The constitutional moments of this simple history of rights which moves from Plato to Nato can be found in most human rights textbooks'" (Douzinas, 2006, p. 623). Human rights histories are complex and tied to power, right and truth (Foucault, 2003); likewise, we can deduce a complexity of the histories of HRE. Nevertheless, for the purposes of this chapter, and for pragmatic reasons, we suggest that it is tentatively acceptable to periodise the development of HRE into four broad phases.

The first, pre-1948 phase, considers the roots of HRE in educations that seem to be linked to an interest in moral education as intrinsic to all the major educational theories, from Plato to Dewey (Kelly, 1995, p. 170). The second phase, 1948–1994, reflects on the formalisation of HRE as an educational effort aimed at legitimising the human rights universals, which are, in turn, products of the frenzied standard-setting processes linked to the establishment of normative international provisions. The third phase (1995–2010), the proliferation of HRE, starts with the proclamation of the United Nations Decade for HRE (A/RES/49/1941995–2004). The decade saw a concerted effort from the international community to canonise HRE into a legitimate and justifiable pedagogical formation and, for the first time, endeavour to provide a structured conceptual framework for HRE. As the legitimacy crisis of the dominant global human rights discourse matured into a full-blown counter-hegemonic distrust, on 19 December 2011, the General Assembly adopted the United Nations Declaration on Human Rights Education and Training (UNDHRET: A/RES/66/137). Ironically, the adoption of the UNDHRET (A/RES/66/137) also represents the beginning of the fourth phase (from 2011), the age of counter-hegemonic distrust and the emergence of CHRE, which we are living today. This periodisation tweaks slightly and builds upon Keet's (2007) previous analyses.

The so-called roots of HRE (pre-1948), the first phase, are in consonance with the origins of the concept of human rights in general, as reflected in the simplistic histories, which Douzinas's critiques (2006). Most scholars trace the derivation of human rights to ancient Greece and Rome (Weston, 1984, p. 258) as embodied in the natural law doctrines of Greek Stoicism, which then and during mediaeval times focused on duties as opposed to rights. Donnelly (2003, p. 71) suggests that the roots of the conceptual meanings of human rights straddle geo-political arrangements and developments across the globe, including Islamic, traditional African and Confucian- Chinese conceptions of 'human rights.' According to Kelly (1995), education for citizenship is one strand through which education for democracy can be pursued in association with personal, social and moral education. When linked with moral education, which is intrinsic to all the major educational theories, HRE has a broad ambit. Compassion-based moral education is reflected in African, Greek and Oriental wisdom (Weil, as discussed in Bell (2002, p. 67). The concepts of justice, love, caring and sharing all form such a central part of a compassion-based moral framework (Bell, 2002, p. 66) that it is safe to deduce that some form of moral education has always been fundamental to traditional African, Greek and other societies. The spread of the Roman Empire (27 BCE to 476 CE), as the historical narrative goes, provided the vehicle for the dissemination of the 'universalising doctrine of Stoic natural law … and the new universal faith of Christianity' (Lloyd, 1991, p. 78). Roman law, Greek philosophy and Christian theology thus conjoin to spawn the 'medieval scholastic doctrine of natural law' (Lloyd, 1991, p. 78), which formed the bedrock of the theory of natural rights of Grotius, Hobbes and Locke in the sixteenth and seventeenth centuries. The period between the seventh and eleventh centuries also witnessed the expansion of the Islamic empire in Africa; the strengthening of egalitarian and democratic traditions (Elfasi & Hrbek, 2003, p. 4), based on Islamic principles; the incorporation of the Sahara and Sudan into the Islamic economic sphere; and the development of an Indian Ocean commercial network.

The 'European renaissance' brought formalised the conviction that human beings have fundamental rights based on an adherence to natural law. This can simplistically be paraphrased as 'law according to the will of God'. Grotius, Hobbes and Locke (Freeman, 2002, pp. 18–22) represent the principal precursory exponents of this notion of human rights, which were later articulated in the English Bill of Rights (1689), the American Declaration of Independence and Bill of Rights (1776 and 1791) and the French Declaration of the Rights of Man and of Citizens (1789). On the African continent, within the context of massive crimes against humanity associated with slaveries and colonialisms, notions of human rights were framed within a resistance framework against colonialism. The formal notions of rights have thus, historically, taken shape in response to colonialism and were fundamentally framed by the experiences related to liberation struggles and the subsequent processes of state formations and nation building.

The second phase, the formalisation of HRE (1948–1994), spans the period from the adoption of UDHR and ends before the beginning of the United Nations Decade for Human Rights Education (UNDHRE) from 1995 to 2005). From the viewpoints of most HRE practitioners, HRE has principally developed since the founding of the United Nations (1945) and the adoption of the Universal Declaration of Human Rights (UDHR 1948) and is generally regarded as a creature of the UDHR. However, the genesis of the formalisation of 'human rights education' can be traced back as far as 1789 when the French National Assembly proclaimed in the preamble to the Declaration of the Rights of Man and of Citizens that this 'declaration being constantly present to the minds of the members of the body social, they may be for ever kept attentive to their rights and their duties'.

This phase witnessed a number of defining events in relation to the development of HRE. First, the concept of HRE became formalised as a right in itself with particular reference points in a number of important international human rights instruments as opposed to the 'loose' educational configurations preceding it.

Second, some of its articulations were captured as legally binding imperatives on nation states. Third, the United Nations, especially through the work of UNESCO, began structuring HRE as a pedagogical formation in its own right. These formulations were, to a large extent, also inhabited by an emerging definitional structure for HRE, which, for many HRE practitioners, represents a distinct category of pedagogical activities that warrants serious consideration and deserves elevated standing within education circles.

Whatever may be said, from 1948 and especially since the 1970s, HRE has developed its own pedagogical spin that became firmly entrenched across the world. The authoritative edited compilation of Andreopoulos and Claude (1997), *Human Rights Education for the Twenty-First Century,* in general reflects the dominant belief that HRE was 'created' by the Charter of the United Nations in 1945 and the UDHR in 1948. The UDHR is regarded as the surrogate of all subsequent human rights provisions and "treated as a quasi-sacred text by its supporters and as a clumsy piece of bad philosophy by its critics" (Freeman, 2002, p. 34). Not only is it the authority on which many other declarations, principles, guidelines, resolutions, recommendations, covenants, conventions and protocols are based, it also represents, for many HRE practitioners, a central curricular and pedagogical text. As a curricular and pedagogical text, most NGOs, independent state agencies and governments themselves, regard the UDHR as the starting point of HRE.

> Whether one is a kindergartener or a professional in the field, human rights education quite often starts at the same place: the Universal Declaration of Human Rights (UDHR). Composed with the leadership of Eleanor Roosevelt and ratified by the full General Assembly of the United Nations in 1948, this document defines, as much as any document can, what human rights are. It seems to be an unspoken standard to begin any article or other text regarding human rights education with a reference to the UDHR; and with good reason. The UDHR is perhaps the single most important document in the creation of a foundation for human rights, and indeed, human rights education. (Campbell, 2001, p. 17)

The above relationship between HRE and international human rights instruments is commonplace and the most dominant. This relationship is hubristic since human rights universals, through diplomatic consensus, call for their own legitimacy to be entrenched through HRE. This relationship has been forged ever since the instructional formulation of the preamble to the UDHR below:

> The General Assembly proclaims this Universal Declaration of Human Rights… to the end that every individual and every organ of society, keeping this Declaration constantly in mind, shall strive by teaching and education to promote respect for these rights and freedoms.

The exact aims of education are outlined in Article 26:

> Education shall be directed to the full development of the human personality and to the strengthening of respect for human rights and fundamental freedoms. It shall promote understanding among all the nations, racial or religious groups, and shall further the activities of the United Nations for the maintenance of peace.

Similar formulations can be found in the International Convention of the Elimination of all Forms of Racial Discrimination (1965) and the International Covenant on

Economic, Social and Cultural Rights of 1966. This configuration of HRE remained dominant throughout the 1970s and the 1980s. These declarationist constructions of HRE view the UDHR as a pre-packaged curriculum framework with the International Covenant on Civil and Political Rights, the International Covenant on Economic, Social and Cultural *Rights* and subsequent instruments as pre- defined syllabi, as if these diplomatic outcomes have been designed for pedagogical purposes. The most striking feature of the development of HRE in this phase is not its formalised construction through United Nations agencies but the speed at which this construction achieved hegemonic status on the back of the international dominance of human rights discourse since the late 1980s. HRE, metaphorically, was hermetically sealed within the parameters and conceptual framework of the United Nations and its agencies.

The third phase, the *proliferation of HRE* (1995–2010), embodied HRE in the proclamation of UNDHRE and the United Nations General Assembly's Plan of Action for the United Nations Decade for Human Rights Education (1995–2004). They reaffirm the tendency to constrain HRE to human rights provisions and direct HRE to analyse human rights problems in congruence with 'human rights standards'. Together with the Montreal Declaration of 1993, the Plan of Action for the UNDHRE (1995–2004) constitutes, for some commentators, a "kind of world-wide educational policy" (Lenhart & Savolainen, 2002, p. 145). The UNDHRE was followed by the United Nations World Programme for Human Rights Education (UNWPHRE), which, at present, consists of three phases: a first (2005–2009), second (2010–2014) and third (2015–2019) phase. Tibbitts (2002, p. 7) also refers to this proliferation of "human rights education programming", while Lenhart and Savolainen (2002, p. 145) speak of HRE as "world-wide educational discourse". This phase includes the 9/11 events and the beginning of the global financial crisis that took shape in 2007/08 around "the triumph of neo-liberalism – that particular brand of free-market fundamentalism, extreme capitalism and excessive greed which became the economic orthodoxy of our time" (Rudd, 2009, p. 1).

Within the processes and activities related to UNDHRE, the declarationist conceptions of HRE calibrated nation-states and organisations to align their frameworks with the definitional features of a United Nations Human Rights Education. This is clearly illustrated in Coysh's (2014, p. 92) study, which also affirms the declarationism of HRE.

> Over the years the UN has increasingly controlled the formation of human rights education discourse by gradually institutionalising and centralising its production. Doing so has not only enabled the UN to control the formation of human rights education discourse by focusing the human rights education language upon the definitions outlined in international instruments, it has also enabled the UN to regulate the operation of the discourse by prescribing how human rights should be disseminated.

As this calibration gained momentum during the third phase of HRE proliferation, the critiques of human rights took a much firmer shape than ever previously. These critiques span a number of decades and are now culminating in an age of counter-hegemonic distrust, the fourth phase in the development of HRE. Because of the productive insights of these critiques, it is hoped that they will bring the possibilities of a CHRE into view. This fourth phase is central to the overall argument of this chapter and the book as a whole and as such, will be argued separately in the following section.

An Age of Counter-Hegemonic Distrust: The Emergence of Critical Human Rights Education (from 2011)

Douzinas (2000, p. 380), in *The End of Human Rights*, argues that human rights have started 'veering away from their initial revolutionary and dissident purposes, as their end becomes obscured in even more declarations, treaties and diplomatic lunches'. HRE, substantively tied to human rights universals, exhibits the same pattern. We thus found it apposite to consider the emergence of a CHRE as rooted in the suffocating heaviness of *declarations*, including the 2011 UNDHRET (A/RES/66/137).

Our understanding of hegemony to mean the manufacturing of consent that is constructed around floating signifiers (Laclau & Mouffe, 1985, p. 112) not only means that human rights discourse can be read as hegemonic, but also that counter-hegemonic possibilities are always resident since these signifiers are open to re-articulation and contestation. Such possibilities are already emerging since a legitimacy crisis exists within the dominant global human rights discourse, which has matured into a full-blown counter-hegemonic *distrust*, with a productive contemporary history. Over the past 15 years, various analyses have highlighted the ways in which human rights are aligned to already existing relations of power and interests, including prevailing economic relations. Mutua (2002, p. 15) has argued that the obsession to universalise human rights stems from the "impulse to universalise Eurocentric norms and values by repudiating, demonising, and 'othering' that which is different and non-European."

The displacement of the other was first operationalised through the practices of the Christian missionary of the previous era who has been replaced by the human rights zealot of the modern era. The critique related to Eurocentric norms correlates with accounts of the relationship between *human rights, globalisation and markets.* Falk contends that there are grounds on which to "reconsider the presumed contradiction between market forces and human rights" (Falk, 2002, p. 73) and this relationship needs to be viewed with scepticism. Baxi's (2002, pp. 119–131) metaphorical notion of "human rights markets" posits the commodification of human suffering (Baxi, 2002, p. 125) in the relationship between human rights and industry markets.[3] He avers that human suffering needs to be commoditised and packaged according to market requirements for human rights entrepreneurs to flour-

[3] For instance, see Tomasevski (2005a) for a comprehensive analysis on *Education as a human right or as a traded service.* Also note Tomasevski's (2005b, p. 237) conclusion on her reflections as the UN Special Rapporteur on the Right to Education from 1998 to 2004: the World Bank is the lead agency in education and does not recognise education as a human right.

ish. Human rights and human suffering, from this perspective, have become a regulated service industry.

In addition to the analyses of human rights markets, considerations of *power* within the human rights discourse have also emerged. Evans's (2001) treatise on the *Politics of Human Rights* highlights the centrality of politics and power in human rights talks within the context of the post-Cold War era and in the age of globalisation, and it exposes the possibilities for understanding rights "as both sustaining existing forms of dominance and providing a powerful tool with which to challenge those forms" (Evans, 2001, p. 34). He further articulates the shortcomings of a fixation with international human rights law (Evans, 2001, p. 55) and demonstrates that human rights are often violated in the "cause of trade" (Evans, 2001, p. 77) and that people who stand in the way of trade-related business 'routinely' lose the right to self-determination and to "freely pursue their economic, social and cultural development" (Evans, 2001, p. 78). Further, in the *Political Philosophy of Needs,* Hamilton (2003) opines that human rights are inherently conservative and tend to entrench the status quo because of their historicity. Linking the natural law theory of Grotius, Hobbes and Locke of the seventeenth, eighteenth and nineteenth centuries, respectively, with the discourse of modern human rights, Hamilton (2003, p. 4) contends that human rights provided both an overarching ideological framework and moral code for guiding the exploitation of territories and peoples.

On a more conceptual level, Brunkhorst (2008, p. 1) postulates

> that every new emancipation, every expansion of democracy and human rights was at the same time a reinvention of exclusion and oppression ... even the present state of inclusion of the other in the new cosmopolitan civil society sometimes appears to be nothing else than the expression of the highly exclusive 'class consciousness of frequent travellers.'

Fine (2010, p. 2) contends that international human rights law should not be perceived an "abstract cosmopolitan ideal against which to measure the actual world, but [that it] rather represents the necessary legal form of contemporary capitalist society and its global reach." Human rights "are Janus-like ... they can emancipate and dominate, protect and control", Douzinas (2010, p. 82) suggests. He also asserts that human rights "have become a means for regulating human life, and so have become tools of public power; ... [they] provide the justification for a new configuration of political, economic and military power" (Douzinas, 2007, p. iii). These scholars generally maintain that human rights facilitate the expansion and legitimation of neoliberal logics; contribute to the reproduction of inequalities and unequal geo-political arrangements; and facilitate the exercise of bio-power and the over-regulation of bodies.

The critiques of human rights come together in Hopgood's (2013) provocative contemporary treatise on *The Endtimes of Human Rights*. Hopgood dismisses rights as 'imperialism in the guise of moralism' (Gearty, 2013). He, according to Landman (2014), argues that the 'sacred metanarrative' of *Human rights* (United Nations codes and conventions) ignores *human rights* (the daily 'organic, localised and self-styled' struggles against oppression). In the wake of its declining moral authority, Hopgood (2013, p. 2) suggests that human rights function as an "ideological alibi to a global system whose governance structures sustain persistent unfairness and blatant injustice"; "it reveals that human rights and liberal capitalism were allies, not enemies" (Hopgood, 2013, p. 13).

An uncritical HRE is complicit in the logic that fuels these critiques and its practical expression in the daily struggles of many people across the globe, demonstrably so. It became imprisoned by its own credulity. Keet has tried to demonstrate this point since 2007 (Keet, 2007) and again in two sets of analyses post the adoption of the UNDHRET (A/RES/66/137) in 2011, essentially arguing that HRE should integrate human rights critiques into the mainstream understanding of human rights as a pedagogical necessity (Keet, 2012, 2014). We have now settled, through the personal process described in the introductory chapter, to argue and advocate for a CHRE that can regenerate the radical transformative potential of human rights and HRE. In the upcoming chapters of this book, we pursue various interpretive schemes more or less associated with Critical Theory and Critical Pedagogy to assert that HRE, in its declarationist format, is incapable of supporting a socially just human rights discourse. To the contrary, it is anti-educational.,

Critical Human Rights Education

A variety of definitions and provisions are compiled in the Office of the High Commissioner for Human Rights' (OHCHR) booklet on *The Right to Human Rights Education.* All these are declarationist in nature. This is confirmed by Article 4 of the 2011 UNDHRET (A/RES/66/137). It states that HRE 'should be based on the principles of the Universal Declaration of Human Rights and relevant treaties and instruments', with a view to raising 'awareness, understanding and acceptance of universal human rights standards and principles, as well as guarantees at the international, regional and national levels for the protection of human rights and fundamental freedoms'. It is precisely at this point, this beginning, where the definitional framework of HRE jettisons the critical.

We use the term 'critical' in this chapter to refer to the necessary distance between HRE and human rights universals that allows for a reflexivity capable of questioning, from a social justice perspective, the assumptions, premises and suppositions of human rights itself and how and why these are exported into the praxis of HRE in the way that they are. The 'critical' is regenerative, aimed at perpetual transformation of, in this case, HRE (see Keet, 2014). We view critique in two ways, as per Delanty's (2011, pp. 88–89) insights: "Firstly, critique takes as its starting point a sense of a problem or crisis in the objective order of society. The second level of critique has a stronger interpretative dimension to it but may be termed reconstructive critique in that its aim is to reconstruct the immanent possibilities in a given situation."

There are different ways in which scholars and practitioners have tried to make sense of human rights praxes and HRE. The first substantive exploration on HRE models was presented by Tibbitts's (2002) work on *Emerging Models of Human*

Rights Education. Tibbitts distinguishes between the values and awareness, accountability and transformational models. Following the intellectual trend set by Tibbitts, Bajaj (2011, p. 489) suggests three ideological orientations that give rise to three HRE categories: HRE for Global Citizenship; HRE for Coexistence; and HRE for Transformative Action. Bajaj (2011, p. 489) links her categories to Dembour's (2010, p. 1) useful model for distinguishing between four schools of thought: "'natural scholars' conceive of human rights as *given*; 'deliberative scholars' as *agreed upon*; 'protest scholars' as *fought for*; and 'discourse scholars' as *talked about*". "While 'protest' scholars may be more likely to align with HRE for Transformative Action, 'deliberative' and 'natural' scholars may be more inclined towards HRE for Global Citizenship" (Bajaj, 2011, p. 489).

For Bajaj (2011, p. 480) "the first model, HRE for Global Citizenship, presents international standards as the ideal". The second model, "HRE for Coexistence presents information related to 'othered' groups, often in post-conflict settings", emphasising "the role of minority rights and pluralism as part of the larger human rights framework, … creating greater empathy and understanding" (Bajaj, 2011, p. 492). In the third model, "HRE for Transformative Action is primarily concerned with understanding how power relationships are structured, and the possibilities for greater collaboration across groups that might effectively result in greater respect for human rights" (Bajaj, 2011, p. 493). On the one hand, it is unclear what kind of human rights for which this model should develop greater respect. It is safe to deduce that she is referring to conventional human rights standards. If this is the case, the 'transformative action' model is a logical impossibility. Rather, this model can best be perceived as working at the borders of human rights standards without crossing into other frontiers. Thus, whereas Dembour (2010) certainly has human rights critiques in mind, Bajaj frames her orientations on the canvas of human rights universals and thus cannot escape the declarationism that has, for the past 15 years, hampered substantive progress in the HRE field. In Bajaj's model, it is the orientation to human rights that fluctuates, while human rights universals are the fixed reference points.

Coysh (2014, p. 89) provides a productive critique of HRE, which "illustrates how the United Nations (UN) has enabled a narrow and manufactured type of human rights education discourse to take shape in practice by validating certain forms of knowledge (institutional, expert, technical) while burying and discounting others (cultural, indigenous, community)". In a carefully crafted analysis, she suggests that the "construction of a global human rights education discourse has therefore relied upon the subjugation of particular types of knowledge … first, by institutionalisation and formalisation of human rights education, so that historical knowledges are buried or masked"; second, "it occurred by subjugating a whole range of different forms of knowledge that were discounted or disqualified as non-conceptual or insufficiently elaborate to have a place" (Coysh, 2014, p. 89). In the main, Coysh (2014) shows how claims of 'transformation' and 'transformative action' in HRE are simply part of a cyclical logic that returns authority to human rights universals, while ignoring the notion of power within the standard generating processes itself. Coysh (2014, p. 108) argues that rather "than widening the scope for social transformation, the dominant discourse of human rights education has in fact narrowed the opportunities for this to take place". With a radical pedagogy in mind, Coysh (2014) wants to root HRE in the following assumptions:

> First, human rights education cannot be detached from its natural community and environment … Second, it is plural and diverse and circulates in a society of difference, rather than as a homogenous state …. Third, human rights education should be learned in terms of different contexts, cultures, people and experiences …. Fourth, it is rooted in people's everyday experiences, aspirations, concerns and needs rather than abstract and intangible concepts …. (Coysh, 2014, pp. 110–111)

While Coysh's (2014) analysis is industrious, her assumptions for a radical pedagogy are surprisingly pedestrian, since these assumptions have been reflected in many HRE formulations and practices from 1995 onwards. Elsewhere, Keet (2010a, pp. 36–37), in an underdeveloped argument, presented five approaches as part of his conceptual analysis of HRE: compliance; political literacy; social cohesion; resistance; and empowerment. This analysis was meant to provide the basis on which to argue for *Critical postmodern pedagogy* as far as HRE is concerned (Keet, 2010b). Admittedly, Keet's arguments (2010b) lacked sophistication and given the weaknesses of his own framings (2012, 2014), he subsequently started framing his engagement with HRE under the rubric of CHRE. Thus, in contrast to the declarationist framing that has brought human rights and HRE to the brink of social justice insignificance, we define CHRE as a pedagogical formation that: first, stands in a critical relationship with human rights universals; second, perpetually revisits the receivable categories of human rights praxes; third, advances a social-justice- oriented human rights practice; and fourth, emphasises human critiques to enrich human rights understanding. CHRE takes seriously Hopgood's (2013) distinction between *human rights* (localised and self-styled struggles) and *Human Rights* (international sacred discourse). The "elitist and sacred nature of Human Rights has its own set of codes and conventions and has become a hermetic community which has little relevance for the every-day struggles for justice taking place at the local level", according to Hopgood (Landman, 2014).

Giroux (1997, pp. 218–225) also provides a way out of Coysh's shortcomings in articulating a set of principles for Critical Pedagogy. We paraphrase and reorganise his analyses in the following way: First, CHRE should be understood as producing and working with human rights knowledge *and* constructing human rights subjects. Second, ethics should be seen as a central concern for CHRE. Third, CHRE needs to focus on the issue of difference in an ethically challenging and politically transformative way. Fourth, CHRE needs a language that allows for competing solidarities and political vocabularies that do not reduce the issues of power, justice, struggle, and inequality to a single script. Fifth, CHRE creates new forms of human rights knowledge that is produced in the space between *Human Rights* and *human rights*. Sixth, CHRE should develop alternatives by combining the languages of human rights critiques and human rights possibilities. Seventh, CHRE needs to develop a theory of human rights practitioners and educators as formative intellectuals who occupy specifiable political and social locations. Eighth, CHRE merges the politics of voice with the primacy of the political.

Giroux's (1997) formulations, if taken up, can contribute to developing a praxis that is engaged with both Critical Social Theory and Critical Pedagogy, but constructively distinctive as Critical Human Rights Education (CHRE) because it takes the critiques of human rights and a critical relationship with human rights universals as its starting points. The way in which rights bearers and human rights subjects are constructed, the power relations that are central to the constitution of these subjects, and the interpretive schemes that make the notion of difference take shape in transformative ways, would be central to CHRE. Additionally, it would be an understanding of human rights as a language of critical hope and possibilities (Keet, 2014), as argued in Chap. 7, where new knowledges and political strategies are generated in the space between *Human Rights* and *human rights.* More than anywhere else, the development of a disciplinary knowledge-base on which basis the autonomy and professionalisation of human rights practitioners (including human rights educators) as formative intellectuals can be advanced, resides in CHRE.

In alignment with Giroux (1997), Keet formulated (2007, pp. 217–228) the following suppositions for a CHRE. First, CHRE is a political activity. HRE as an instrument of human rights colonialism has been pre-packaged for delivery across vast and diverse cultural, political and economic spaces, buttressed by an epistemology of diplomatic consensus. Acknowledging itself as a political activity within which various power-knowledge relations are embedded, CHRE might, as a first step towards an alternative construction, see how certain alignments and calibrations further an agenda of critical social justice and real empowerment, and how other alignments militate against such possibilities. Second, CHRE should be anti-declarationist and based on a substantive and dramatic inversion in relation to the dominant grammar of HRE. In essence, this principle argues that human rights universals[4] and instruments should not provide the conceptual directives for HRE, but rather be viewed as part of all the discourses that are subjected to critical analyses within HRE. Such an approach would open up the conceptual spaces so that the human rights experiences of the marginalised, the subalterns and the micro-politics of people's struggle for survival become human rights instruments in themselves. An HRE that is grounded in declarationism must forfeit its claims to being 'experiential', 'participatory' or 'emancipatory' and relinquish the post-fix of 'education'. The reasons are obvious. HRE cannot be experiential because declarationism determines that all experiences are pre-packaged to suit the 'configuration' of HRE in international instruments. There is very little in this 'dominant' HRE discourse and practice that remotely represents the hope of a 'critical pedagogical engagement'.

Third, CHRE requires an alternative pedagogical language that is more than a regurgitation of international, regional and national human rights provisions. This language must be rooted in the notion of human wrongs. There is a conceptual difference between a 'human wrong' and a 'human rights violation'. A 'human wrong' constitutes an instinctive registration of a negative and degrading 'human experience'. A human rights violation is a deviation from a regulatory principle. 'Human wrongs' are constructed within the context of needs and compassion, while 'human

[4] See the Donnelly-Gibb exchange in Egendorf (2003): *Human Rights: Opposing Viewpoints.*

rights violations' are composed on the basis of non-compliance with stated regulations or laws, a technical or administrative deviation, inaction, or professional.

Conclusion

An alternative configuration of HRE as a Critical Human Rights Education will remain incomplete (see also, Chap. 11). Its perpetual incompleteness registers with the function of critique; that is, the systematic construction of new possibilities that open up towards different futures along social justice lines. Human rights educators should acknowledge that the conceptual and practical tools of dominant and conventional forms of HRE are inadequate to respond to both the challenges and critiques of human rights. As the steady growth of human rights critiques indicate: we are in the age of counter-hegemonic distrust; an age partly brought about by a declarationist HRE. Baxi (1994, p. 30), 20 years ago, foresaw this development and had already then called for HRE "to simultaneously engage in understanding and undermining the new world in the process of becoming …", and it "is on this perspective that the various formulations of the 'objectives' of HRE, in the United Nations discourse, bare themselves to full view and summon HRE endeavours to beyond their untruth". The United Nations discourse should be summoned to and beyond its own untruths; through which the falsehoods of a declarationist HRE is called to account by HRE itself. Baxi, in a sense, had, at the time, already formulated the founding principle of a CHRE. In an uncanny way, he (1994, p. 30) framed the "critiques of human rights as sites of resistance to HRE", from where counter-hegemonic sentiments and logics are sourced. It is this resistance, via human rights critiques, which form the basis on which a CHRE should take shape. Baxi (1994, p. 29) also warned against 'market- friendly' and 'trade-related' human rights, which demand from HRE a rational critique of capitalist democracies and neoliberal logics. This has been forestalled by a declarationist HRE. On the basis of these starting points and practical principles specified earlier, which are rooted in an analysis of the unjust human-rights-related arrangements on local and global levels, there is a real chance for *Critical* Human Rights Education to contribute to developing a socially just, counter-hegemonic project and contribute more productively to achieving the broader purposes of education.

References

Andreopoulos, G. J., & Claude, R. P. (Eds.). (1997). *Human rights education for the 21st century*. Philadelphia: University of Pennsylvania Press.

Bajaj, M. (2011). Human rights education: Ideology, locations, and approaches. *Human Rights Quarterly, 33*(2), 481–508.

Baxi, U. (1994). *Human rights education: The promise of the third millennium?* Paper presented to U.N. Member States and Non-Governmental Organisations in the occasion of the launching of the U.N. Decade for Human Rights Education. Retrieved from http://eric.ed.gov/?id=ED409221

Baxi, U. (2002). *The future of human rights*. New Delhi, India: Oxford University Press.

Bell, R. H. (2002). *Understanding African philosophy. A cross-cultural approach to classical and contemporary issues*. New York: Routledge.

Boltanski, L., & Chiapello, E. (2007). *The new spirit of capitalism*. London: Verso.

Brunkhorst, H. (2008). *The crisis of legitimisation in the world society* [PDF file]. Retrieved from http://www2.warwick.ac.uk/fac/soc/sociology/staff/emeritus/robertfine/home/teachingmaterial/humanrights/pdfreadings/brunkhorst-the_crisis_of_legitimation_of_human_rights.pdf

Campbell, M. A. (2001). *Getting it right: Exploring the conception and presentation of human rights in education*. Unpublished paper. Retrieved from http://www1.umn.edu/humanrts/edumat/gettingitright.pdf

Coysh, J. (2014). The dominant discourse of human rights education: A critique. *Journal of Human Rights Practice, 6*(1), 89–114.

Delanty, G. (2011). Varieties of critique in sociological theory and their methodological implications for social research. *Irish Journal of Sociology, 19*(1), 68–92.

Dembour, M. B. (2010). What are human rights? Four schools of thought. *Human Rights Quarterly, 32*(1), 1–20.

Donnelly, J. (2003). *Universal human rights in theory and practice*. New York: Cornell University Press.

Douzinas, C. (2000). *The end of human rights: Critical legal thought at the turn of the century*. Oxford, UK: Hart Publishing.

Douzinas, C. (2006). Left or rights? In T. Campbell (Ed.), *Review of rights: A critical introduction. Journal of law & society*. Oxford, UK: Blackwell Publishing Ltd.

Douzinas, C. (2007). *Human rights and empire. The political philosophy of cosmopolitanism*. Abingdon, UK: Routledge-Cavendish.

Douzinas, C. (2010). *Adikia: On communism and rights*. Retrieved from http://criticallegalthinking.com/2010/11/30/adikia-on-communism-and-rights/

Douzinas, C. (2013). *Philosophy and resistance in the crisis*. Cambridge, UK: Polity Press.

Egendorf, L. K. (2003). *Human rights: Opposing viewpoints*. San Diego, CA: Greenhaven Press.

Elfasi, M., & Hrbek, I. (Eds.). (2003). *General history of Africa (Vol. 3) Africa from the seventh to the eleventh century*. Cape Town, South Africa: ABC Press.

Evans, T. (2001). *The politics of human rights. A global perspective*. London: Pluto Press.

Falk, R. A. (2002). *Human rights horizons. The pursuit of justice in a globalising world*. London: Routledge.

Fine, R. (2010). *Political argument and the legitimacy of international law: A case of distorted modernisation* [PDF file]. Retrieved from http://www2.warwick.ac.uk/fac/soc/sociology/staff/emeritus/robertfine/home/teachingmaterial/humanrights/pdfreadings/fine_political_argument_and_ the_legitimacy_of_international_law.pdf

Ford, P., Johnston, B., Mitchell, R., & Myles, F. (2004). Social work education and criticality: Some thoughts from research. *Social Work Education, 23*(2), 185–198.

Foucault, M. (2003). *Society must be defended: Lectures at the college de France* (pp. 1975–1976). New York: Picador.

France: Declaration of the Right of Man and the Citizen. (1789, August 26). Retrieved from http://www.refworld.org/docid/3ae6b52410.html

Fraser, N. (2009). *Scales of justice*. New York: Columbia University Press.

Freeman, M. (2002). *Human rights*. Cambridge, UK: Polity Press.

Gearty, C. (2013). *Conor Gearty on an impassioned attack on 'imperialism disguised as moralism'*. Retrieved from http://www.freenewspos.com/news/article/c/889060/today/the-endtimes-of-human-rights-by-stephen-hopgood

Giroux, H. (1997). *Pedagogy and politics of hope: Theory, culture and schooling*. Oxford, UK: West View Press.

Goodale, M. (2006). Towards a critical anthropology of human rights. *Current Anthropology, 47*(3), 485–509.

Gündoğdu, A. (2015). *Rightlessness in an age of rights. Hannah Arendt and the contemporary struggles of migrants*. New York: Oxford University Press.

Hamilton, L. A. (2003). *The political philosophy of needs*. Cambridge, UK: Cambridge University Press.

Hopgood, S. (2013). *The endtimes of human rights*. Ithaca, NY: Cornell University Press.

Keet, A. (2007). *Human rights education or human rights in education*, Doctoral dissertation. Retrieved from http://upetd.up.ac.za/thesis/available/etd- 06192007-130614/unrestricted/00front.pdf

Keet, A. (2010a). A conceptual typology of human rights education and associated pedagogical form. *Journal for Human Rights Education, 1*, 30–41.

Keet, A. (2010b). *Human rights education: A conceptual analysis*. Saarbrücken, Germany: Lambert Academic Publishers.

Keet, A. (2012). Discourse, betrayal, critique: The renewal of human rights education. In C. Roux (Ed.), *Safe spaces: Human rights education in diverse contexts* (pp. 7–28). Rotterdam, The Netherlands: Sense Publishers.

Keet, A. (2014). Plasticity, critical hope and the regeneration of human rights education. In V. Bozalek, B. Leibowitz, R. Carolissen, & M. Boler (Eds.), *Discerning critical hope in educational practices* (pp. 69–81). New York: Routledge.

Kelly, A. V. (1995). *Education and democracy*. Liverpool, UK: Paul Chapman Publishing.

Khoja-Moolji, A. (2014). Producing neoliberal citizens: Critical reflections on human rights education in Pakistan. *Gender and Education, 26*(2), 103–118.

Laclau, E., & Mouffe, C. (1985). *Hegemony and socialist strategy: Towards a radical democratic politics*. London: Verso.

Landman, T. (2014). *Social magic and the temple of human rights*. Retrieved from http://www.todd- landman.com/tag/endtimes-of-human-rights/

Lenhart, V., & Savolainen, K. (Eds.). (2002). Editorial introduction. Special issue on education and human rights. *International Review of Education, 48*(3–4), 145–158.

Lloyd, D. (1991). *The idea of law*. London: Penguin Books.

Lohrenscheit, C. (2002). International approaches in human rights education. *International Review of Education, 48*(3–4), 173–185.

Malabou, C. (2008). *What should we do with our brains?* New York: Fordham University Press.

Mutua, M. (2002). *Human rights. A political and cultural critique*. Philadelphia: University of Pennsylvania Press.

Rudd, K. (2009, February 20–29). The global financial crises. *The Monthly (Australian Politics, Society & Culture)*.

Tibbitts, F. (2002). Understanding what we do: Emerging models for human rights education. *International Review of Education, 48*(3–4), 159–171.

Tomasevski, K. (2005a). Globalising what: Education as a human right or as traded service? *Indiana Journal of Global Legal Studies, 12*(1), 1–78.

Tomasevski, K. (2005b). Has the right to education a future within the United Nations? A behind-the-scenes account by the special rapporteur on the right to education 1998–2004. *Human Rights Law Review, 5*(2), 205–237.

United Nations. (1966). *International covenant on economic, social and cultural rights*. Retrieved from http://www.ohchr.org/en/professionalinterest/pages/cescr.aspx

Weston, B. H. (1984). Human rights. *Human Rights Quarterly, 6*(3), 257–283.

Chapter 3
The Political and Pedagogical Renewal of Human Rights Education

Introduction

The last few decades, as we outlined in the previous chapter, have witnessed the evolution of human rights education (HRE) into a field that sources its currency from a perceived consensus on the universalism of human rights and their moral power (Keet, 2012). Since the adoption of the United Nations Universal Declaration of Human Rights (UDHR) in 1948, the rhetoric of human rights has become so powerful and universal that has been "elevated to political correctness where a denial of them taints the innocent philosophical sceptic" (Knowles, 2003, p. 133). As Baxi (1997) has also argued, "the language of rights nearly replaces all other moral languages" and "emerges as the only ideology-in-the-making, enabling both legitimation and delegitimation of power and anticipatory critiques of human rights features" (p. 1). As Keet has written in the past, "…pedagogically speaking, HRE does not have a dynamic, self-renewing, and critical orientation towards human rights. Consequently, an unreflexive form of HRE masquerading as its radical-productive opposite becomes dominant […] Thus, now more than ever, HRE is in need of critique and renewal" (2012, p. 8). The basis of this renewal lies in our ability to articulate human rights and human rights education along the lines of a critical engagement that is neither caught up in human rights idolatry, nor is conservative and uncritical. Thus, this chapter begins our exploration of various possibilities for responding to the challenges outlined in the first two chapters by engaging in a critical consideration of human rights and its implications for HRE.

In particular, this chapter takes up Foucault's politics of human rights and suggests that it may constitute a valuable point of departure for the renewal of HRE not only because it rejects the moral superiority of humanism—the grounding for the dominant liberal framework of international human rights—but also because it makes visible the complexities of human rights as illimitable and as strategic tools for new political struggles (Golder, 2011). Enriching human rights critiques has

M. Zembylas, A. Keet, *Critical Human Rights Education*, Contemporary Philosophies and Theories in Education 13,
https://doi.org/10.1007/978-3-030-27198-5_3

important pedagogical implications for HRE, precisely because these critiques prevent the dominance of unreflexive and unproductive forms of HRE that lead toward a declarationalist, conservative and uncritical approach. Foucault's "critical affirmation" (Golder, 2011, p. 286) of human rights—that is, an approach which is neither a full embrace nor a total rejection—provides a critique that can be disruptive to the conventional approach to HRE (Al-Daraweesh, 2013) and creates openings that could renew HRE, both politically and pedagogically.

Overview of Critiques to the Conventional Approach to Human Rights Education

As noted in Chap. 2, historically speaking, UNESCO and Amnesty International have been most influential in the conceptualization of HRE (Tibbitts, 2002). Although in the first few decades after the UDHR, efforts to define HRE were limited to cognitive learning in formal school settings, in later decades the conceptualisation of HRE had extended to include critical thinking skills and empathy not only in school-based education but also in non-formal and informal settings. The general goal of all HRE remains the integration of human rights standards and practices into people's daily lives. However, over the years, human rights have ended up to be presented, through HRE, as monolithic truths derived at by a questionable epistemology that assumes a universal conception of human rights as representative of all traditions (Al-Daraweesh, 2013; Al-Daraweesh & Snauwaert, 2013; Keet, 2012; Zembylas, 2014).

In particular, Al-Daraweesh (2013) argues that there has been gradually constructed a 'conventional approach to human rights education' which is based on a singular conceptualisation of human rights as representative of all other conceptualizations. This epistemological tendency is grounded, according to Okafor and Shedrack (2001), in three orthodoxies that are viewed as constitutive of the broader human rights discourse as well as the mainstream HRE discourse and practice: the heaven-hell binary, the one-way traffic paradigm, and the abolitionist paradigm. Each of these orthodoxies is briefly discussed below because they show the gradual construction of the conceptualisation of human rights as dogmatic truths.

The first orthodoxy, the heaven-hell binary, basically splits the world into two types of societies: the one "hellish" and the other "heavenly", that is, one part which respects human rights and the other which violates them. This typology of states—expressed in terms of heaven and hell—constructs Western societies as heavenly places, while third world countries are "virtually constituted by incessant epidemics of the most horrendous sorts of human rights violations" (Okafor & Shedrack, 2001, p. 566). The existence of the heaven-hell binary, according to Okafor and Shedrack, is a result of grounding human rights knowledge on the Western tradition. As other contemporary critiques highlight, human rights have become over the years essentialised and universal norms, when their history indicates that human rights are a

Western concept grounded in liberal views and serve the interests of Western powers (e.g. Mutua, 2002) acting in neo-colonial terms (Baxi, 2007; Spivak, 2004). In a rather polemic tone, Mutua (2002) argues that interpretations of human rights are not neutral but they are very much embedded in cultural and political assumptions, and writes that 'The grand narrative of human rights contains a subtext which depicts an epochal contest pitting savages, on the one hand, against victims and saviours, on the other' (2002, p. 10). Human rights discourses, then, function as a subtle form of neo-colonialist crusade, where "civilised" nations must teach "primitive savages" the proper way of living and behaving. The main problem with the use of this binary, suggest Okafor and Shedrack (2001), is that it contributes to the alienation of many addresses of HRE experience because the human rights message is often occluded by the operation of this binary.

The second orthodoxy, the one-way traffic paradigm, is grounded in the idea that current HRE applications are mainly dependent on a Western conceptualisation of human rights. Thus the focus of HRE becomes the transmission of human rights knowledge from heaven to hell. The first evidence that Okafor and Shedrack (2001) offer to show that this paradigm exists is "that almost all the energies of the Western human rights movement....is devoted to human rights activism in the Third World" (p. 576), resulting in blindness in the recognition of human rights violations in many parts of the Western world. This "hierarchical pedagogy", as Okafor and Shedrack call it, is based on a one-way traffic from the West to the rest of the world, in which the western view remains "uncritically proselytized without benefiting from" (p. 575) other views on human rights and HRE. Okafor and Shedrack outline the negative implications for HRE wondering, "how can a people feel the kind of 'ownership' of a human rights movement if they have had no input regarding the validity of the basic philosophical foundations of the human rights corpus, or as to the relevance of the priorities of the movement to their own lived experience?" (p. 576).

Finally, the third orthodoxy, the abolitionist paradigm, "understands a major task of the human rights movement as the abolishment of local cultural practices that contravene the dictates of international human rights law" (Okafor & Shedrack, 2001, p. 584). In this manner, cultural traditions are considered as an obstacle to HRE. The abolitionist paradigm is problematic as a basis for HRE, argue Okafor and Shedrack, because it leads to approaches that are decontextualised, overly ethnocentric and disrespectful. Hence, it is suggested that practitioners and scholars in HRE must rethink the content of HRE to move beyond these orthodoxies (Al-Daraweesh, 2013).

After this brief discussion of the orthodoxies in mainstream HRE discourse and practice an apparent question is the following: What are the pedagogical consequences of these orthodoxies in the conceptualisation of HRE? One important consequence that is documented in the HRE literature is the emphasis on teaching the articles of human rights from the UDHR as universal truths—hence a 'declarationalist' approach— and how this approach limits the pedagogical value of HRE and most importantly its transformative possibilities. In fact, according to Keet (2012), the 'institutionalization' of HRE over the years—namely, the inclusion of human rights in structured and often highly formalized curricula, textbooks and materials—has contributed to the spread of the declarationalist approach. The declarationalist approach is usually grounded in a perceived consensus on human rights (as) universals and refrains from reflections on how human rights and their critiques are integrated into HRE efforts. Also, Sliwinski (2005) explains that the preferred curriculum strategy often follows a standard formula, beginning from the basic article of the UDHR, followed by specific case studies of oppression—usually about distant places and different peoples. The problem with this formula is that it "offers a largely normative approach in which the steady re-articulation of this curricular strategy is combined with a justification of human rights education as a universal method for interpreting specific cultural violence" (pp. 221–222). It is not hard to see, then, how such a conceptual framing of HRE might lead to a perception of human rights as a sacred metanarrative discourse (Hopgood, 2013)—namely, a view of human rights as a revered set of universal norms.

However, the implications of the conventional or a declarationalist approach to HRE need to be further explored and unpacked, if human rights educators want to facilitate the transformative radicality of human rights and HRE. If human rights educators learn to take human rights as universal principles, they will fail to adopt a self-renewing and critical orientation towards both human rights and HRE. For this reason, we suggest that the language of human rights and the practices of HRE must remain in a space of ongoing contestation and debate so that HRE will not be caught up either in human rights idolatry or in a conservative and uncritical orientation. In other words, HRE should be engaged with human rights critiques, using them for a productive renewal not only of human rights but also of HRE approaches. And here is precisely where Foucault's political engagement with human rights may prove valuable in efforts to enrich human rights critiques and contribute to the renewal of HRE. Our goal in the next part of the chapter is to discuss Foucault's approach to human rights in order to show later (in the last part of the chapter) how this approach contributes to a multiperspectival understanding of human rights that is valuable for the constant renewal of HRE. The idea of a multiperspectival understanding of human rights is deeply significant to this book, and the chapters that follow work to expand the variety of potential theoretical perspectives in this regard.

Foucault's Approach to Human Rights

Michel Foucault is not often read as a theorist of human rights (Golder, 2011), yet the interpretation of his late engagement with human rights and with rights politics more generally has stirred some interesting debates in recent years. On the one hand, there is a tendency to read Foucault's works in the 1970s, and especially his genealogies of the subjectivity, of discipline, and of biopolitics, as proposing a critique of rights discourse (e.g. Barret-Kriegel, 1992). According to this view, Foucault is perceived to have a problem not only with the language of rights (Patton, 2004), but also with the metaphysical assumptions of (human) rights discourses as well as the usefulness of rights as political instruments (Golder, 2011).

On the other hand, Foucault's works of the late 1970s and early 1980s on ethics and the technologies of the self are perceived as re-introducing a liberal humanist notion of subjectivity and, with that, an 'embrace' of human rights (e.g. Paras, 2006; Wolin, 2006; see Golder, 2010a for a discussion on recent interpretations of Foucault's engagement with human rights). Thus, Foucault's increasing concern with human rights is equated with his 'return' to humanist principles. As Golder comments on this common interpretation of Foucault's engagement with human rights: "This belated 'embrace' of human rights as a principle of political action eventually sees Foucault accept the political limitations of his previous anti-humanist critiques of the subject and articulate some kind of common humanity or essence as a ground of political action" (2010b, p. 653).

Against these common interpretations, however, there is the view that Foucault's engagement with human rights should be read along the lines of a "critical affirmation", that is, "neither a full embrace nor a total rejection of human rights" (Golder, 2011, p. 283). Foucault's critical engagement with human can be best understood as an *anti-humanist* one, as Golder (2010a, 2010b) suggests. Golder explains that what Foucault offers us in his later work in which he begins to engage much more extensively (and, indeed, sympathetically) with human rights, "is less a revision of his views on 'man' or humanism but rather the outlines of a critical engagement with human rights, with-in and against existing human rights, in the name of a necessarily unfinished humanity" (2010b, p. 653). In our discussion below, we seek not to engage in the debates whether Foucault has 'really' embraced human rights or whether he remains an anti-humanist until the very end. Our aim, instead, is to provide some evidence on Foucault's stance on rights and argue that his engagement with human rights provides indeed a point of departure to problematise the conceptualisation of human rights and HRE in ways that might contribute to their renewal. Crucially, Foucault's sustained suspicion of the idea of an atemporal and universal human essence is echoed in contemporary critiques of human rights and HRE that look for ways to overcome human rights foundationalism (e.g. see Keet, 2010, 2012).

Foucault on Rights

In his engagement with rights in the 1970s, Foucault offers a sustained critique of liberal rights because he thought that liberal rights failed to impede the most important power relations (Pickett, 2000). For example, in *Discipline and Punish* Foucault (1991) describes a decisive transformation of power that took place in the eighteenth century with the rise of various forms of liberties. As he points out:

> The general judicial form that guaranteed a system of rights that were egalitarian in principle was supported by these tiny, everyday, physical mechanism, by all those systems of micro-power that are essentially non-egalitarian and asymmetrical that we call the disciplines. [...] The real, corporal disciplines constituted the foundation of the formal, juridical disciplines. [...] The "Enlightenment," which discovered the liberties, also invented the disciplines. (p. 222)

As a result of the parallel development of various mechanisms of normalisation and discipline (e.g. in asylums, military barracks, hospitals, schools, prisons and so forth), Foucault observes that regimes of rights both 'mask' and enable disciplinary projects, thus facilitating and naturalising certain relations of power at the same time as rights claim to emancipate (see Brown, 1995). In other words, Foucault is suspicious of how rights discourse has become complicit and constitutive of modern technologies of power (Golder, 2011). As he writes:

> [T]he theory of sovereignty, and the organization of a legal code centered upon it, have allowed a system of right to be superimposed upon the mechanisms of discipline in such a way as to conceal its actual procedures, the element of domination inherent in its techniques, and to guarantee to everyone, by virtue of the sovereignty of the State, the exercise of his proper sovereign rights. (Foucault, 1980, p. 105)

That is, not only appeals to rights fail to acknowledge the workings of power relations in society, but also they seem to reinforce the sovereignty which supposedly they contest. Furthermore, precisely because rights are incapable of restricting the most important sites of normalisation and discipline, they are in fact becoming irrelevant, according to Foucault, as the rights held by individuals do nothing to combat the spread of modern power (Pickett, 2005).

And yet while Foucault provides this thorny critique of the discourse of rights, he also provides comments and ideas that seem to assert a certain politics of rights (Golder, 2011). Foucault himself admits that his critique "does not mean that we have to get rid of what we call human rights" (Hunt, 2004, p. 42). However, where he speaks positively of rights (in his later work), Foucault suggests a new form of right "one which must indeed be anti-disciplinarian" (Gordon, 1994, p. xxxi). As Foucault (2003) suggests, "[W]e should not be turning to the old right of sovereignty; we should be looking for a new right that is both antidisciplinary and emancipated from the principle of sovereignty" (p. 40). What this implies is that "concepts of rights can exist and be created without requiring foundational juridical premises: they can be created and affirmed through invention and struggle" (Gordon, 1994, p. xxxi.). If this new form of right is to "indeed be anti-disciplinarian", it must be capable of blocking disciplinary tactics such as hierarchical observation, confession, and surveillance and should encourage new ethical self-formations (Pickett, 2000, 2005). As Foucault explains elsewhere, "We have to promote new forms of subjectivity through the refusal of this kind of individuality [linked to the state] which has been imposed on us for several centuries now" (Foucault, 1983a, p. 216).

In his later work from the mid-1970s onwards, Foucault makes references to several rights—such as the right to asylum, the right to suicide, the right to health, the right to a fair trial, the right to choose one's own sexuality and other rights (Pickett, 2005)—which have led some of his biographers to suggest that he 'embraces' human rights. Paras (2006), for example, argues that Foucault embraces the advocacy of human rights as part of his late work on subjectivity in which he abandons his strong anti-humanist position. Pickett (2005), on the other hand, wonders whether Foucault invokes human rights principles as a pragmatic response to the political demands of the age of rights. But one cannot but wonder whether it's more productive to focus on what exactly Foucault's approach might bring to the critique of human rights—without dismissing, of course, the value or relevance of exploring the question whether he remains an anti-humanist until the very end or not. In response to this question, Golder (2011) presents Foucault's thinking on rights through three inter-related figures that not only reiterate his anti-humanist position throughout his work, but most importantly argue that Foucault's deployment of human rights in the name of an unfinished humanity is indeed productive, critically affirmative, and opens new human possibilities. Each of these three figures is briefly discussed below in order to build on these ideas and show their implications in the efforts for the renewal of HRE.

The first figure is that of the ungroundedness and illimitability of rights. The key point here is that, "For Foucault, rights cannot be based upon some timeless and immutable essence of humanity but are in fact a function of particular power-knowledge formations which themselves configure the human" (Golder, 2011, p. 287). Elaborating on Foucault's approach, Golder further explains that a form of humanism that posits an essentialist notion of the human is unnecessary when it comes to human rights. For example, as Foucault warns in a late interview:

> What I am afraid of about humanism is that it presents a certain form of ethics as a universal model for any kind of freedom. I think that there are more secrets, more possible freedoms, and more inventions in our future than we can imagine in humanism as it is dogmatically represented on every side of the political rainbow: the Left, The Center, the Right. (quoted in Martin, 1988, p. 15)

The assertion of rights, according to Foucault, needs to remain unfounded upon some metaphysics of humanity; on the contrary, rights claims should remain a contested territory because this would allow the generation of new rights in the future. As he writes elsewhere: "One must guard against reintroducing a hegemonic thought on the pretext of presenting a human rights theory or policy" (Foucault, 2000, p. 472). Therefore, from this perspective, suggests Golder (2011), "Foucault's insistence upon the contingency of the human emerges not as a liability but rather as a critical promise, as the unstable yet necessary condition of possibility for any and all rights claims" (p. 289).

The second figure is that of rights as the strategic instruments of political struggle (Golder, 2011). The key point here, according to Golder, is that for Foucault rights are political because they are made and unmade, and "crucially, the terms of their un/making betray particular exclusions, erasures and disavowals which themselves reflect particular political aims, projects and alliances" (2011, p. 290). As Foucault puts it: rights are "both grounded in history and decentered from a juridical universality" and "they are strongly marked by a relationship of property, conquest, victory, or nature. It might the right of his [the subject's] family or race, the right of superiority or seniority, the right of triumphal invasions, or the right of recent or ancient occupations" (2003, p. 52). This idea highlights Foucault's ongoing concern for the consequences of rights; this is why he insists that the openness and contingency of rights constitute a critical promise rather than their tarnishing.

As political tools, then, rights can be used strategically to deconstruct or (re) construct different social and political visions (Brown, 2004). If one perspective devalues rights, explains Golder (2011), then their reconstruction from another perspective might open up both a politically richer and a more self-reflexive (e.g. less legalistic, less moralistic) rights discourse. Rights, therefore, can be instruments in the service of political projects. At the same time though, it is important to remember how Foucault acknowledges that political subjects (who use rights as tools) are also constituted through rights. In this sense, the effect of rights is not only restrictive but also productive because deploying rights can contest existing social practices and constitute "a process of self-critique in which new forms of being are installed in given emanations of rights" (Golder, 2011, p. 294). The deployment of Foucauldian rights, then, is strategic because they are invoked as tools for critical reflexivity, resistance and disruption of the power relations and taken for granted assumptions about rights.

Finally, the third figure of Foucault's approach is the idea of rights as a mechanism for bringing about changes to and within community, and even constructing new formations of community (Golder, 2011). In his effort to affirm rights while avoiding the 'blind alley' our rights have become (Blasius, 1994), Foucault makes a call for a "relational right" (1997, p. 158). As he says in an interview: "Rather than arguing the rights are fundamental and natural to the individual, we should try to imagine and create a new relational right that permits all possible types of relations to exist and not be prevented, blocked or annulled by impoverished relational institutions" (ibid.). Foucault's appeal to relational right avoids recourse to a claim about what is normal, while still relying on some claims about human beings, yet without putting forward an essentialist conception of human nature that would be the basis for normalisation (Pickett, 2000). This 'performative' assertion of a right, as Golder (2011) calls this, constitutes a point of departure through which the values, assumptions and beliefs of a political community can be altered and (new) rights created. A new relational right, then, aims to use rights discourse to create spaces for new forms of relation (community) between individuals, while avoiding the atomistic individualism of many liberal conception of rights (Pickett, 2005). In the last part of the chapter, we turn to the implications of Foucault's approach to human rights in the efforts to renew HRE.

Implications of Foucault's Approach for the Renewal of HRE

As we have suggested so far in this chapter, Foucault's approach to human rights emphasizes the importance of rights while at the same time refusing the metaphysical determinations of the human upon which rights are often grounded. In particular, Foucault's approach, writes Golder (2010b),

> insists upon the necessary plurality of 'the human' and what goes to constitute it, and the consequent contingency and constitutive instability of any form of human rights. Human rights are not simply read off the metaphysical face of humanity but are particular historico-political emanations, the shifting expression of the needs and incidents of membership in particular political communities. (p. 662)

Building on both the work of Foucault and subsequent interpretations of his approach, we argue that this sort of thinking on human rights has several implications for human rights discourses and creates important openings to (re)conceptualise human rights (education) as a contingent and contestable field. We will outline Foucault's contributions toward this direction without evading some possible criticisms of his proposition for celebrating the creation of new rights (e.g. see Pickett, 2000, 2005) as well as considering the affirmations of his approach by others (e.g. see Golder, 2010a, 2010b, 2011, 2013). But first, we want to discuss three implications that offer possibilities toward the efforts for the renewal of HRE.

First of all, by rejecting an essentialist human nature, Foucault opens spaces for acknowledging that foundationalist categories of rights need to be constantly contested and not taken for granted. As noted earlier, rights function where power does and therefore legal 'truths' are always connected with power; that is, rights are linked to a set of rules and power relations that embody those rules. This idea implies that human rights discourses do not necessarily have to rely on a metaphysical and essentialist conception of human rights; rather human rights may be viewed as contingent, unstable and incomplete, always situated in webs of power relations. Invoking new rights, therefore, means the creation of new rights against existing disciplinary mechanisms.

Foucault's approach aids HRE in enlarging the scope of its interpretive inquiry to understand the meaning of diverse conceptualisations of human rights. For example, in the context of an interpretive approach to HRE (e.g. see Al-Daraweesh and Snauwaert, 2013), the central consideration is in how learners construct human rights understandings from various perspectives. Thus learners delve into the social practices, moral systems and power relations that pertain to concepts of rights, focusing on the ways in which humanity in different cultures shares similar or different perspectives on human rights. Compared to traditional liberal understandings of human rights, an approach of HRE that is informed by Foucauldian views opens spaces for marginal types of cultures and peoples in ways that liberal approaches have not been concerned with. Consequently, Foucault's approach has the potential to enrich HRE by engaging the learner in a comparative interpretation and assessment of human rights understandings (e.g. see Keet, 2010); this comparison encourages an attitude of openness and criticality.

Secondly, Foucault's approach to human rights invokes a critical and strategic engagement with human rights (Golder, 2010b). This idea suggests that engaging with human rights is not limited to either a celebration or an embrace of formal human rights achievements. Rather, as Golder writes, Foucault's approach "imports a constant *ethic of self-critique* and awareness of the occlusions and elisions of human rights discourse itself" (2010b, p. 663, original emphasis). As such, there is not a (naive) satisfaction that human rights are respected or protected, because there are ongoing struggles for human rights. Foucault's approach, then, in our view, highlights the importance of viewing rights as strategic 'tools' in the service of political struggles for (new) rights.

In relation to the pedagogical implications of this idea for HRE, again a critical and interpretive pedagogy (Al-Daraweesh & Snauwaert, 2013) has a number of characteristics that could produce narratives about human rights which are less exclusionary and perhaps more critical concerning their regulatory elements such as: focus on the cultural, social, historical and political nature of HRE; emphasis on understanding rights as tools that may reinforce or interrupt social practices or forms of power; recognition of the multiple perspectives of human rights concepts; critical inquiry into the assumptions that are taken for granted in local and international conceptions of human rights (education); and finally, acknowledgement that each and every conceptualisation of human rights is partial and incomplete, therefore, what is required is "a critical pedagogy based on hermeneutics to provide a complex approach to understanding the relationship between the self and the 'other' as evident in human rights conceptualisations" (Al-Daraweesh & Snauwaert, 2013, p. 410).

Thirdly, Foucault's arguments point to the limitations of the juridical form of rights and highlight the advantages of taking a self-consciously political approach on human rights. This idea does not imply that all power is evil or all regulations must be rejected as unacceptable. Rather, Foucault warns us not to uncritically accept the 'juridico-discursive' language of legitimation. The deployment of juridical form of rights is, for Foucault, like everything else, not good or evil in itself; it is to be constantly critiqued as dangerous of establishing certain 'fictions' (see Foucault, 1983b). Foucault's approach is political because it acknowledges that human rights can be a powerful political discourse through which different power relations can be established or challenged. In particular, Foucault argues that rights can be utilized politically so that new relations rights are invented to promote a more inclusive sense of community.

Once again, in terms of the pedagogical implications of the Foucauldian idea to constantly invent new 'relational rights', an approach for HRE that is reflective of the notion of 'relational rights' pays attention to the relational understanding of human rights and HRE. Adami (2014), for instance, explores a 'relational approach' in HRE, emphasising the learning of human rights through narratives in relations, that is, an approach which moves away from identity politics and essentialist perspectives of the human subject toward how peoples and cultures construct and enact unique relations through narratives. Thus a plurality of narratives on human rights, suggests Adami, frees individuals from their limited perspective on the world and on what human rights might mean in the world. Likewise, Al-Daraweesh (2013) proposes a 'relational paradigm' of HRE, that is, the development of a theoretical framework for HRE that considers how "all elements of meaning in a given situation have reference to one another and derive their significance from this reciprocal interrelationship in a given frame of thought" (p. 45). In other words, an approach of HRE that is relational and carves out spaces for new forms of relation recognizes the importance of considering human rights conceptualisation in relation to the moral, cultural, historical, and political system from which the meaning of rights emerges.

Our account on the implications of Foucault's approach to human rights would have been incomplete, if it did not consider some possible limitations. For example, Pickett (2000, 2005) suggests that by avoiding a 'basic' corpus of rights, and instead celebrating the creation of new (e.g. relational) ones, the Foucauldian approach could lead to an endless proliferation of rights claims and counterclaims. In addition, there is danger that this move away from an essential corpus of rights could weaken the status of any rights claims. As Pickett puts it, the Foucauldian understanding of rights is threatened with ineffectiveness against modern power. Finally, another challenge is the possibility that the increase in asserted rights could lead to rights conflict, that is, the idea that the duties required by specific rights in a particular context might be incompatible. Needless to say, these concerns have also important implications for our HRE approach, because by failing to recognize possible limitations in any approach to HRE we could end up replacing one normalised approach with another.

Admittedly, there are limitations in Foucault's approach to human rights but it would be unfair to set more demanding standards of assessing Foucault's approach to human rights than those which exist for the liberal approach. As Pickett (2000, 2005) acknowledges, the mere existence of rights conflict is not a decisive shortcoming because it is something which exists for the liberal approach and for any approach toward human rights for that matter; the important point, he argues, is the effectiveness of our approach. In our view, then, Foucault's scepticism to the determination of human being is important politically, strategically, and pragmatically for the *promise* of human rights and the sustained potential for their renewal, rather than any shortcomings from demanding 'too many' rights. Besides, the decision of which (new) rights to invoke is a political and strategic decision; therefore, some risks are unavoidable (see also Golder, 2010b).

Consequently, we argue that a pedagogical approach in HRE inspired by Foucault's approach on human rights—yet one which is critically conscious of its potential limitations—will be still less likely to degenerate into a relativistic or (politically) naive conceptualisation of human rights within particular historic-political communities. To the extent that Foucault's ideas inspire a critical and interpretive approach to HRE, then its contribution is that it offers teachers and learners the 'tools' to construct a *multiperspectival understanding* of the concept of human rights, and then *perform* it in politically strategic ways. A multiperspectival understanding of human rights is grounded in the three ideas we discussed earlier, that is: it rejects essentialist views of human nature and rights; it invokes a critical and strategic engagement with human rights; and, it acknowledges the limitations of the juridical form of rights and highlights the advantages of historicising different perspectives of human rights. We want to suggest, therefore, that a multiperspectival understanding of the concept of human rights and its enactment in ways that inaugurate new political arrangements and relationalities cannot guarantee, yet it is very likely that it may enable a sustained renewal of HRE.

Concluding Remarks

In this chapter we have, as part of our overall project to develop alternative interpretive schemes, attempted to draw on Foucault's approach to human rights and argue that his ideas can be valuable in the renewal of HRE that we will advocate throughout this book. We are in agreement with Golder's (2011) interpretation of Foucault's stance on rights that Foucault "aimed to deploy rights discourse critically in the service of a range of different political commitments and engagements but that the quality of his late affirmation of rights cannot be reducible to a simply embrace, defence or acceptance of the existent norm" (p. 286). Foucault's approach is important because it departs from standard legalistic discourses of rights and opposes liberal political idioms (in which contemporary human rights discourses are grounded); rather he adopts an unfinished process of critical affirmation of rights as both a political and a strategic stance that creates space for the renewal of human rights. It is this resistance to the determination of human beings and human rights that constitutes a valuable contribution of Foucault in the field of HRE. To construct the *critical* HRE that we suggest in this book—one which moves away from a declarationalist, conservative, and uncritical framework—human rights educators need to engage in relentless human rights critiques. To interrupt the operation of HRE as a habituated action guided by normative ideologies of human rights, critiques such as Foucault's are needed to remind us of the insistence on unsettling essentialist determinations of who we are or which reading of human rights ought to be universally adopted. In the same way that Foucault's critique makes more visible the multiperspectival nature of human rights that is central to Critical Human Rights Education, Arendt and Rancière provide conceptual pathways for an agonistic, non-consensual, aporetic account of HRE. This the topic of the next chapter.

References

Adami, R. (2014). Rethinking relations in human rights education: The politics of narratives. *Journal of Philosophy of Education, 48*(2), 293–307.

Al-Daraweesh, F. (2013). Human rights and human rights education: Beyond the conventional approach. *In Factis Pax, 7*(1), 38–58.

Al-Daraweesh, F., & Snauwaert, D. (2013). Toward a hermeneutical theory of international human rights education. *Educational Theory, 63*(4), 389–411.

Barret-Kriegel, B. (1992). Michel Foucault and the police state. In T. J. Armstrong (Ed.), *Michel Foucault: Philosopher* (pp. 92–98). London: Harvester Wheatsheaf.

Baxi, U. (1997). The promise of the third millennium. In G. Andreopoulos & R. Claude (Eds.), *Human rights education for the 21st century* (pp. 142–154). Philadelphia: University of Pennsylvania Press.

Baxi, U. (2007). *Human rights in a posthuman world.* New Delhi, India: Oxford University Press.

Blasius, M. (1994). *Gay and lesbian politics: Sexuality and the emergence of a new ethic.* Philadelphia, PA: Temple University Press.

Brown, W. (1995). *States of injury: Power and freedom in late modernity*. Princeton, NJ: Princeton University Press.

Brown, W. (2004). "The most we can hope for": Human rights and the politics of fatalism. *The South Atlantic Quarterly, 103*(2/3), 451–463.

Foucault, M. (1980). In C. Gordon (Ed.), *Power/knowledge: Selected interviews and other writings (1972–77).* New York: Pantheon Press.

Foucault, M. (1983a). The subject and power. In H. Dreyfus & P. Rabinow (Eds.), *Michel Foucault: Beyond structuralism and hermeneutics* (pp. 208–226). Chicago: University of Chicago Press.

Foucault, M. (1983b). On the genealogy of ethics. In H. Dreyfus & P. Rabinow (Eds.), *Michel Foucault: Beyond structuralism and hermeneutics* (pp. 229–252). Chicago: University of Chicago Press.
Foucault, M. (1991). *Discipline and punish: The birth of the prison.* (A. Sheridan, Trans.). Harmondsworth, UK: Penguin.
Foucault, M. (1997). The social triumph of the sexual will. In P. Rabinow (Ed.), *Essential works of Foucault 1954–1984* (*Ethics, Subjectivity and Truth*) (Vol. 1, pp. 157–162). Harmondsworth, UK: Penguin.
Foucault, M. (2000). The moral and social experience of the poles can no longer be obliterated. In J. Faubion (Ed.), *Power. Essential works of Foucault 1954–1984* (Vol. 3, pp. 465–473). New York: The New Press.
Foucault, M. (2003). *Society must be defended: Lectures at the Collège de France 1975–76.* (D. Macey, Trans.). London: Allen Lane.
Golder, B. (2010a). Foucault and the unfinished human of rights. *Law, Culture and the Humanities, 6*(3), 354–374.
Golder, B. (2010b). What is an anti-humanist human right? *Social Identities, 16*(5), 651–668.
Golder, B. (2011). Foucault's critical (yet ambivalent) affirmation: Three figures of rights. *Social & Legal Studies, 20*(3), 283–312.
Golder, B. (2013). Foucault, rights and freedom. *International Journal for the Semiotics of Law, 26*(1), 5–21.
Gordon, C. (1994). Introduction. In J. Faubion (Ed.), *Power. Essential works of Foucault 1954–1984* (Vol. 3, pp. xi–xli). New York: The New Press.
Hopgood, S. (2013). *The endtimes of human rights*. Ithaca, NY: Cornell University Press.
Hunt, L. (2004). The 18th century body and the origins of human rights. *Diogenes, 51*(3), 41–56.
Keet, A. (2010). *Human rights education: A conceptual analysis*. Saarbrücken, Germany: Lambert Publishers.
Keet, A. (2012). Discourse, betrayal, critique: The renewal of human rights education. In C. Roux (Ed.), *Safe spaces: Human rights education in diverse contexts* (pp. 7–27). Rotterdam, The Netherlands: Sense Publishers.
Knowles, D. R. (2003). Political philosophy. In J. Shand (Ed.), *Fundamentals of philosophy* (pp. 326–350). London: Routledge.
Martin, R. (1988). Truth, power, self: An interview with Michel Foucault. In L. H. Martin, H. Gutman, & P. H. Hutton (Eds.), *Technologies of the self: A seminar with Michel Foucault* (pp. 9–15). Amherst, MA: University of Massachusetts Press.
Mutua, M. (2002). *Human rights: A political and cultural critique*. Philadelphia: University of Pennsylvania Press.
Okafor, O. C., & Shedrack, A. (2001). Re-imagining international human rights education in our time: Beyond three constitutive orthodoxies. *Leiden Journal of International Law, 14*, 563–590.
Paras, E. (2006). *Foucault 2.0: Beyond power and knowledge*. New York: Other Press.
Patton, P. (2004). Power and right in Nietzsche and Foucault. *International Studies in Philosophy, 36*, 43–61.
Pickett, B. (2000). Foucaultian rights? *The Social Science Journal, 37*, 403–421.
Pickett, B. (2005). *On the use and abuse of Foucault for politics*. Oxford, UK: Lexington Books.
Sliwinski, S. (2005). Thinking without banisters: Toward a compassionate inquiry into human rights education. *Educational Theory, 55*(2), 219–230.
Spivak, G. (2004). Righting wrongs. *The South Atlantic Quarterly, 103*(2/3), 523–581.
Tibbits, F. (2002). Understanding what we do: Emerging models for human rights education. *International Review of Education, 48*(3–4), 159–171.
Wolin, R. (2006). Foucault the Neohumanist? *The Chronicle of Higher Education, 53*(2), B12.
Zembylas, M. (2014). Human rights and religious education in the contentious context of conflict-troubled societies: Perspectives from human rights education. *Journal of Beliefs and Values: Studies in Religion & Education, 35*(3), 303–314.

Chapter 4
Towards an Agonistic Account of Human Rights Education

Introduction

The previous chapter explored the possibilities of Foucault's 'critical affirmation' of human rights. The idea of this kind of affirmation—neither a full embrace nor a total rejection—points to an approach that refuses certainties or absolutes—full embrace or total rejection. This approach is apparent in Hannah Arendt's work on human rights, which, along with Jacques Rancière's critique of her work, we take up in this chapter in order to give an agonistic account of HRE. This makes a contribution to discussions in earlier chapters about the need for a renewal of HRE by suggesting that the paradoxes of human rights—such as the disparity between the reality of the human condition and the abstract ideal of human rights—can be politically and pedagogically invigorating by rethinking human rights in agonistic terms and formulating more robust practices of HRE.

Arendt addressed the disparity between the reality of the human condition and the abstract ideal of human rights, which is frequently discussed in our age of counter-hegemonic distrust, after the Second World War. In *The Origins of Totalitarianism* (1951/1968), she observed that the 'rights of man' proved to be illusory when the massive population displacements rendered millions of people 'stateless'. Arendt argued that stateless people found themselves in the difficult condition of rightlessness as they lost not only their citizenship rights but also their human rights. The idea of human rights came apart, according to Arendt, because it proved difficult for stateless people to claim their rights by virtue of being born human. In her analysis of this disparity, Arendt offered one of the most powerful criticisms of human rights and suggested that, given this paradoxical situation, there is a right more fundamental than the rights of justice and freedom: the 'right to have rights', that is, the right to belong to a political community.

Arendt's critical analysis of human rights has provoked interesting scholarly debates over the years. While some scholars have turned to her critique to grapple

M. Zembylas, A. Keet, *Critical Human Rights Education*, Contemporary Philosophies and Theories in Education 13,
https://doi.org/10.1007/978-3-030-27198-5_4

with the challenging problems posed by the continuing plight of non-citizens to the existing normative frameworks of human rights, others have utilized her approach to rethink politics of human rights in relation to practices of claiming rights (Gündoğdu, 2011). However, there have also been several criticisms of Arendt's political and ontological framing of human rights (e.g. Balibar, 2007; Benhabib, 2004). One of the most powerful criticisms has been offered by Rancière (2004) who argues that Arendt's analysis of human rights is politically paralyzing (Schaap, 2011). Rancière rejects Arendt's (Aristotelian) distinction on which her whole argument on the 'right to have rights' is grounded, namely, the attachment of 'the human' to mere life and 'the citizen' to the good life. This distinction is problematic, according to Rancière, because it assumes that 'the human' in human rights is a life deprived of politics. Instead, Rancière conceives of 'the human' in human rights as the political struggle to *enact* equality in *praxis* and contest political exclusion through this enactment of equality (Schaap, 2011).

This chapter takes up Arendt's 'aporetic' framing of human rights (Gündoğdu, 2011) as well as Rancière's critique and suggests that reading them together may offer another way to re-envision human rights and HRE along the lines discussed throughout this book—not only because they make visible the perplexities of human rights, but also in that they call for an *agonistic* understanding of rights; namely, the possibility to make new and plural political and ethical claims about human rights as practices that can be evaluated critically rather than taken on faith (Hoover, 2013). In particular, this chapter complements the work of writers such as Schaap (2011), Keet (2010) and Hoover (2013), in considering the implications of an agonistic account inspired by Arendt and Rancière's engagement with human rights, especially in terms of how such an account makes possible openings for critical and transformative manifestations of HRE.

The Need for the Renewal of HRE

In Chaps. 1 and 2, we advocated that it is time to develop a *Critical* Human Rights Education (CHRE) that can regenerate the radical transformative potential of HRE, asserting in this manner that HRE, in its declarationist format, is incapable of responding to local complexities and needs, especially those that take into consideration social justice demands. As we suggested, CHRE is understood as a pedagogical formation that: first, stands in a critical relationship with human rights universals; second, perpetually revisits the receivable categories of human rights praxes; third, advances a social-justice-oriented human rights practice; and fourth, emphasizes human critiques to enrich human rights understanding. Our understanding of the 'critical' in CHRE is in relation to Giroux's (1997) notions of critical pedagogy, articulating a set of principles such as: developing a language for human rights that allows for competing solidarities and political vocabularies that do not reduce the issues of power, justice, struggle, and inequality to a single script; creating new forms of human rights knowledge that promote political transformation; and developing a theory of human rights practitioners and educators as formative intellectuals.

Along similar lines, Bajaj, Coslaghi, and Mackie (2016) use the term 'Transformative Human Rights Education' (THRED) to denote "forms of human rights education that take into consideration the distinct social locations and forms of marginalization faced by different groups in order for educational strategies to be more holistic, relevant and effective" (p. 15). Bajaj and her colleagues outline a number of key principles of THRED that define its goal, pedagogy, context, approach, process and outcomes (ibid., pp. 4–30). In general, THRED is understood as a participatory co-investigation of existing social issues using human rights as a critical framework. Both the notions of 'critical' and 'transformative' emphasize the ideas of keeping human rights open to interpretation and highlight human rights as a dialectical process that recognizes challenges such the disparity between the reality of the human condition and the abstract ideal of human rights. Mainstream or declarationist approaches of HRE have put this particular challenge under the carpet for a long time; thus what is suggested via the critical and transformative forms of HRE is precisely to develop new theoretical and practical insights of dealing with this challenge.

One of the most widespread manifestations of this challenge is the contemporary plight of non-citizens and refugees in relation to the existing normative frameworks of human rights, and particularly the entanglements between citizenship and human rights (Benhabib, 2004). In educational terms, this challenge is further complicated when HRE is translated into or depends heavily on education for citizenship (Hung, 2012). As such, writes Hung, human rights are often considered equal to citizenship and thus human rights education can be replaced by citizenship education or human rights are conflated with citizenship rights. Kiwan (2005) has argued that there is a divergence between citizenship education and human rights discourses in that the former is located within a particular frame of reference, while the latter within a universal one. Hung (2012) adds that there is a fundamental, often hidden, difference between 'being human' and 'being a citizen':

> The confusion of citizen and human being is quite common and may potentially lead to a neglect of the private, idiosyncratic and individualized lived experience of individuals. This may enhance indifference and exclusion of the people who are taken as unqualified citizens. [...] The 'unconditional' (or fully qualified) citizens are often taken equivalent to perfectly complete or full human beings and the 'conditional' citizens and non-citizens as imperfect, deficient and unqualified human beings. (p. 38)

Arendt's and Rancière's insights in the upcoming sections will help us problematize the political and ontological underpinnings in this construction of 'the human' and 'the citizen' and enable us to theorize the implications for developing critical and transformative forms of HRE.

Arendt's Aporetic Inquiry on Human Rights

Arendt's (1951/1968) point of departure for her critique of human rights is the puzzling condition of the stateless people after Second World War; these people found themselves deprived of not only their citizenship rights but also their human rights. Arendt finds this paradoxical, because according to the natural law tradition, we are supposed to have universal rights by virtue of our human nature, regardless of whether we belong to a particular political community such as a nation-state. However, given that the declaration of the 'rights of man' coincided with the emergence of the nation-state, the 'rights of man' came to stand for 'national rights'. Therefore, Arendt (1951/1968, p. 299) tells us, human rights could not be enforced outside the prevailing international system organized around the nation-state and nationality; hence, people who lost their citizenship rights—deprived of their home and legal status and found themselves in concentration camps—also lost their human rights.

In her reaction to this paradoxical situation, Arendt (1949) argues that attempts to frame a new bill of human rights were unsuccessful, because they failed to pay attention to the one human right that the plight of the stateless seemed to reveal, namely, "the right to have rights", that is, "the right to belong to a political community" (p. 37). To respond to this problem, explains Gündoğdu (2011), Arendt undertakes an *aporetic* inquiry on the perplexities of human rights. Her analysis is aporetic, according to Gündoğdu, because it is focused on the paradoxes arising from our conventional assumptions of ordinary concepts, while she resists resolving these paradoxes by turning to an absolute principle or conclusive truth. "The goal of Arendt's aporetic inquiry," writes Gündoğdu,

> is not to demonstrate that human rights are either void or tautological [...] but instead to open a critical space for their reevaluation. [...] Arendt's critique highlights that human rights lose their meaningfulness without practices of scrutinizing our conventional assumptions about them. Only such practices can alert us to how these assumptions [...] stand in the way of a new articulation that would allow human rights to be more responsive to crises inaugurated by unprecedented forms of injustice. (2011, p. 9)

In particular, Gündoğdu (2011) discusses two ways in which aporias figure in Arendt's analysis of human rights. Discussing her analysis is valuable for the purposes of the present article not only because they show Arendt's efforts to highlight that aporetic inquiry into human rights is fundamentally important for their continuing renewal, but also because there are ongoing debates on the grounding of human rights till nowadays.

The first way in which aporia figures in Arendt's analysis of human rights is how human rights give rise to perplexities because of their ultimate groundlessness. These perplexities, for example, can be seen especially in the tensions pervading the formulations of rights in the 1789 Declaration of The Rights of Man. Aporia is manifested in the scope of rights, that is, whether they are universal or particular: if they are 'rights of man', they are universal regardless of whether someone or not belongs to a political community; if they are 'rights of citizen' then they are rights guaranteed by particular communities. Arendt rejects the temptation to turn to an absolute principle or conclusive truth to resolve these perplexities, because an absolute ideal would rely on an abstract human being who seemed to exist nowhere; such a notion would also evade the importance of political community for guaranteeing human rights (Gündoğdu, 2011). As Gündoğdu explains: "When Arendt's critique is read as an aporetic inquiry [...] the lack of foundations is not a problem awaiting a solution: it is indeed in tune with a mode of thinking that refuses to establish final resolutions for the political and ethical dilemmas arising from the groundlessness of human rights" (p. 11). The ongoing debates between the universal and the particular in human rights discourses demonstrate that the perplexities arising from the groundlessness of these rights are still not easy to overcome.

But Arendt's resistance to invoking a normative framework to resolve the perplexities of human rights is also motivated by a practical concern (Gündoğdu, 2011). Adopting an absolute principle or conclusive truth would give the illusion of a stable authority, thus turning our attention away from questions of how human rights can be politically secured through institutions and structures. Arendt's (1951/1968) argument that we are not born equal, but become so as members of political groups suggests that human rights are in constant need of political practices and institutions that would guarantee them. This tension between human rights and institutional structures established to protect them underscores the second way in which aporia figures in Arendt's analysis of human rights (Gündoğdu, 2011). Arendt (1951/1968) cites the rise of national consciousness during the last 200 years as an example of how the 'nation' turned into a new absolute, thus hijacking the representative functions of the 'state'; 'nationalism,' tells us Arendt, has made 'citizens' into 'nationals' (ibid., p. 230), making it more difficult to turn the 'rights of man' into a site of political struggle for those who are not nationals. Briefly put, explains Gündoğdu (2011), this aporetic inquiry "suggests that, although some institutional structures might be more promising in terms of offering effective guarantees for equal rights, no institutional form, including a denationalized, postnational or cosmopolitical one, will fully resolve the tensions between rights and their institutional protections" (p. 12).

Arendt's aporetic inquiry into human rights makes two important contributions to debates on the perplexities of human rights and to discussions about the renewal of HRE. First, it highlights that, despite the political promises and risks of human rights, the constant rethinking and reexamination of human rights and their conditions of possibility in practice, as a response to aporias, is a necessity. In other words, Arendt insists that the deeply embedded paradoxes, tensions, and aporias manifested in binary terms (e.g. man/citizen, universal/particular, natural/historical) that are characteristic of any politics of human rights can be the starting point for their renegotiation and renewal. As it will be argued later in this chapter, this claim is not dissimilar from the call for the renewal of human rights and HRE made recently by several scholars. The way Arendt develops her critique as an aporetic inquiry that is not resolved, but leaves open different possibilities and trajectories shows precisely an example of the potential of thinking human rights and HRE anew.

Second, the aporias Arendt explores "are not ahistorical contradictions dooming human rights to an ontological destiny from the beginning; instead, they are political and ethical dilemmas that are shaped and transformed significantly by historically *contingent* events and conditions" (Gündoğdu, 2011, p. 15, original emphasis). In other words, Arendt's analysis of the perplexities of human rights raises important political and ethical questions that cannot be answered by resorting to an ontological essentialism of human rights; there are ongoing struggles how to invoke, claim and exercize human rights in different socio-historical and political settings. In the next section, we will see that Rancière (2004) makes a different claim arguing that Arendt's inquiry entails serious ontological and political traps. Yet, for the time being it is important to remember that the notion of historical contingency is at the core of recent scholarship in HRE emphasizing how the contextualization and critical interpretation of human rights aids HRE in enlarging its scope of inquiry (Al-Daraweesh & Snauwaert, 2013; Zembylas, Charalambous, Charalambous, & Lesta 2017; Zembylas, Lesta, Charalambous, & Charalambous, 2016).

Rancière's Criticisms of Arendt's Views

Arendt's analysis of the perplexities of 'the rights of man' makes an important presupposition: her claim, that a premordial 'right to have rights' is needed, entails that it is only within a political community that human beings can realize a fully human life. This provides the background of Rancière's (2004) criticisms of Arendt:

> She makes them [Rights of Man] a quandary, which can be put as follows: either the rights of the citizen are the rights of man—but the rights of man are the rights of the unpoliticized person; they are the rights of those who have no rights, which amounts to nothing—or the rights of man are the rights of the citizen, the rights attached to the fact of being a citizen of such or such constitutional state. This means that they are the rights of those who have rights, which amounts to a tautology… Either a void or a tautology, and, in both cases, a deceptive trick, such is the lock that she [Arendt] builds. (p. 302)

For Rancière, then, Arendt's analysis is politically paralyzing and her conception of the political is problematic (Schaap, 2011), because it is only by virtue of political organization that an artificial human equality is established. According to Arendt, the political is public communicative action between human beings who interact as equals; without the institutions of a political community to ensure rights, humans not only do not have specific rights, but they are no humans (Balibar, 2007). Rancière finds Arendt's conception of the political deeply problematic because she limits understanding of the right to have rights to one dependent on membership of political institutions: we only become human by virtue of the legal status of personhood within a political community.

More importantly, Arendt invokes the right to have rights as a primordial human right: the right never to be excluded from political community (Schaap, 2011). As Schaap explains: "This leads to a puzzle: if human rights can be said to exist only insofar as they are the product of political association, what is the ground of the right to have rights? If to be deprived of citizenship is to be rightless, on what basis might a rightless person claim a right to have rights" (p. 27). In either case, notes Hoover (2013), human rights only become effective rights when they are remade as the rights of citizens within a political community. In Rancière's view, then, Arendt constructs an 'ontological trap' by attaching 'the human' to mere life and 'the citizen' to the good life, for if human rights are reducible to citizenship rights, they are redundant; if human rights are independent of membership to a political community, they amount to nothing (Schaap, 2011). As such, Arendt's ontological trap, Schaap explains, "leads at best, to a depoliticized account of human rights and, at worst, to the justification of an anti-political humanitarian politics" (ibid., p. 29).

In other words, Arendt makes the (Aristotelian) distinction between political and non-political modes of activity, assuming that human rights struggles can only exist within political institutions. In order to be recognized as a speaking being, one must participate in politics, acting and speaking within a community of equals (Schaap, 2011). On the one hand, the distinction between political and non-political modes of activity entails the danger of establishing an ontological social division. On the other hand, Schaap points out, Arendt's conception of the political within this frame does not take into account that those who are considered to lack speech—because they might lack legal personhood—can actually struggle for the right to speech as political animals. It is for this purpose that Rancière (2004) finds deeply troubling Arendt's inability to recognize the political agency of stateless people.

In particular, for Arendt (1951/1968) the plight of stateless people is "not that they are not equal before the law, but that no law exists for them; not that they are oppressed, but that nobody wants to oppress them" (p. 293). Rancière (2004) finds "plainly contemptuous" (p. 299) the tone of Arendt's statement, "as if these people were guilty of not even being able to be oppressed, not even worthy of being oppressed" (ibid.). Notwithstanding Rancière's misconstruction of Arendt's tone (Schaap, 2011, p. 33), he makes a good observation when he points out that "we must be aware of what is at stake in this statement of a situation and status that would be 'beyond oppression,' beyond any account in terms of conflict and repression, or law and violence" (Rancière, 2004, p. 299). The conceptualization of a 'state beyond oppression', says Rancière, is a problematic consequence of Arendt's rigid opposition between the realm of politics and the realm of private life. Consequently, for Rancière, "the human in human rights does not necessarily correspond to a form of life, bare or otherwise. Rather, the human is a litigious name that can be invoked to assert a fundamental quality" (Schaap, 2011, p. 23).

Therefore, while Arendt understands rights as a precondition for politics because they institutionalize an artificial equality, for Rancière "politics is fundamentally about contesting political exclusion by *enacting* equality" (Schaap, 2011, p. 23, original emphasis). On Rancière's account, human rights emerge through political action and speech that seek to enact equality as speaking subjects and demonstrate inequality within the social order: "the Rights of Man are the rights of those who have not the rights that they have and have the rights that they have not" (Rancière, 2004, p. 302). From Rancière's perspective, then, stateless people—to go back to the example that is being raised throughout the chapter—demonstrate their equality by acting *as if* they had the same rights as those with citizenship rights. Hence for Rancière, there is no need to suggest as a precondition a particular notion of the human; there "is no man of the Rights of Man" (2004, p. 305), as he writes.

In response to Arendt's assumptions about the difference between man and citizen, Rancière concludes that, "The very difference between man and citizen is not a sign of disjunction proving that the rights are either void or tautological. It is the opening of an interval for political subjectivization" (2004, p. 304). Although Rancière's emphasis on the enactment of praxis resembles Arendt's practical concerns, it differs in terms of its underlying assumptions about the relation between the human and the political and of equality as a condition of possibility for politics (Schaap, 2011, p. 34). Arendt's aporetic analysis of human rights, according to Schaap, makes it difficult to account for how stateless people might claim the right to have rights, because for Arendt politics is possible only within a political community in which equality is first recognized as a precondition. In contrast, Rancière starts from equality as an axiom of politics; it is precisely the assumption of anyone's equality with everyone that gives rise to politics. Consequently, politics entails the enactment of equality in situations of inequality (Schaap, 2011).

An Agonistic Account of HRE

Considered together, Arendt's and Rancière's critiques suggest that the aporias, perplexities and paradoxes emerging from the disparity between the reality of the human condition and the abstract ideal of human rights offer two important insights in the project of renewing HRE. First, abandoning legislative and transcendent justifications of human rights and accepting their contingency in the world do not have to be understood in negative terms, as is usually the case, but rather as a point of departure for rethinking human rights beyond binary terms (e.g. man/citizen, universal/particular, natural/historical). In the face of crisis as that of stateless people, Arendt shows how conventional accounts relying on these binaries render human rights either void or tautological in Rancière's terms (Gündoğdu, 2011). This paradox can be addressed in HRE by embracing, for example, a critical hermeneutical approach as opposed to a declarationist and juridical one (e.g. see Al-Daraweesh & Snauwaert, 2013; Zembylas et al., 2017, 2016). This approach—which draws from critical and hermeneutical theories—emphasizes the importance of grounding the conceptualization of human rights in cultural and historical interpretation. This implies that while it is valuable for learners to become aware of the notion of human rights as global, it is equally important for learners to explore how human rights are locally conceptualized and embraced in light of diverse cultural traditions. (We come back to this approach and its practical implications later in this section).

The second insight is that the 'failings' of human rights—as identified, for example, in the disparity between the reality of the human condition and the abstract ideal of human rights— are indicative of the lack of engagement with how human rights are used politically (Hoover, 2013). What both Arendt and Rancière emphasize is an understanding of human rights politics as based on *praxis* (Schaap, 2011). But they depart from each other, as Schaap notes, in that Rancière's radical politics of equality goes beyond Arendt's conception of politics as the actualization of a particular human potential; Rancière's politics challenges inequality in the name of an equality of anyone with everyone—established through the process of political contestation. Equality "has no substantive content but only makes sense in the particular context of social inequality that it challenges," explains Schaap (2011, p. 39). In relation to the implications of this idea for HRE, it can be argued that Arendt's aporetic critique and Rancière's radical politics of equality offer a rearticulation of human rights (and HRE) in political terms. This suggests that human rights are rendered meaningful again insofar as they pay attention to "the multiple, equivocal and contingent effects of human rights as a discourse characterized by aporias" (Gündoğdu, 2011, p. 19) within specific cultural and historical settings.

Taking into serious consideration the above insights requires a conceptual renewal of not only the politics of human rights (Hoover, 2013) but also HRE too. Moving away from a view of human rights and HRE as juridical and declarationist, this renewal adopts what some theorists have recently called an *agonistic* understanding of rights (e.g. see Honig, 1995, 2008; Hoover, 2013; Schaap, 2011). As Hoover suggests, "An agonistic approach to rights accepts that rights claims will remain political, which is to say partial and contestable, but it also embraces the conflict that those political claims generate rather than seeing it as an unfortunate condition to be overcome" (2013, p. 947). This approach offers an alternative to declarationist and juridical approaches of HRE that often treat human rights in universal or legislative terms. It may be also argued that declarationist and juridical approaches do not only essentialize human rights but they also depoliticize them insofar as they fail to draw attention to the political struggles that claim these rights within specific political communities.

An agonistic account of HRE, then, takes into account Arendt's and Rancière's critiques, which suggest that rights are meaningless if they are decontextualized and depoliticized. Therefore, learning *about*, *through*, and *for* human rights (United Nations General Assembly 2011) needs to be critical and transformative, namely, it needs to take into consideration the distinct social locations and forms of inequality faced by different groups in order for educational strategies to become more holistic, relevant, and effective (Bajaj, Cislaghi, & Mackie, 2016). This implies that HRE scholars and practitioners, rather than overlooking the politics of human rights and HRE or claiming that HRE is compromised by its politicization, need to ask how human rights teaching and learning can foster an understanding of human rights that recognizes their political contestation, as opposed to merely accepting a universal and juridical authority.

The contribution, therefore, of an agonistic account of HRE is that it approaches human rights not as universal principles expressed in declarations, but rather through the lens of what Delanty (2011) calls a 'reconstructive critique', namely, an engagement with human rights that encourages their ongoing reconstruction. This implies that educators, trainers, activists and learners of human rights in formal, non-formal and informal settings try to make sense of human rights in practice, as an open-ended process, just as Rancière would suggest. This engagement with human rights should be recognized as always incomplete and transforming—in complex ways that defy any imposition of idealist or essentialist perspective of human rights. Encouraging this agonistic perspective of human rights in HRE makes it impossible to teach or learn about human rights as an expression of a legislative framework. Rather, it opens up our understanding of the different trajectories in which human rights can develop, and have developed historically and culturally.

A practical example of an agonistic perspective in HRE that has potential to reconstruct human rights is Al-Daraweesh and Snauwaert's (2013) critical and hermeneutical approach and its recent 'translation' into pedagogical praxis by Zembylas et al. (2017, 2016). According to Al-Daraweesh and Snauwaert (2013), the critical hermeneutical approach in HRE.

> constitutes a third conceptualization of human rights that seeks to reconcile the debate between universalists and cultural relativists. While accepting the basic tenets of antifoundationalism, particularism, perspectivalism, and historicism, this middle way rejects the most radical and nihilistic [...] position of the cultural relativists [...]. This third way holds to the normative power of injustice and human rights while being grounded in cultural interpretation. (2013, p. 395).

In practice, reconciling universalist and cultural relativist conceptualizations, can be translated into the following elements (Al-Daraweesh & Snauwaert, 2013, p. 410) of a pedagogy that is framed within a critical hermeneutical approach (see also Chap. 3): it focuses on the cultural, social, political and historical nature of HRE (historicization); it offers learners the tools to understand the concept of human rights in context (contextualization); it draws strength from the idea of multiple perspectives on HR (multiperspectivity); it takes a critical stance toward human rights as they are conceptualized/interpreted locally (criticality); and it recognizes that human rights conceptualizations are partial and incomplete (partiality). Working within an agonistic account, we find these elements helpful in formulating not only what a critical hermeneutical approach entails in pedagogical praxis, but also how HRE can exceed the declarationist and juridical discourses and practices, reconnecting human rights claims with Arendt's recommendation to constantly rethink human rights or Rancière's insight to pay attention to the political contestations of human rights.

The critical and hermeneutical approach has been recently 'translated' into pedagogical praxis by Zembylas et al. (2017, 2016). 'Adopting' this approach in practice implies two important ideas: first, the idea that learners have opportunities to interpret human rights rather than merely accept them as universal and absolute truths—a practice that takes place in the form of a dialogue between the learner and the specific sociohistorical context with its own complexities and sensitivities. Pedagogically, this orientation suggests the use of more empowering and transformative methodologies (Tibbitts, 2017), that is, teaching practices which are oriented toward the cultivation of agency in learners with the explicit aim of personal and social transformation. Second, the critical hermeneutical approach promotes a critical understanding of diverse manifestations of human rights; this involves, for example, questioning certainties and established ideas, recognizing the role of power relations, and highlighting the controversies around hegemonic discourses on human rights. This critical and interpretive orientation towards human rights contributes to the recognition of certain prejudices within and across different perspectives. Again, pedagogically speaking, this approach has the potential to aid the development of curricular and pedagogical approaches that enlarge the scope of human rights inquiry by legitimizing sociohistorically sensitive understandings of human rights and HRE, thus enriching an agonistic human rights understanding and praxis.

In research conducted by one of us and his team in Cyprus (Zembylas et al., (2017, 2016), it is documented how this approach constituted a completely new and unfamiliar pedagogical practice for the teachers who implemented it. It constituted a novel pedagogical tool for taking HRE to a deeper level, where a more holistic, critical, and multiperspectival understanding of human rights could take place, compared to the declarationalist approach that these teachers had implemented in the past. In particular, this approach seemed valuable to explore the complexity of human rights in conflictual situations such as the context of divided Cyprus, because it provided space to recognize human rights violations from the perspectives of both sides involved in the conflict. The implementation of this approach in practice shows that rupturing the dominance of certain pedagogical practices of HRE means taking seriously local realities and finding ways for HRE not to be decontextualized from its local community and environment. This is precisely the agonistic element that needs to be emphasized in HRE practices, namely, engaging learners in a critical, open-ended dialogic process with regard to the complex cultural, political and social representations of human rights and their implications in everyday life.

Conclusion

In conclusion, adopting an agonistic account of HRE enables the cultivation of 'critical responsiveness' (Hoover, 2013) towards diverse manifestations of human rights; this involves paying attention to the paradoxes, aporias and tensions around discourses and practices of the human rights regime. As Hoover notes, "critical responsiveness encourages those who support existing human rights to remain mindful of the exclusions […] and to attend to the harms they fail to address. And most importantly, it focuses on the use of human rights as tools of creative political action that can fundamentally upset the social order" (2013, p. 952). An agonistic perspective aids the development of curricular and pedagogical approaches that enlarge the scope of human rights inquiry by legitimizing sociohistorically sensitive and critical understandings of human rights and HRE.

At the same time, it is important to remember that any attempt to provide alternative manifestations of HRE—such as an agonistic account—will always be incomplete; yet, as we concluded in Chap. 2, this perpetual incompleteness registers with the function of critique, opening new possibilities for different futures along social justice lines. Arendt and Rancière are *praxis* philosophers concerned with the conditions of possibility for the disclosure of new social worlds (Schaap, 2011). Similarly, an agonistic account of HRE is a praxis-based orientation of HRE that advances critical and transformative forms of HRE; as noted earlier in the chapter, such forms of HRE encourage a critical engagement with human rights and perpetually revisit the idea of human rights, while advancing a human rights pedagogical practice grounded in principles of equality and social justice.

It is time for human rights educators to acknowledge the inadequacy of conceptual and practical tools of dominant and conventional forms of HRE grounded in declarationist and juridical frameworks to respond to contemporary challenges and critiques of human rights. With its equivocal and contingent understanding of aporias, an Arendtian critique of human rights indicates the vital importance of rearticulating these rights, whereas Rancière enables human rights educators to recognize that human rights are above all political struggles. This fundamental contingency and contestability of human rights is one of the most valuable lessons for HRE; we must keep this alive in our (re)thinking to avoid treating human rights as an idol (Hoover, 2013) or an ideology rather than a tool for social transformation. In the South African case study that is discussed in the subsequent chapter, the employment of human rights as idol and ideology - the fetishisation of human rights - in the absence of an integrated critique of human rights, opens up pathways for the emergence of a kind of neoliberal pedagogy that is closely aligned to the conversion of human into capital rights.

References

Al-Daraweesh, F., & Snauwaert, D. (2013). Toward a hermeneutical theory of international human rights education. *Educational Theory, 63*(4), 389–411.

Arendt, H. (1949). "The rights of man": What are they? *Modern Review, 3*(1), 24–37.

Arendt, H. (1951/1968). *The origins of totalitarianism* (edition if not the first?). New York: Harcourt.

Bajaj, M., Cislaghi, B., & Mackie, G. (2016). *Advancing transformative human rights education: Appendix D to the Report of the Global Citizenship Commission*. Cambridge, UK: Open Book Publishers.

Balibar, E. (2007). (De)constructing the human as human institution: A reflection on the coherence of Hanna Arendt's practical philosophy. *Social Research, 74*(3), 727–738.

Benhabib, S. (2004). *The rights of others: Aliens, residents and citizens*. Cambridge, UK: Cambridge University Press.

Delanty, G. (2011). Varieties of critique in sociological theory and their methodological implications for social research. *Irish Journal of Sociology, 19*(1), 68–92.

Giroux, H. (1997). *Pedagogy and politics of hope: Theory, culture and schooling*. Oxford, UK: West View Press.

Gündoğdu, A. (2011). "Perplexities of the rights of man": Arendt on the aporias of human rights. *European Journal of Political Theory, 11*(1), 4–24.

Honig, B. (1995). Toward an agonistic feminism: Hannah Arendt and the politics of identity. In B. Honig (Ed.), *Feminist interpretations of Hannah Arendt* (pp. 135–166). University Park, PA: Pennsylvania State University Press.

Honig, B. (2008). The time of rights: Emergent thought in an emergency setting: The paradox of politics. In D. Campbell & M. Schoolman (Eds.), *The new pluralism: William Connollly and the contemporary global condition* (pp. 85–120). Durham, NC: Duke University Press.

Hoover, J. (2013). Towards a politics for human rights: Ambiguous humanity and democratizing rights. *Philosophy & Social Criticism, 39*(9), 935–961.

Hung, R. (2012). Being human or being a citizen: Rethinking human rights and citizenship education in the light of Agamben and Merleau-Ponty. *Cambridge Journal of Education, 42*(1), 37–51.

Keet, A. (2010). *Human rights education: A conceptual analysis*. Saarbrücken, Germany: Lambert Academic Publishing.

Kiwan, D. (2005). Human rights and citizenship: An unjustifiable conflation? *Journal of Philosophy of Education, 39*(1), 37–50.

Rancière, J. (2004). Who is the subject of the rights of man? *South Atlantic Quarterly, 103*(2/3), 297–310.

Schaap, A. (2011). Enacting the right to have rights: Jacques Rancière's critique of Hannah Arendt. *European Journal of Political Theory, 10*(1), 22–45.

Tibbitts, F. (2017). Evolution of human rights education models. In M. Bajaj (Ed.), *Human rights education: Theory, research, praxis* (pp. 69–95). New York: Bloomsbury.

United Nations, General Assembly. (2011). *United Nations declaration on human rights education and training* (GA 66/127, Art. 2, paras. 1–2). Geneva, Switzerland: United Nations.

Zembylas, M., Charalambous, P., Charalambous, C., & Lesta, S. (2017). Toward a critical hermeneutical approach of human rights education: Universal ideals, contextual realities and teachers' difficulties. *Journal of Curriculum Studies, 49*(4), 497–517.

Zembylas, M., Lesta, S., Charalambous, C., & Charalambous, P. (2016). Toward a critical hermeneutical approach in human rights education: Transformative possibilities and the challenges of implementation. *European Education, 48*(2), 137–157.

Chapter 5
Capital Rights: Human Rights Education and Neoliberal Pedagogies

Introduction

The premise underlying this book is that human rights critiques are key to the renewal of HRE, and the revitalisation of human rights itself. The slow take up of these critiques has, amongst other developments, exposed HRE to neoliberal and capital alignment, as discussed in Chap. 2. Without these critical resources, it also became ensnared by the neoliberalism's stealth revolution (Brown, 2015). That is, in the absence of an analysis of how neoliberalism has transformed rights into capital rights and the subject of rights into little capitals, HRE will inevitably operate as neoliberal pedagogies. Moreover, to facilitate such operation, human rights function as a central discourse in producing a phantasmal reality within which HRE can be incorporated as a means for neoliberal expansion.

This chapter explores how inequality and rights violations in the context of South Africa are legitimated and discursively organised by the prevailing discourses on Human Rights and Transformative Constitutionalism (HR&TC) which are furthered by HRE. Focusing on the notions of HR&TC as idolatry that generate a fictitious narrative of inclusive socio-economic and cultural-political progress in the 'aftermath' of apartheid in South Africa, we suggest that this argument may also extend to the global human rights and HRE discourses. 'Mainstream' HRE (see Chap. 3) does not have the praxes-related resources to escape the logic of neoliberal pedagogies and thus cannot work against the economisation of rights and its conversion into capital rights. Consistent with our overarching project on CHRE in this book, we suggest critique as a strategy to work against idolatry for HRE to contribute to developing antidotes to the production of this phantasmal reality.

Constitutional and human rights idolatry was always destined to become a dominant social and political organising theme in post-1994 South Africa. Regarded as the "birth certificate of the new South Africa" (Ebrahim & Miller, 2010, p. 111), the interim and final Constitution (1993, 1996) conjoin a past of indescribable suffering

M. Zembylas, A. Keet, *Critical Human Rights Education*, Contemporary Philosophies and Theories in Education 13,
https://doi.org/10.1007/978-3-030-27198-5_5

for most South Africans with a future rooted in rights, reconciliation and democracy.[1] This past refers to the well-documented, systematic repression of black people through colonialism and apartheid. The deepening of internal and external resistance during the 1970s and 1980s, together with international pressure and worsening economic conditions, forced the last apartheid regime to unban political parties on 2 February 1990, which was likely more in line with the logics of 'interest convergence theory' (Bell, 1980) than an authentic social justice impulse. Nelson Mandela's release on 11 February 1990 soon followed. The talks and negotiations between the apartheid state and the liberation movements that started in 1990 gave form to the interim Constitution in November 1993. The first democratic elections took place on 27 April 1994 and the final Constitution was adopted towards the end of 1996.

The Constitutional Court (CC), with a history tightly linked to the Bill of Rights[2] in both the interim and final Constitutions, came into being in 1994. The final interpretative authority concerning constitutional matters rests with the

[1] See epilogue of the Interim Constitution (Act 200 of 1993). The salutation of the Promotion of National Unity and Reconciliation Act (no 34 of 1995) states:

> […] the Constitution of the Republic of South Africa (Act 200 of 1993), provides a historic bridge between the past of a deeply divided society characterised by strife, conflict, untold suffering and injustice, and a future founded on the recognition of human rights, democracy and peaceful co-existence for all South Africans, irrespective of colour, race, class, belief or sex; [...] it is deemed necessary to establish the truth in relation to past events as well as the motives for and circumstances in which gross violations of human rights have occurred, and to make the findings known in order to prevent a repetition of such acts in future; [...] the Constitution states that the pursuit of national unity, the well-being of all South African citizens and peace require reconciliation between the people of South Africa and the reconstruction of society; [...] the Constitution states that there is a need for understanding but not for vengeance, a need for reparation but not for retaliation, a need for ubuntu but not for victimisation; [...].

The preamble of the final Constitution (Act 108 of 1996 which commenced on 4 February 1997) reads as follows:

> [...] We therefore, through our freely elected representatives, adopt this Constitution as the supreme law of the Republic so as to: heal the divisions of the past and establish a society based on democratic values, social justice and fundamental human rights; lay the foundations for a democratic and open society in which government is based on the will of the people and every citizen is equally protected by law; improve the quality of life of all citizens and free the potential of each person; and build a united and democratic South Africa able to take its rightful place as a sovereign state in the family of nations.

[2] As it is pointed out:

> The notion of a bill of rights for South Africa can be traced back to an ANC document from the early 1920s. The Freedom Charter of 1955 carried the idea forward. In the following decades, the idea of an entrenched bill of rights received support from liberal academics and judges. The question of who would enforce it, however, was left open. This void was debated at a conference organised by the Constitutional Committee of the ANC in 1991. What emerged was a commitment to a Constitutional Court in a hybrid continental form, similar to that of Germany: able to hear cases by direct access, as well as by referral and on appeal.
> [http://www.constitutionalcourt.org.za/site/thecourt/history.htm, accessed on 12 October 2018].

CC. Furthermore, the Human Rights Commission Act (no 54 of 1994) eventuated in the establishment of the South African Human Rights Commission (SAHRC) on 2 October 1995, tasked with the promotion, protection and monitoring of human rights. The Act, setting up the Truth and Reconciliation Commission (TRC), was assented to in July 1995 and commenced in December 1995. The TRC's first meeting took place on 16 December 1995.[3] The TRC's final report was submitted to 'democratic' South Africa's first president Mandela in October 1998; the codicil to the report was submitted to Mbeki, Mandela's successor, in March 2003. The TRC viewed its mandate in human rights terms—not only in relation to accountability for past human rights violations, but also in relation to building a future human rights culture within which the ongoing project of reconciliation may be located.[4]

This triad of mechanisms, the CC, TRC and SAHRC, together with other independent bodies supporting constitutional democracy[5] and the constitution itself, emerged as the 'formal framers' of the rights discourse post-1994, within the context

[3] Regarding the work of the TRC:

The work of the TRC was accomplished through three committees: Human Rights Violations (HRV) Committee investigated human rights abuses that took place between 1960 and 1994. Reparation and Rehabilitation (R&R) Committee was charged with restoring victims' dignity and formulating proposals to assist with rehabilitation. Amnesty Committee (AC) considered applications for amnesty that were requested in accordance with the provisions of the Act. In theory the commission was empowered to grant amnesty to those charged with atrocities during Apartheid as long as two conditions were met: The crimes were politically motivated, and the whole truth was told by the person seeking amnesty. No one was exempt from being charged. Even ordinary citizens, members of the police could be charged and, most notably, members of the African National Congress, the ruling party at the time of the trial, could also be charged. Out of a total of 7112 petitioners, 5392 people were refused amnesty, and 849 were granted amnesty (there were a number of additional categories, such as *withdrawn*). The commission brought forth many witnesses giving testimony about the secret and immoral acts committed by the Apartheid Government, the liberation forces including the ANC, and other forces for violence that many say would not have come out into the open otherwise. On October 28, 1998 the Commission presented its report, which condemned both sides for committing atrocities. [https://www.sahistory.org.za/article/truth-and-reconciliation-commission-trc-0, accessed on 15 October 2018].

[4] See TRC final report (n.d.):

Reconciliation is a process which is never-ending, is costly and often painful. For this process to develop, it is imperative that democracy and a human rights culture be consolidated. Reconciliation is centred on the call for a more decent, more caring and more just society. It is up to each individual to respond by committing ourselves to concrete ways of easing the burden of the oppressed and empowering the poor to play their rightful part as citizens of South Africa.

[5] As Zajda and Ozdowski (2016, p. 103) explain:

The 'State Institutions Supporting Constitutional Democracy' – known as the Chapter 9 Institutions, after their place in the Constitution – consist of the Public Protector (PP), the Auditor General (AG), the Electoral Commission (IEC), the South African Human Rights Commission (SAHRC), the Commission for Gender Equality (CGE), and lastly, the Commission for the Protection of the Rights of Cultural, Religious and Linguistic Communities. These institutions are independent of government, subject only to the Constitution and the law, and report annually to Parliament.

of a "sea-change in global politics and the rise of human rights as the archetypical language of democratic transition" (Wilson, 2001, p. 1).[6]

Transformative Constitutionalism and Human Rights as Idolatry

During the second part of the 1990s, as constitutionalism, reconciliation and rights became the lexicon of South African 'speak', especially in proper, elite settings of power, Klare (1998) published his seminal article, *Legal Culture and Transformative Constitutionalism.* In this text, Klare (1998) defines transformative constitutionalism (TC) as

> a long-term project of constitutional enactment, interpretation, and enforcement committed (not in isolation, of course, but in a historical context of conducive political developments) to transforming a country's political and social institutions and power relationships in a democratic, participatory, and egalitarian direction. Transformative constitutionalism connotes an enterprise of inducing large-scale social change through nonviolent political processes grounded in law.

Van Marle (2009, p. 286) suggests that Klare's contribution is "probably the article most frequently quoted article by South African legal scholars in the field on constitutional law." According to Madlingozi (2017), it is "discourse-setting" (p. 128). As Christiansen (2010) also states, "South Africa is the most frequently discussed example of this form of transformative constitutionalism" (p. 576), perceiving the CC's praxes as efficacious from a social justice perspective:

> Generous rights interpretation, expansive remedial power, broad jurisdiction, and permissive access rules are the tools of the South African Constitutional Court that allow it to serve the transformative goals of the post-apartheid Constitution. The Court's procedural and interpretive characteristics empower it to serve as the pinnacle institution of a country committed to transformative constitutionalism and substantive justice. The Constitutional Court is, of course, not sufficient for the task of national transformation—no court or judicial system could be—but its willingness to experiment with its authority is a lesson for all courts. (p. 613)

Here, the CC emerged as the apex institution *for* TC. Regarded originally as a South African brand, TC is now seen as a Southern paradigm (Hailbronner, 2017, p. 527), increasingly spanning the Global South as a form of legal praxes. Further, some argue that "The Constitution has set itself the mission to transform society in the public and private spheres," that it is a "transformative constitution" (Davis & Klare,

[6] A revived language of liberal democracy became increasingly prevalent in the mid-1980s, and was accentuated by the demise of the former Soviet Bloc and the rise of ethno-nationalist conflict in the Balkans. Since 1990, nearly all transitions from authoritarian rule have adopted the language of human rights and the political model of constitutionalism, especially in Latin America and the new states of Eastern Europe. The end of the Cold War and the threat of irredentist nationalism led many intellectuals in Europe from a variety of political traditions to promote human rights and a return to the Enlightenment project.

2010, p. 404). No doubt, despite conceptual, legal-methodological, implementation and socio-cultural limitations, there are sufficient indications that the Constitution and the CC can indeed be transformative (Baxi, 2008; Davis & Klare, 2010; Hailbronner, 2017; Liebenberg, 2010) and have been key in steering the country within the parameters of its founding values. Some of these limitations include a "traditional legal culture" that may "constrain the transformative project," and jurists that "continue to deploy traditional methods of legal analysis" are some of the concerns (Davis & Klare, 2010, p. 509) raised. Additional concerns include:

> the absence thus far of a coherent exploration of the Constitution's values or an explicit and sustained effort to develop new legal methodologies appropriate to transformative constitutionalism; the reluctance to interrogate the distributive consequences of private law rules in the routines of economic life; the emergence of a neo-liberal strand in constitutional application; and the lack of critical sharpness with respect to separation-of-powers issues. (Davis & Klare, 2010, p. 509)

The genre within which these limitations are framed does not challenge the 'idea' of TC itself. Rather, the limits of its success are ascribed to culture, tradition and praxes, not the notion itself. However, it seems that we have an "impulse for idolatry," constitutional interpretation as "dependent upon the (usually tacit) assumption of a transcendent authority akin to a religious enterprise" (see Smith, 1993, p. 587). Thus, legal research and praxes curved towards TC look as if entangled in a sacred, self-referential configuration that legitimate one another through the dominant human right discourse in South Africa.

There has emerged then, in a certain sense, the risk of two co-constitutive secular religions: HR&TC. In both cases, within the logic of idolatry, it appears that human principles can possibly be elevated into unquestioned absolutes (Ignatieff, 2000, p. 341). The South African research and socio-political spaces and everyday discourses undoubtedly exhibit elements of these.

Marx (1887) once explored the religious and mystical character of "the fetishism of commodities and the secret thereof" (p. 47), where the "phantasmagoric process is going to constitute the premise of the discourse on fetishism, in the analogy with the 'religious world'" (Derrida, 1994, p. 199). Based on the work of Walter Benjamin (1892–1940), who was a member of the Frankfurt School of Critical Theory, Martel (2011, p. xiii) describes the phantasmagoria as a "miasma of false, idolatrous forms of reality base on our misreading of the world and its objects";

> [...] which overwrites our lives, our very reality with its meanings and truths, its great, organising narratives and promises of salvation. The phantasmagoria amounts to a mass practice of idolatry, a practice of misreading and misattributing meaning to the signs that compose the world with profound theological, political, and linguistic consequences. (Martel, 2011, p. xii)

'The best constitution in the world'[7] is a commonplace reference to the South African Constitution as the most unreserved statement of idolatry, a shaping narrative that forebode the inclusive story of progress best captured in the National

[7] As Madlingozi (2017, p. 149) writes: "Post-1994 fetishisation of human rights accords with the deification of the Constitution. This deification is seen in the way the Constitution is often evoked and invoked as the 'best constitution in the world.'"

Development Plan as the strategic chart of the country's polity (Madlingozi, 2017, p. 125). This 'best' is tied to the 'different': "The South African Constitution is *different* – it is a transformative constitution" (Davis & Klare, 2010, p. 404), and there is sufficient evidence to suggest that it overwrites our lives, discursively and materially. For instance, Madlingozi (2017, p. 125) refers to transformative constitutionalism's master frame of social justice within mainstream legal thought, whilst Rafudeen (2016, p. 225–226) interprets the South African polity as "primarily animated by human rights norms." In the South African setting, as we witness massive systemic and everyday violations of human rights, HR&TC is ironically called on as the main, almost ontological reference points of South African body-politic. There seems to be a fetish-like, "quasi-religious and quasi-magical" relation (Blaettler, 2012, p.32) with HR&TC.

From Human Rights to Capital Rights, to Neoliberal Pedagogies

The critique of human rights has grown into a prolific body of knowledge as discussed in Chap. 2. The same holds true regarding works on the limits of democracy and constitutionalism (Dean, 2009). The purpose of these labours at the limits *of* and *with* critique is the opening up of possibilities. In this instance, aptly captured by Van Marle's (2009) notion of TC *as/and* critique as

> an approach to the Constitution and law in general that is committed to transforming political, social, socio-economic and legal practices in such a way that it will radically alter existing assumptions about law, politics, economics and society in general. I distinguish this approach from other approaches aimed at change, for example those which pursue substantive equality or socio-economic rights which are premised on a liberal politics and liberal approaches to law. Although transformative constitutionalism by its nature is a project rooted in law, I do not regard it as limited to law and legal enquiry. (p. 2)

An interesting possibility is taking shape through Van Marle's (2009) argument: TC as subversive and dissident that may allow the Constitution as the hegemonic signifier (Madlingozi, 2017, p. 125) to reframe itself and its fundamental, organising notions. Within the parameters of critical legal theory, Van Marle's (2007) earlier work suggests that "that there is a danger that law, monumental constitutionalism and human rights embody another spectacle" (p. 411), which may feed the South African 'imagination' to the "detriment of the ordinary, the way people actually live and, more pertinently, the complexities of life" (p. 411).

Madlingozi (2016) advances the argument further towards a decolonial notion of *constitutionness*, as opposed to the "hegemonic constitutional project" that promises human rights to all (p. 5), paradoxically excluding the victims of settler colonialism from the 'benefits' of TC. Madlingozi (2016) thus returns, in some ways to the argument he made 15 years ago: legal and rights discourses create "false consciousness and thus hinder genuine democracy and justice" (Madlingozi, 2003, p. 15) because "people are fooled into believing that what should be, already is"

(Madlingozi, 2003, p. 23). Based on Ramose's (2001) work, Madlingozi (2016) argues for the idea of constitutionness "because this pursuit for inclusion, cohesion and 'standing together' is an open and never-ending quest towards ceaseless unfolding and wholeness; that is, towards national being-becoming" (p. 16).

The kind of 'imagination' and 'false consciousness' that Van Marle (2007) and Madlingozi (2003) touch upon, respectively, link up with the impulses associated with the phantasmagoria that returns us to the politics that itself (the phantasmagoria) suggests. This circular arrangement is fuelled by the "fetishisation of human rights, deification of the Constitution, and veneration of civil society" that ultimately perpetuate a neo-liberal and neo apartheid praxes of social justice (Madlingozi, 2017, p. 135).

Within HR&TC as idolatry, that is, as fetishised, particular discourses of rights, reconciliation and democracy are mobilised via public institutions and social systems to generate the mask of an inclusive narrative of progress that normalises the existence and growth of deep socio-economic inequalities, poverty and exclusion. This normalisation, as part of the phantasmagoria's almost totalising influence can in part be explained by Madlingozi's (2014) three categories of critiques against human rights discourses. First, he claims, the Marxist and neo-Marxist critiques hold that "the legalism of rights can induce a false consciousness whereby radical demands are transmuted into [sterile] 'human rights' claims." Second, the critique on a tactical level argues that "in liberal democracies the human rights discourse has so much currency as the only legible script of emancipation that once deployed, inevitably, it over-shadows other radical discourses that speak to problems of political economy, and so on" (Madlingozi, 2014); it has, for instance, displaced a properly formulated project on decolonisation in South Africa. The third category of critiques suggests that "in historically white supremacist societies, Euro-American modernist constitutions like that of South Africa simply perpetuate whiteness as a system of privilege" (Madlingozi, 2014) within which the new black elite are captured.

Through the idolatry of HR&TC, the phantasmagoria "has such a strong hold on our political imagination that it has become almost impossible to invent alternative forms of politics that can bring to light different understandings of equality, freedom, justice and emancipation" (Gündoğdu, 2015, p. 15). This imprisonment of thought and action, as well as the coyness of HR&TC as critique, neoliberal jurisprudence, tightly knitted into the idea of liberal democracy, "has transformed the operation of rights, both the subject of rights and the field in which rights operate" (Brown in Cruz and Brown, 2016, p. 72). Brown further elucidates:

> Let me try to be concrete: what has neoliberalism done most fundamentally? It has economised everything and everyone, it's rendered everything as a market and it's rendered everything we do as market action. When rights are adjudicated through that frame, human beings get figured as little capitals, and all of civic and political life gets rendered as market spheres. That means that rights increasingly get allocated not as civil rights, not as civil liberties, not as rights to empower the disempowered, but as capital rights. (Brown in Cruz and Brown, 2016, p. 72)

For Brown (2005) "neoliberalism is not simply a set of economic policies" (p. 39). Rather, it "carries a social analysis that, when deployed as a form of governmentality, reaches from the soul of the citizen-subject to education policy to practices of empire" (Brown, 2005, p. 39). Neoliberal rationality "involves *extending and disseminating market values to all institutions and social action*" (p. 40, original emphasis), by "developing institutional practices and rewards for enacting this vision"; building institutions, policies and discourse appropriate to its rationality; and the "dissemination and institutionalisation of such rationality" by "law, policies and political institutions" (Brown, 2005, p. 40).

The state adopts for itself the indices of neoliberal rationality to measure its success which legitimates and justify itself, no longer in terms of its historical mission, but with reference to economic growth (p. 42). Thus, the state itself, including the law, is "animated by market rationality" (Brown, 2005, p. 42). Through the state, "neoliberalism normatively constructs and interpellates individuals as entrepreneurial actors measured by their capacity for 'self-care'" (Brown, 2005, p. 42):

> Correspondingly, a 'mismanaged life,' the neoliberal appellation for failure to navigate impediments to prosperity, becomes a new mode of depoliticising social and economic powers and at the same time reduces political citizenship to an unprecedented degree of passivity and political complacency. The model neoliberal citizen is one who strategises for her- or himself among various social, political, and economic options, not one who strives with others to alter or organise these options. A fully realised neoliberal citizenry would be the opposite of public-minded; indeed, it would barely exist as a public. (Brown, 2005, pp. 42–43)

The state, law, education (including HRE), and market are all coordinated in the project of making the neoliberal subject through policy and regulation where the state "leads and controls subjects without being responsible for them [...] Neoliberal subjects are controlled *through* their [supposed] freedom" (ibid.) under liberal democracy.

For Koelble (2003), these are inevitable developments: "The new South African democracy is part and parcel of the encompassment process of circulatory capitalism, in its financial and rhetorical form, which has engulfed most parts of the globe since 1973" (p. 145):

> The political emancipation that took place symbolically in 1994, was part of a much larger global movement towards the realisation of an ideology of human freedom, market reform and universal rights that is intrinsically connected to the circulatory, some might add predatory, form that capitalism has taken. (ibid.)

This state of affairs then gave rise to what Bond (2000) regards as an 'elite transition' in South Africa during the 1990s, 'from apartheid to neoliberalism'. Other analyses of South African neoliberal juggernauts include the work of Cornish-Jenkins (2015), Schutte (2017), and Bond (2018). Thus, leaving the huge socio-economic inequalities largely untouched, the main feature of socio-economic rights post-1994 came to be its commodification (Madlingozi, 2007) (i.e., the conversion of human rights into capital rights). It is thus no surprise that "poor communities have started organising themselves in order to challenge the government's neoliberal policies as well as marginalisation from structures of governance" (Madlingozi, 2007).

It follows then, within a political and socio-economic milieu of HR&TC as idolatry in South Africa, that both legal and human rights praxes have played a productive role over the past two decades to provide the conditions for neoliberal subjectivity to become hegemonic. In the case of HRE, its uncritical treatment of human rights universals provided the link between the logics of capital, neoliberalism, neo-conservatism and the new right, whilst masquerading as its radical opposite. HRE has also been key in inventing the 'finished', 'neo-liberal' rights-subject *without* rights. Herein lies a key link between capital rights, HRE and neoliberal pedagogies; with HRE playing a constitutive in the production of the phantasmagoric.

The point here is that HR&TC as idolatry are by nature phantasmagoric. Stated differently, or as Madlingozi (2017, p. 146) would have it, the Constitution is deified, and human rights are fetishised. As such, they have structured the conditions for the dominion of neoliberalism because critique and the capacity to engage the delusion of the phantasmagoria are absent. The deficiency of critique makes the phantasmagoric reality so totalising that even left-oriented social justice practitioners and human rights activists "are endowed with a secret desire for capitalism to succeed" (Martel, 2011, p. xii). And, by extension, for the neoliberal logic to trump.

HRE, displaced from critique, has evolved into a burgeoning, conservative and uncritical pedagogical formation over the past three decades (see Chap. 2). Instead of facilitating the transformative radicality of human rights, the dominance of this approach undercuts the pedagogical value of HRE. It also diminishes its resistance for inscription into the neoliberal configurations within the context of liberal democracies. Thus, an intrinsic compatibility between liberal democracy, the conversion of human rights into capital rights and the neo-liberal subject as a human rights citizen emerges. Stated differently, human rights are *incorporated*. Moreover, HRE advances a form of human rights that are systematically depoliticising politics, as Neocosmos (2006) argues. Brown (in Cruz and Brown 2016) further warns that "not only can rights be depoliticising, not only can they be economised, that is transformed through a neoliberal economisation of their meaning and of their venue, but they can also simply be grabbed by anyone for anything" (p. 73).

HRE as a producer of neoliberal citizens has been confirmed by Khoja-Moolji's (2014) study in Pakistan; this is probably a worldwide trend. In a recent South African based study on HRE research among doctoral students, Simmonds and Du Preez (2017, p. 19) find

> that researchers often uncritically accept the fundamental nature of human rights and how it influences the way human rights education is conceptualised. Possibly, these studies remain school-based and fundamentally descriptive and uncritical because many of the doctoral candidates approach the topic with a 'how-to-solve-the-problem-mentality'.

Such research that points to the general uncritical orientation within HRE suggests an opening up, a susceptibility, toward neoliberal pedagogies. However, one has to wonder now that we have handed HR&TC over to the phantasmagoria via idolatry and fetishism, whether HRE has any other option but to be sucked into neoliberal pedagogies. Given this captivity, it seems to us, at this historical moment, that the conventional rights discourse has run out of steam as a tool for a radical project of social justice. Instead, as a matrix of discipline and regulation, it may be producing docile bodies.

Such arguments around the disempowering spin-offs of transitional justice (TJ)[8] and human rights praxes are commonplace in South Africa. In the context of TJ practices with South Africa, Madlingozi argues (2010) that the TJ industry, especially that which is part of the "international human rights movement/community" (pp. 212–213), could be accused of producing a racially inferior and politically disempowered subject. Regarding human rights, Madlingozi aligns himself with Neocosmos's (2006) insights: "human rights discourse is part of a project to substitute emancipatory politics based on active citizenship with 'statism', that is, politics of demobilisation and passivity reliant on 'state-delivery' or delivery by other institutions" (p. 357).

In the South African setting, TJ, TC and human rights are interconnected discourses. They, firmly within the grasp of the phantasmagoria, share a linguistic universe around the Constitution, the master signifier. TJ, entrepreneurially formulated, folds trauma, pain and rights alike into capital and produce professionals, academics and victims in the image that serves its market industry (Madlingozi, 2010). In the case of human rights, Baxi (2006, p. 216), more than a decade ago, has already studied the shift from human rights movements to human rights markets. Human rights entrepreneurs, as in the case of TJ, "commodify human suffering to package and sell it in terms of what the markets will bear" (Baxi, 2006, p. 223).

The notions of markets, commodities and capital analogous to the TJ and human rights industries now position us to argue that the absence of critique in mainstream HRE is not coincidental or accidental. The lack of critique within TC, TJ and human rights is a function of idolatry and perhaps a paucity of conviction, which in turn left HRE open for neoliberal conscription. Such enlistment is rooted by human rights, together with TJ and TC, firmly within the phantasmagoria where neoliberalism reigns; amplified by modern, connexionist capitalism.

Conclusion

In an earlier publication (Zembylas & Keet, 2018; for more on this, see Chap. 1), we formulated the idea of 'double critique' within the HRE field: critique of human rights praxes, and critique of its subject matter and content. We were, in a sense, while paraphrasing Paipais (2014, p. 374), trying to present a double critique of human rights praxes in general, and of HRE in particular to bring it to its limits, "in

[8] Transitional justice is understood here as

> a response to systematic or widespread violations of human rights. It seeks recognition for victims and promotion of possibilities for peace, reconciliation and democracy. Transitional justice is not a special form of justice but justice adapted to societies transforming themselves after a period of pervasive human rights abuse. In some cases, these transformations happen suddenly; in others, they may take place over many decades. [https://www.ictj.org/sites/default/files/ICTJ-Global-Transitional-Justice-2009-English.pdf accessed on 17 October 2018].

thinking that there is no alternative to what is" for some alternative to open up. All significant critical theory is this *drive*: incessantly encircling the impossibility of something existing "outside what is" and in the very thinking of this, the production of a certain 'excess' or 'gap' (Paipais, 2014, p. 374), an opening, a possibility of regeneration. Furthermore, again reiterating Paipais (2014, p. 360) as he mobilises Zizek's insights, double critique is tied to the political that designates the "moment of openness, of undecidability when the very structuring principle of society, the fundamental form of the [human rights] social pact is called into question."

The crux of our argument is that the sluggish uptake of *the critical* within human rights praxes has provided fertile, non-resistive grounds for human rights push-backs. In other words, an instrumentalised, uncritical conception of rights would always have opened itself up to incorporation and conscription into capital. In this sense critique can be viewed as a social justice-oriented cushion. As human rights are called into question, double critique renders its assumptions visible: "to bring into view that which is obscured when there is no critical outside", as Williams (2009, p. 629) argued some time ago. Human rights, therefore, is forced to test its own language. Also, double critique, as Mignolo (2006) would have it, is subsequently a way of moving towards decoloniality. This move, in the case of human rights, is towards its own outside as ways to animate human rights beyond its codified limits; beyond its staleness; so as to continuously reinvest rights with social activism.

Rebughini (2018, p. 11) brings the notion of critique as developed by the canonical work of Kant, Hegel, Marx, and their numerous twentieth-century interpreters, in conversation with the American pragmatism (of James, Dewey, and Mead) where "critical agency can be associated with the creativity of seeking innovative solutions, rather than with rejection of and opposition to a given social order". However, we argue that Rebughini (2018) does not give sufficient credit to the praxis of emancipation as formulated within critical theories of all sorts, including those which have guided activist practices across the world for many decades. What she does offer, however, is the possibility to develop the capacity.

> to produce critique by imagining the 'new', denying the 'given' and coping with the constraints […] from everyday life experiences". [It] is the work of love, justice, imagination and actualisation; […] [where] critique can arise from the creation of alternatives generated by internal and unpredictable transformations. (Rebughini, 2018, p. 16)

Rebughini further argues that critical agencies have an unstable openness and incompleteness that, despite their fragility, try to catch up "with the right moment, where resistance and creativity, unveiling and redemption can meet" (ibid.).

Critique, in critical situations such as what we are experiencing today across the world in terms of social justice pushbacks, has the obligation of driving human rights to its limits. At these limits, we empty out all redemptive possibilities, to produce a gap for an alternative to emerge. This is what Benjamin (Martel, 2011) had in mind. To wit, the phantasmic nature of human rights folded into liberal democracy, transformative constitutionalism and neoliberal configurations produce a battery of fantasies around the pursuit of socio-economic equality, human dignity, non-discrimination, social solidarity, and so on. Within these fantasies, well-aware of how they are constituted within the phantasmagoria, HRE and human rights institutions source the justification of their practices. Only those whose lines of sight are obscured by idolatry will not concede to the failures of conventional human rights practices against the backdrop of massive global and local inequalities, the massive expansion of human precarity, the conservatisation of politics in the Global North—tagged by tragically powerful new waves of intra- and inter- state racism, race-populism, bigotry, every day fascisms and ethno-nationalisms across the globe, and so forth.

Failures, as Martel (2011, p. 26)) argues, is an asset for Benjamin in the strategy of the antidote: "tools of combating the phantasmagoria [...] like an antidote (a term Benjamin employs) our subjection to and participation in the phantasmagoria can become the basis for resistance." Once we acknowledge the fallen world of human rights, "where there is nothing but idolatry", dissidence and resistance are required to "subvert the phantasmagoria and to use its own effects against itself. By such means, the absolute certainty that the phantasmagoria is real, natural, and historical can be dispelled or disturbed" (Martel, 2011, p. 26), thereby working against its fantasies.

As is the case, South Africa's post-1994 fantasies were, and still are, necessary to hold the idea of a 'new' nation together. However, the need for such phantasms has too easily slid into idolatry "in an effort at 'self-representation,' [whereby] these visions interfere with or even replace any sense of a community's material existence" (Martel, 2011, p. 248). Such existence is soaked with the reality of human rights subjects without rights. The purpose of the antidote is to disclose this reality, digging, through critique, deeper into the delusions of rights because we are already imprisoned in its cave (Martel, 2011, p. 258).

On the South African scholarly-activist scene, the consistent, lucid work of Madlingozi (2003, 2010, 2014, 2016, 2017), in revealing the poverty of thought and the limits of our imaginations to break through the fetishisation of HR&TC and TJ, is attempting to make visible the everyday violations, ruin, damage and human harm that is veiled by these idolatrous discourses. In is also in his work that the struggles of communities such as those mobilised under the *Abahlali baseMjondolo*[9] *movement are rendered legible, as an antidote to the phantasmagoria.*

The conversion of human to capital rights tied to the emergence of neoliberal pedagogies is a function of HRE, conventionally understood. This kind of HRE is

---

[9]The *Abahlali baseMjondolo* (Shack Dwellers) movement

began in Durban, South Africa, in early 2005. Although it is overwhelmingly located in and around the large port city of Durban it is, in terms of the numbers of people mobilised, the largest organisation of the militant poor in post-apartheid South Africa. Its originary event was a road blockade organised from the Kennedy Road settlement in protest at the sale, to a local industrialist, of a piece of nearby land long promised by the local municipal councillor to shack dwellers for housing'.[http://abahlali.org/a-short-history-of-abahlali-basemjondolo-the-durban-shack-dwellers-movement/ accessed on 26 October 2018].

central to the project of human rights and constitutional idolatry and the phantasmagoria. The new battleground for Critical HRE, as reflected in Madlingozi'work, is the development of antidotes rooted in human rights critiques that may resist neoliberal pedagogical conscriptions. Critique must, as one of its functions, assist us to work against our tendency for idolatry, to disclose and "render legible the communities that gather in the wake of such a fetish" (Martel, 2011, p. 3).

The preceding chapters put forward, both in broad and specific terms, the varieties of critique that can be mobilise for more productive human rights praxes. This chapter suggests that the absence of such critiques, in the case of South Africa, has lead us down the path of human rights and constitutional idolatry that coupled neoliberalism, capital rights and neoliberal pedagogies together within HRE programming. Such idolatrous discourses has masked the human suffering HRE is meant to respond to. In a sense, HRE, in South Africa, is lost, incorporated. One way of retrieving it would be through the antidotes to the phantasmagoria which presupposes a much stronger expression of *Critical* HRE. The next chapter takes further our engagement with the dominant liberal discourse as it relates to the affective dimensions of HRE.

References

Baxi, U. (2006). *The future of human rights*. Oxford, UK: Oxford University Press.

Baxi, U. (2008, April 27–29). *Preliminary notes on transformative constitutionalism*. Paper presented at the BISA conference on Courting Justice II, New Delhi, India.

Bell Jr., D. A. (1980). Brown v. Board of Education and the interest-convergence dilemma. *Harvard Law Review, 93*(3), 518–533.

Blaettler, C. (2012). Phantasmagoria: A profane phenomenon as a critical alternative to the fetish. *Image & Narrative, 13*(1), 32–47.

Bond, P. (2000). *The elite transition: From apartheid to neoliberalism in South Africa*. London: Pluto Press.

Bond, P. (2018, February 27). Cyril Ramaphosa relaunches neo-liberalism. *ZNET*. Retrieved from https://zcomm.org/znetarticle/cyril-ramaphosa-relaunches-neo-liberalism/

Brown, W. (2005). *Edgework: Critical essays on knowledge and politics*. Princeton, NJ: Princeton University Press.

Brown, W. (2015). *Undoing the demos: Neoliberalism's stealth revolution*. New York: Zone Books.

Christiansen, E. (2010). Transformative constitutionalism in South Africa: Creative uses of constitutional court authority to advance substantive justice. *Journal of Gender, Race and Justice, 13*, 575–614.

Cornish-Jenkins, H. (2015). Despite the 1994 political victory against apartheid, its economic legacy persists. *South African History Online*. Retrieved from https://www.sahistory.org.za/article/despite-1994-political-victory-against-apartheid-its-economic-legacy-persists-haydn-cornish-

Cruz, K., & Brown, W. (2016). Feminism, law, and neoliberalism: An interview and discussion with Wendy Brown. *Feminist Legal Studies, 24*(1), 69–89.

Davis, D. M., & Klare, K. E. (2010). Transformative constitutionalism and the common and customary law. *South African Journal on Human Rights, 26*(3), 403–509.

Dean, J. (2009). *Democracy and other neoliberal fantasies: Communicative capitalism and other left politics*. Durham, NC: Duke University Press.

Derrida, J. (1994). *Specters of Marx: The state of the debt, the work of mourning and the new international*. New York: Routledge.

Ebrahim, H., & Miller, L. E. (2010). Creating the birth certificate of a new South Africa. In L. E. Miller & L. Aucion (Eds.), *Framing the state in times of transition: Case studies in constitution making*. Washington, DC: United States Institute of Peace Press.

Gündoğdu, A. (2015). *Rightlessness in an age of rights: Hannah Arendt and the contemporary struggle of migrants*. Oxford, UK: Oxford University Press.

Hailbronner, M. (2017). Transformative constitutionalism: Not only in the global south. *American Journal of Comparative Law, 65*(3), 527–565.

Ignatieff, M. (2000, April 4–7). *Human rights as idolatry* (The Tanner lecture on human values). Princeton University.

Khoja-Moojli, S. (2014). Producing neoliberal citizens: Critical reflections on human rights education in Pakistan. *Gender and Education, 26*(2), 103–118.

Klare, K. E. (1998). Legal culture and transformative constitutionalism. *South African Journal on Human Rights, 14*, 146–188.

Koelble, T. (2003). Building a new nation: Solidarity, democracy and nationhood. In D. Chidester, P. Dexter, & W. James (Eds.), *What holds us together: Social cohesion in South Africa* (pp. 143–172). Cape Town, South Africa: HSRC Press.

Liebenberg, S. (2010). *Socio-economic rights. Adjudication under a transformative constitution*. Claremont, CA: Juta.

Madlingozi, T. (2003, September 5–7). *The significance of critical legal studies' rights critique for Africa: Exposing the dangers and limitations of the human rights discourse*. Paper presented at the Critical Legal Conference, Johannesburg, South Africa.

Madlingozi, T. (2007). Post-apartheid social movements and the quest for the elusive 'new' South Africa. *Journal of Law and Society, 34*(1), 77–98.

Madlingozi, T. (2010). On transitional justice entrepreneurs and the production of victims. *Journal of Human Rights Practice, 2*(2), 208–228.

Madlingozi, T. (2014). *There is no 'outside the law': How can social movement use the law to bring about social change* [Web log comment]. Retrieved from http://thinkingafricangos.blogspot.com/2014/05/there-is-no-outside-law-how-can-social.html

Madlingozi, T. (2016). *On settler colonialism and post-conquest constitutionness: The decolonising constitutional vision of African nationalists of Azania/South Africa* [Drat paper]. Retrieved from http://www.academia.edu/33747352/On_Settler_Colonialism_and_Post-Conquest_Constitutionness_The_Decolonising_Constitutional_Vision_of_African_Nationalists_of_Azania_South_Africa

Madlingozi, T. (2017). Social justice in a time of neo-apartheid constitutionalism: Critiquing the anti-black economy of recognition, incorporation and distribution. *Stellenbosch Law Review, 28*(1), 123–147.

Martel, J. R. (2011). *Textual conspiracies: Walter Benjamin, idolatry, and political theory*. Ann Arbor, MI: The University of Michigan Press.

Marx, K. (1887). *Capital: A critique of political economy*. Moscow, Russia: Progress Publishers.

Mignolo, W. (2006). Introduction to double critique: Knowledges and scholars at risk in post-Soviet societies. *South Atlantic Quarterly, 105*(3), 479–500.

Neocosmos, M. (2006). Can a human rights culture enable emancipation? Clearing the theoretical ground for the renewal of a critical sociology. *South African Review of Sociology, 37*(2), 356–378.

Paipais, V. (2014). Between politics and the political: Reading Hans. J. Morgenthau's double critique of depoliticisation. *Millenium: Journal of International Studies, 42*(2), 354–375.

Rafudeen, A. (2016). A South African reflection on the nature of human rights. *African Human Rights Law Journal, 16*, 225–246.

Ramose, M.B. (2001). An African perspective on justice and race. *Polylog: Forum for Intercultural Philosophy, 3*. Retrieved from http://them.polylog.org/3/frm-en.htm#s7

Rebughini, P. (2018). Critical agency and the future of critique. *Current Sociology, 66*(1), 3–19.

Schutte, G. (2017, May 25). Masses shackled by neoliberalism. *IOL*. Retrieved from https://www.iol.co.za/pretoria-news/masses-shackled-by-neoliberalism-9339621

Simmonds, S., & Du Preez, P. (2017). Discourses shaping human rights education research in South Africa: Future considerations. *South African Journal of Higher Education, 31*(6), 9–24.

Smith, S. D. (1993). Idolatry in constitutional interpretation. *Virginia Law Review, 79*(3), 583–631.

Van Marle, K. (2007). The spectacle of post-apartheid constitutionalism. *Griffith Law Review, 16*(2), 411–429.

Van Marle, K. (2009). Transformative constitutionalism as/and critique. *Stellenbosch Law Review, 20*(2), 286–301.

Williams, J. A. (2009). Unholy matrimony? Feminism, orientalism, and the possibility of double critique. *Signs, 34*(3), 611–632.

Wilson, R. A. (2001). *The politics of truth and reconciliation in South Africa: Legitimising the post-apartheid state*. Cambridge, UK: Cambridge University Press.

Zajda, J., & Ozdowski, S. (2016). *Globalisation, human rights education and reforms*. Dordrecht, The Netherlands: Springer.

Zembylas, M., & Keet, A. (2018). *Entanglements and regenerations: Critical human rights, citizenship and democracy education*. London: Bloomsbury.

Chapter 6
Political Depression, Cruel Optimism and Pedagogies of Reparation

Introduction

It is increasingly argued, as we have also done in this book, that Human Rights Education (HRE) is problematic in the way it adopts a liberal discourse that legitimates human rights as universal values, while it ignores the political conditions of oppression, suffering, and injustice (Al-Daraweesh & Snauwaert, 2013; Coysh, 2014; Keet, 2010, 2012; Zembylas, 2016; see Chaps. 2 and 5). In addition to critiques concerning the declarationalist form of HRE, which sees all human rights truths as emerging solely from instruments such as declarations (Keet, 2012, p. 22) and tends to discount other forms of knowledge (Coysh, 2014, pp. 89–90), there have also been concerns about the formulation of a pedagogical approach that often treats human rights violations in ahistorical and sentimental ways rather than within a framework that inspires action and activism (Sliwinski, 2005; Zembylas, 2016; see also, Amsler, 2011; Zembylas, 2013). In the previous chapter we explored, in relation to the South African case study, how the idolatrous discourses around human rights that generate political depression and inaction as part of the phantasmagoria, also reveal the possibilities of the antidote. These concerns point to the *affective* aspect of human rights, human rights violations and HRE. This chapter takes up the issue of sentimentality and political depression, while the next two chapter also deal with issues related to affect, in order to try and counter rationalist ideas about human rights and HRE that strip it of its affective dimension.

An important critique of the dominant liberal discourse of human rights is grounded in what Berlant (2008) has called 'the unfinished business of sentimentality', that is, the way sentimentality is being *used* in public spheres simply to generate emotions that aim to touch audiences about human rights violations; the unfinished business is that sentimentality in itself rarely leads to action for social change. As Cvetkovich (2012) points out in a statement that refers in general about

M. Zembylas, A. Keet, *Critical Human Rights Education*, Contemporary Philosophies and Theories in Education 13,
https://doi.org/10.1007/978-3-030-27198-5_6

the dominant liberal discourse of human rights, but one which could easily apply to 'the dominant discourse of HRE' (Coysh, 2014, p. 89):

> [...] the history of human rights is frequently told as though it begins with the Universal Declaration as a response to the Second World War. Moreover, the popular origins of this highly sanctioned form of emotional politics need to be more fully acknowledged so as to better explain its tensions and failures. In contexts ranging from the testimony of truth and reconciliation commissions, to Amnesty International reports, to documentary films that explore human rights abuses, liberal models by which representation of suffering is presumed to have a salutary effect on an audience that is removed culturally and geographically [...] are pervasive. There are many different variations on these strategies, but they rarely include a critical perspective on the presumed transparency of representation. (Cvetkovich, 2012, p. 9)

The patterns emerging from critiques of discourses on human rights and HRE—that is, the uncritical advancement of human rights universals as an uncontested social good; the sentimental and liberal approach to suffering; and the ahistorical, apolitical and acritical practice of human rights and HRE without considering how human rights are tied onto socio-political conditions such as neoliberalism[1]—are situated within a wider context of social and political experiences that Cvetkovich (2012) has called 'political depression'. Political depression is the sense that customary forms of political response— including activism, HRE, and even some forms of critical analysis—are no longer working either to change the world or to make us feel better. Importantly, the concept of political depression is not meant to be depressing or paralysing; on the contrary, according to Cvetkovich, the goal is to depathologise 'negative' affects (e.g. anger, disappointment, disillusionment) that are often associated with depression so that they can be seen as a possible resource for political action and transformative work.

The linkage between depression and political failure is relevant to HRE and contemporary efforts for its critical renewal, because depression as "a cultural and social phenomenon rather than a medical disease" (Cvetkovich, 2012, p. 1) is related to long-term histories of human rights violations that have ongoing impacts at the level of everyday life. The portrayals of human rights as a set of universal facts and HRE as a practice that is packaged within global UN structures are inevitably embedded within a particular affective politics. This affective politics fails to uncover the tensions and failures of the human rights paradigm and pathologizes negative affects expressed about the political failure of human rights around the world. An HRE that is truly 'critical' and goes beyond a liberal and sentimental approach toward human rights needs to critique the cultural, social, political and affective conditions that make possible the perpetuation of rights violations. In fact, we want to borrow Berlant's (2011) term of 'cruel optimism' and go as far as to

---

[1] Given the multiplicity of theorisations of 'neoliberalism' and its emerging definitions over time, this term is deployed here in a broad manner to denote emphases on productivity, economic liberalization policies, and the significance of the individual. (For a summary of different arguments on the relationship between human rights and neoliberalism, see Chap. 5; also see Moyn, 2014). In education, these neoliberal policies are exemplified, for example, through high stakes testing, accountability, standards, and audit regimes (e.g. see Taubman, 2009).

argue that an enduring attachment to an ahistorical, apolitical and acritical approach in HRE would amount to a form of 'cruel optimism', that is, an attachment to compromised conditions of possibility, despite evidence that this approach actually becomes an obstacle to the flourishing of a CHRE.

The present chapter, then, focuses on the following questions: How might a theorisation of political depression be relevant to efforts that aim to renew criticality in HRE? In which ways can a 'critical' HRE go against cruel optimism and turn our attention to important ethical, political and affective questions on human rights? Can the negativity of political depression become a site for HRE pedagogies that are 'reparative'? This chapter, then, turns to how a form of CHRE can be enriched through pedagogies that are 'reparative' (Sedgwick, 2003), that is, pedagogies which attempt to address representations of suffering and human rights violations within a frame that takes into consideration histories of violence, oppression, and social injustice, without falling into the trap of sentimentality.

'Political Depression' and Its Affective Implications for Understanding Human Rights Violations

Generally speaking, depression is more often than not 'read' through a medical model that constructs it as a psychological disorder. There is, however, an emerging literature in various fields about how medical models have contributed to the 'medicalisation' and 'pathologisation' of social problems (Flatley, 2008; Horowitz & Wakefield, 2007). These critiques maintain that mental states are never purely 'individual' or 'psychological', but rather reflect social, political and historical realities (Ahmed, 2004, 2010; Berlant, 2004, 2011; Cvetkovich, 2003, 2012). Thus, labels such as 'depression' often become justifications for the exclusion and persecution of individuals and groups who do not fit with a normative agenda—all in the name of ideals such as happiness and health.[2]

In the psychoanalytic tradition, Melanie Klein (1984) was one of the theoreticians who took great interest in articulating the 'depressive position' (Kristeva, 2001; Sedgwick, 2003). In particular, Klein refers to the 'paranoid position' being always in oscillation with the depressive position in children's intra-psychic developmental processes. Contrary to Freud and Lacan, Klein argues (see Kristeva, 2001) that for the infant there is a paranoid position—marked by hatred, envy and anxiety—"a position of terrible alertness to the dangers posed by the hateful and envious part-objects that one defensively projects into" (Sedgwick, 2003, p. 128). By contrast, the depressive position is an anxiety-mitigating situation experienced by the infant only briefly, according to Klein; this is the position from which it is possible for the infant or adult to use his or her own emotional resources to 'repair' the hateful and envious part-objects. From the infantile depressive position—coincident

[2] See Farley (2014) for a psychoanalytic understanding of depression in curriculum and pedagogy.

with the process in which the child mourns the loss of love objects (e.g. mother's breast)—comes the desire to make reparation, that is, to make good on the injuries done to the loved objects. Reparation, then, becomes the means through which feelings of hatred, envy and anxiety are reduced and displaced, making the possibility to love possible at separation; this is why love is among Klein's names for the reparative process, as Sedgwick points out. (We come back to reparation later in the chapter).

In recent years, the so called 'affective turn' (Clough, 2007) in the humanities and social sciences has developed some of the most innovative and productive theoretical ideas, bringing together psychoanalytic perspectives, political theories and critical social analysis. The affective turn marks "critical theory's turn to affect" (p. 2), as Clough writes, "at a time when critical theory is facing the analytic challenges of ongoing war, trauma, torture, massacre, and counter/terrorism" (ibid.). This scholarship emphasizes that what is felt "is neither internally produced nor simply imposed on us from external ideological structures" (Rice, 2008, p. 205), but rather affects and emotions cannot be thought outside the complexities, reconfigurations and re-articulations of power, history and politics (Athanasiou, Hantzaroula, & Yannakopoulos, 2008). Thus the affective turn highlights how psychic elements of relationality as responses to suffering, violence and trauma are entangled with historical, cultural, social and political norms and conventions (e.g. the human rights paradigm).

One of the most powerful articulations of the affective turn is Cvetkovich's (2012) reconceptualisation of depression in order to depathologise it and to relate it not to individual medical symptoms, but to wider social and political conditions such as neoliberalism, human rights violations, historical trauma, racism, colonialism and violence. Cvetkovich justifies her turn to this sort of analysis asserting that "political depression might explain the current explosion of interest in trauma studies and public cultures of memory" (p. 127). As she further explains:

> The limits of political representation and legal recognition in eliminating racism require not only new visions for the future but the affective energy to sustain disappointment. The turn to public cultures of memory that address transnational histories of genocide, colonization, slavery, and diaspora stems from the need to connect with histories of trauma that have not yet been overcome. Epidemics of depression can be related (both as symptom and as obfuscation) to long-term histories of violence that have ongoing impacts at the level of everyday emotional experience. (2012, p. 7)

More generally, Cvetkovich argues that "histories of geographic and political dispossession can usefully illuminate what gets called depression" (p. 25), and "Depression […] is thus a way to describe neoliberalism and globalization, or the current state of political economy, in affective terms" (p. 11). Put differently, this reconceptualisation of depression as political is nicely captured in the following question: "What if depression […] could be traced to histories of colonialism, genocide, slavery, legal exclusion and everyday segregation and isolation that haunt all of our lives, rather than to biochemical imbalances?" (p. 115). Arguing for a cultural and political history of depression that is neither universalising (people throughout history have suffered from depression) nor individualising (depression as the result of individual psychic troubles or biochemical imbalances), Cvetkovich suggests that depression is better described as the product of a sick culture (Rand, 2015).

Beyond describing depression as political, it is important to also delve deeper into an analysis of the affective implications of political depression. In general, depression is characterized by Cvetkovich (2012) as an impasse, "being at a 'dead end' or 'no exit' [...] a state of being stuck [...] both literal and metaphorical, that requires new ways of living or, more concretely, moving" (pp. 20, 26). The material dimensions of being stuck can literally shut down or inhibit movement, says Cvetkovich, while as a theoretical concept, impasse suggests that things have no future. The affective dimensions of impasse are often associated with feelings of dispossession and sadness and a sense of powerlessness to do anything to change the state of being stuck. Importantly though, while the theorisation of political depression recognizes feelings of dispossession and sadness, it also resists calls for therapeutic solutions that would sentimentalize or supposedly 'overcome' the sufferings of the present—e.g. by commemorating the sufferings of the past. Cvetkovich makes a strong point that her suggestion is not that political depression and the affects associated with it will eventually be converted into a positive experience. Rather, she wants "to avoid a public culture of trauma that substitutes the horrors of the past for a less dramatic but no less disturbing present" (p. 131), and warns that "trauma histories can become in their own way an exercise in self-indulgence, a substitution of the melodrama of the past for the everyday weariness of the present" (p. 132). This "everyday weariness of the present" is a pertinent description of education, culture and politics in many conflict and post-conflict societies such as Israel, Northern Ireland, and Cyprus (see Bekerman & Zembylas, 2012) in which there is a fixation on the "public culture of trauma" that is fixed in commemorating the sufferings of the past. Therefore, Cvetkovich views the affects associated with political depression —e.g. inertia, despair, if not apathy and indifference—as sites of departure for new community formations—that is, for reparative relations, to use Klein's term—that go beyond sentimental and melodramatic configurations.

For our interests in reconceptualising a CHRE, then, by reading political depression through oppression, social injustice and colonisation, our attention shifts to a 'materialist' (Berlant, 2011) understanding of the everyday experiences of human rights violations. Several theorists, especially feminist scholars, have for many years suggested that oppression is often carried out at an affective level (Ahmed, 2000; Boler, 1999; Lorde, 1984; Young, 1990). These theorists have argued that power relations work through affect and shape individual and social bodies, thus analyzing a social and cultural phenomenon such as depression requires attention to the ways in which affects (re)produce dominant social and political hierarchies and structures, forms of oppression, and exclusions (Pedwell & Whitehead, 2012). When connections between depression and political structures (such as systematic human rights violations) are disavowed, "then one's individual biological or psychological pathology is offered as an explanation for the bad feelings that might legitimately arise from larger social ills" (Rand, 2015, p. 174). Analysing oppression as a 'public feelings project' linked to the legacies of colonialism, slavery and racism, argues Cvetkovich (2012), does not only offer alternatives to a psychologised or pathologised understanding of depression, but also produces new vocabularies of hope that avoid naïve optimism—a form of optimism that fails to address the difficult legacies of the past and is too easily sentimentalised.

Therefore, historicising and politicising—rather than psychologising—human rights violations enables the formulation of theories of human rights and HRE that bring violence and oppression to their historical roots. To take one example, it has been suggested that a better understanding of the negative affects associated with racism and the melancholic attachments to loss would need to make visible not only the social bases of these attachments, but also their creative, political aspects (Eng & Kazanjian, 2003). This would imply that melancholy's negativity could in fact be productive, as Cvetkovich (2012) asserts, and an important corrective to a naïve politics of hope, if loss becomes the point of departure for a new sense of community. This sense of community is not constituted in terms of 'overcoming' loss through any therapeutic process or seeking redemption— because one cannot 'work through' unimaginable acts of violence (Eng & Kazanjian, 2003)—but in terms of pointing out injuries as an affirmation of a renewed politics of solidarity and empathy, while taking into consideration material/structural conditions of inequality. The challenge, then, is to dwell in the sadness of witnessing human rights violations, without seeking 'sentimental optimism' (Da Costa, 2014) or immediate redemptions, yet without losing the promise of optimism at all. In the next part of the chapter, the affective implications of historicizing human rights violations are further explored through the notion of 'cruel optimism', focusing on what this move might imply for HRE.

The Affective Politics of 'Cruel Optimism' and the Consequences for HRE

Berlant (2011) examines our desires for things that are not good for us, arguing that the historical present is marked by relations of 'cruel optimism'. Cruel optimism exists "when something you desire is actually an obstacle to your flourishing" (p. 1). Berlant has in mind attachments to varied objects and ideals ranging from love and the good life to political projects such as human rights, peace or patriotism. "Why," she asks, "do people stay attached to conventional good-life fantasies […] when the evidence of their instability, fragility and dear cost abounds?" (p. 3). The reason, she says, is because "the loss of what's not working is more unbearable than the having of it" (p. 27). This is precisely why these visions are not merely inconvenient or tragic but rather cruel; cruel optimism, Berlant asserts, is the condition of maintaining an attachment to a problematic object or ideal *in advance* of its loss. Berlant situates her analysis in theorizations of political depression, suggesting that the politically depressed position is manifested in the difficulty of detaching from life-building modalities that are no longer doing their job and that indeed become obstacles to the flourishing of the subjects whose optimism drives them (pp. 27, 227).

To gain a deeper understanding of cruel optimism and its implications in contemporary human rights discourses requires an analysis of the modes through which affective attachments are constituted and perpetuated despite disappointments. Berlant (2011) suggests that these attachments become collective, historical and shared; they are "structures of relationality" (p. 13) within the impasse of the present. We might experience disappointments, she says, but powerful structures compel our attachments to sources of disappointment. Yet, this disappointment should not be interpreted as a "symptom of error, a perversion, damage, or a dark truth: optimism is, instead, a scene of negotiated sustenance that makes life bearable" (p. 14). Optimistic attachments to ideals—e.g. human rights ideals—keep us going despite disappointments that our visions (e.g. a more just world) are not materialized. These affective attachments keep us going because their potential loss is a double loss, according to Berlant (2011): of a particular attachment, and of the fantasy of the attachment as such. In the fact of this overwhelming loss, people often stay tethered to bad lives and unrealizable ideals that exhaust and defeat them. This defeat in turn means that disappointments sustain modes of relationality by engendering cruelly optimistic relations. The great significance of Berlant's analysis for our discussion here is that it provides an account of the multiple affective registers of collective life that keep people loosely knotted together despite disappointments; that is, "the process of knotty tethering to objects, scenes, and modes of life that generate so much overwhelming yet sustaining negation" (p. 52). Berlant traces the ways habits begin to formulate and function through repetition that sustain affective attachments in the everyday and enable the affective conditions that may disrupt or foreclose normalization. An obvious question at this point is the following: What are the consequences of this analysis in exploring the enduring sustenance of the dominant discourse of human rights and HRE?

First of all, Berlant's (2011) intention to "track the becoming general of singular things" (p. 12) turns our attention to the 'ordinariness' of suffering and trauma in the everyday rather than thinking in terms of grand notions of trauma. This concern about the ordinariness of suffering and trauma has important implications for thinking about the normativity of violence—as well as the violence of normativity— that sustains human rights violations at the micro-political level. The perspective on trauma and suffering as ordinary suggests the usefulness of paying attention to the "affective infrastructure" (Berlant, 2011, p. 49) of the ordinariness of trauma, because this perspective focuses "on the spreading of symbolizations and other inexpressive but life-extending actions throughout the ordinary and its situations of living on" (ibid.). Therefore, human rights violations are not to be found in some distant countries with a 'questionable record' on human rights (Sliwinksi, 2005), but rather in oppressive infrastructure of local institutions, laws, and everyday practices. A history of any contemporaneous moment, then, involves analyzing how suffering is diffused through the ordinary and makes all of us complicit to its perpetuation. "Survival in the present of an ordinary collective life suffused with a historic and historical crisis to which we are always catching up," writes Berlant, "is *the way we live now*" (2011, p. 59, original emphasis).

Furthermore, when one considers the ongoing affective attachments to particular discourses of human rights and HRE, one cannot help but join Berlant (2011) in asking the following: "How and why does this attachment persist? Is it out of habit? Is it in hopes of the potentiality embedded in the political as such? Or, from a stance of critical engagement, an investment in the possibility of its repair?" (p. 227). While Berlant does not provide any definite answers to these questions, she suggests that the point of departure is taking affective attachments seriously and analyzing their consequences in maintaining a regime of cruel optimism. This is what happens, she says, when our

> modes of orientation and having a feeling about it confirm our attachment to the system and thereby confirm the system and the legitimacy of the affects that make one feel bound to it, even if the manifest content of the binding has the negative force of cynicism or the dark attenuation of political depression. [...] The exhausting repetition of the politically depressed position that seeks repair of what may be constitutively broken can eventually split the activity of optimism from expectation and demand. (p. 227)

In other words, cruel optimism eventually makes optimism itself a source of survival that is disassociated from expectations of what can be achieved. For example, considering the historical roots of colonialism, oppression, and racism and their association with ongoing human rights violations, one wonders for how long the dominant universal-liberal model of human rights—which portrays human rights as universal facts grounded in liberal views of rights—will continue to ignore the political conditions of injustice (Baxi, 2007; Donnelly, 2003; Douzinas, 2000, 2007)? Wouldn't this political failure of expectations amount to a form of cruel optimism, because of the attachment to compromised conditions of possibility?

It is striking how these moments of optimism are 'institutionalised' by universal-liberal discourses of human rights often through deploying sentimental pedagogies of affective recognition (Zembylas, 2016). These sentimental pedagogies—such as, for example, the reading of sad and sentimental stories of horrendous suffering which move us to pity, patting ourselves on back, and then resuming our ordinary life—are *used* to establish affective connections, but they are deeply problematic because they create superficial feelings of empathy and solidarity with those who suffer (Kaplan, 2005), while ignoring material/structural conditions of inequality. The belief that a liberal approach of human rights or a sentimental approach of HRE will somehow make things better constitutes, in our view, an instance of cruel optimism, because it focuses our attention on fantasies that are unachievable. More importantly, both of these approaches divert our attention from valuable political questions such as, to paraphrase Berlant's questions quoted earlier: How and why do attachments to a liberal framework of human rights and the dominant discourse of HRE persist? Is it out of habit? Is it in hopes of the potentiality embedded in these practices as such? Or, are they conducted in hopes of their repair? What form can this repair take in order to be critical, compassionate yet not 'cheap sentimentality' (Arendt, 1994, p. 251)? The next part of the chapter turns to exploring how the notions of political depression and cruel optimism can help our struggle of "treading water" (Berlant, 2011, p. 10) in efforts to regenerate HRE.

The Promise of Human Rights Education and Its Critiques

As noted in previous chapters, despite the overproduction of human rights instruments after 1948, the extent of human rights violations all over the world raises the question whether the rhetoric of human rights remains simply an empty and abstract moral ideology (Keet, 2009) that contributes to the climate of political depression rather than working against it. As seen throughout the book, various critiques of human rights in recent years have raised "the problematic consequences of the *desire* for universal human rights," (Hoover, 2013, p. 935) by asking questions not only about the philosophical justification of universal moral rights, but also about the consequences of a supposed universalism of human rights and especially the failure of the human rights paradigm to consider the political conditions of injustice as well as the alignment of the human rights paradigm with neoliberal arrangements (Malabou, 2008). Given that cruel optimism exists when the desire—in this case, the desire for universal human rights—constitutes an obstacle to a pragmatic and critical address of human rights violations, it would not be an exaggeration to claim that certain discourses of human rights may function as cruel optimism.

Human rights are treated as universal and uncontested social good, without pausing to consider how they may be tied onto the global, neoliberal stage on which massive human rights violations are performed. Building on Douzinas's (2013) argument about the 'imprisonment' of human rights in neoliberalism, we have reiterated in this book that the legalistic human rights paradigm has limited the promise of human rights within a regulated and packaged frame. As we already mentioned in Chap. 5, neoliberalism and the legalistic model of human rights gave rise to 'human rights markets' and the commodification of human suffering (Baxi, 2002). There, however, we were discussing it in relation to capital, while here we are interested in the fact that this commodification is generally performed through a traded service that posits sentimentalised images and narratives. Human suffering is commoditised and affectively packaged according to market requirements for human rights entrepreneurs to flourish; human rights and human suffering, from this perspective, have become a regulated service industry. For example, in the contemporary world, people are not sold commodities but the promise of certain feelings e.g. happiness (Ahmed, 2010).

The problematic issue here, of course, as noted in earlier chapters, is not human rights critiques per se, but rather how HRE is historically attuned to the uncritical advancement of human rights universals and its failure to reflect on the consequences of the liberal-declarational model promoted (Al-Daraweesh & Snauwaert, 2013; Coysh, 2014; Keet, 2012; Zembylas, 2014). Al-Daraweesh (2013) argues that there has been gradually constructed a 'conventional approach to human rights education' which is based on a singular conceptualization of human rights as representative of all other conceptualizations. Furthermore, HRE is problematic, argues Coysh (2014), because "Over the years the UN has increasingly controlled the formation of human rights education discourse by gradually institutionalizing and centralizing its production. Doing so [...] it has also enabled the UN to regulate the operation of the discourse by prescribing how human rights should be disseminated" (p. 92). The Universal Declaration of Human Rights, then, has become the blueprint for an HRE curriculum (Lohrenscheit, 2002), by "subjugating a whole range of different forms of knowledge that were discounted or disqualified as nonconceptual or insufficiently elaborate to have a place" (Coysh, 2014, p. 94).

As we have been arguing throughout this book, if human rights educators simply take for granted human rights as universal principles, they will most likely fail to adopt a critical orientation towards both human rights and HRE. In particular, treating human rights as universal principles may have two important consequences. First, this orientation may lead towards a juridical address of human rights in which human rights learning is limited to their presentation as universal legal entitlements for all. A juridical approach fails to capture the local cultural and political complexities of human rights abuses around the world and may inadvertently lead learners to adopt a rationalist perspective. Second, the conventional or a declarational approach to HRE may end up cultivating a 'cheap sentimental' approach to human rights, because even if students are moved from learning about horrendous human rights abuses, this learning does not necessarily lead to a more compassionate response (Sliwinski, 2005). As Sliwinski points out, it may be too much to expect from human rights educators and learners to respond directly to human rights violations, yet the issue of affect and sentimentality cannot be ignored because it interferes with learning about human rights and their violation (see also Abrams, 2011; Zembylas, 2016). In other words, the aim is to gain a notion of human rights learning that moves away from a set of universal principals to a critical inquiry of human rights violations (Adami, 2014) in a way though that touches learners affectively yet not superficially.

Rupturing the dominance of certain forms of HRE means engaging in a systematic and sustained critique of HRE that formulates pedagogically a CHRE. In this chapter, then, we build on efforts in previous chapters to theorize a form of CHRE, by engaging with the concepts of political depression and cruel optimism, to advance the following two major arguments. First, CHRE needs to be rooted in people's everyday experiences, aspirations, concerns and needs (Coysh, 2014), and it is important that it pays attention to the 'ordinariness' of suffering and trauma in the everyday and its affective implications, rather than abiding by abstract and intangible concepts of universal human rights. This conceptualisation of CHRE stands in a critical relationship with human rights universals, while it historicizes human rights violations through a turn to deconstructing the affective politics of these violations. This 'materialist' conceptualization of CHRE produces new vocabularies that could promote 'critical hope' in HRE (see Chap. 7) as a 'reparative' response to cruel optimism.

Second, CHRE needs to advance a social justice-oriented human rights pedagogical practice that develops a language that allows for competing solidarities and political vocabularies that do not reduce the issues of power, justice, struggle, and inequality to a single script (see Chap. 5). Oftentimes, 'packaged' HRE programs reduce social justice to solidarity, while neglecting material/structural conditions of inequality (Zembylas, 2016).[3] This critique highlights the failure to acknowledge the systemic (social, economic, juridical) inequalities and deficiencies of the political system that hinder the implementation of human rights in the first place. Again, while critique is necessary, it is not sufficient and requires new and critical vocabularies of affect; these new vocabularies of affect not only expand the field of HRE but also transform its pedagogies. Therefore, CHRE needs to be a deeply 'reparative' pedagogical formation, if it is going to 'repair' or 'recover' a transformative and productive dialectic of human rights discourse and praxis. The last part of the paper begins to sketch the meaning and contours of this *reparative* pedagogical formation of CHRE.

Reparative Pedagogies in CHRE

The late queer theorist Eve Sedgwick (2003) is one of the first scholars who theorized the term 'reparative' in what she called 'reparative reading', a critical practice that begins from a politically depressed position and seeks repair of what may be broken. Building on Klein's theorization, Sedgwick carves out a 'reparative position' that picks up the fragments of the 'depressive position' to construct a sustainable life. Through reparation, which is largely accomplished through love, according to Klein, the loved object is restored; the ability to make reparation, then, is considered an important quality of healthy life, love, and a foundation for security and trust as the child grows. More generally, reparation becomes a form of restoration and repair against the potential of harming others (Todd, 2003).

Importantly, the reparative position for Sedgwick is not just a critical mode but more generally a *practice*, a way of life that creates productive openings that enable us to redeem the impasse of political depression or the cruel optimism of some of our social or pedagogical interventions. Reparative position, then, is not merely a critical practice of "making visible [...] the hidden traces of oppression and persecution" (Sedgwick, 2003, p. 141), but it is affectively driven and "undertakes a different range of affects, ambitions, and risks" (ibid., p. 150). Critique remains necessary but it is not sufficient, because it requires new vocabularies at the affective level (Berlant, 2011; Cvetkovich, 2012). As Cvetkovich emphasizes, reparative position creates space for strategies beyond those that have been critiqued as melodramatic or sentimental; it critiques liberal forms of affect and takes on the vocabularies of tolerance, diversity and multiculturalism as connected to certain affects that

---

[3] By 'packaged' programs, we remind the reader that we refer to sets of guidelines and practices that are packed together as a collection of activities for human rights teaching and learning. Although these packages offer valuable ideas for promoting human rights, the danger is to utilize these activities in a decontextualized and unsystematic manner that overlooks the social injustices associated with ongoing human rights violations in particular settings. Examples of such 'packaged' programs are: *Compasito* (Council of Europe, 2009a), and *Human Rights Education in the School Systems of Europe, Central Asia and North America: A Compendium of Good Practice* (Council of Europe, 2009b).

are inadequate to, or too conveniently packaged, the difficult legacies of historical trauma, loss, and massive human rights violations. How might an understanding of the notion of reparation be useful in formulating critical pedagogies of HRE—that is, pedagogical practices which enable teachers and students to respond critically and productively to stories of suffering, trauma and human rights violations without idealizing or sentimentalizing these stories?

So far, the term reparation has been used in the work of educational scholars of psychoanalytic origin (e.g. see Britzman 2000; Kelly, 2004; Simon, 2005; Tarc, 2011, Todd, 2003) to formulate what may be called 'reparative pedagogies'—in the plural, because there are potentially many forms of pedagogical practices that can be reparative. This work theorizes the intrapersonal dynamics of psychical reparation through learning from terrible traumatic histories of others. For example, Britzman (2000) focuses on how pedagogical encounters with trauma can offer hope and reparation rather than being stuck in despair and the work of memorializing loss (pp. 33–35). She is concerned with how the curriculum can be organized in a way that does not provide closure but rather possibilities to repair traumatic experiences. Kelly (2004) builds on Britzman's work, emphasizing that understanding how reparation works is essential for a teacher if she or he is to avoid a colonial position in the classroom. "[S]pecifying the context of reparative teaching—what is means to teach across social and cultural differences *in this place*," writes Kelly, "raises issues about the particularity of the repressed history that has not been confronted and has not been mourned effectively" (p. 164).

Simon (2005) uses the notion of reparation in his work on historical remembrance to discuss the ethical demands to response to unimaginable experiences of trauma and loss. Similarly, reparation accompanies Todd's (2003) efforts to respond to stories of suffering, arguing that while reparation has a moral orientation, it cannot fully explain the state of ethical responsibility demanded. As she explains, the point she wants to make is "how it is that *I am* [feeling a sense of reparation] and do not merely feel responsible for an other in light of my guilt. In other words, how are students' utterances of guilt speaking about their own suffering" (ibid., p. 107). Finally, Tarc (2011) theorizes "the intrapersonal and inter-political dynamics of psychical and social reparation" (p. 350), advancing the idea of what she calls 'reparative curriculum'—an attempt to develop and sustain reparative relations in the context of education. Drawing on psychoanalytic and curriculum theory to analyze processes of psychical and social reparation, Tarc extends Britzman's (2000) work through using Butler's theorization to suggest that psychical theories of reparative learning might supplement calls for political and ethical interventions in histories of trauma.

Here we want to extend this analysis by theorising reparative pedagogies as constituted politically through which the urge for reparation is an important aspect of grounding HRE in the 'ordinariness' of suffering and trauma in the everyday, while advancing a social justice-oriented human rights pedagogical practice. In other words, reparative pedagogies in CHRE are essentially critical pedagogies that reconceptualize reparation as both psychical and socio-political work (Zembylas, 2014) of interpreting traumatic histories and seeking just responses through action and activism. Reparative pedagogies are also critical pedagogies in that they enable the use of one's own and others' resources to 'repair' the depressive position of cruel optimism in articulating possible 'responses' to everyday forms of oppression, injustice, and human rights violations.

Importantly, reparative pedagogies in CHRE make no claim to authorizing or bringing closure to articulations of oppression, injustice, and human rights violations. Reparative pedagogies resist idealizing, even implicitly, any program of HRE. As Berlant (2011) puts it forcefully: "How would we know when the 'repair' we intend is not another form of narcissism or smothering will? Just because we sense it to be so?" (p. 124). Todd (2003) also warns us of the dangers of claims about reparation that cannot explain the state of responsibility in responding to stories of suffering; that is, feeling responsible is not the same as being responsible. In other words, reparative pedagogies are not enough in inspiring or constituting ethical responsibility in the classroom; much more work is needed to be done to move from a reparative position to actions that are reparative.

Britzman (2000) would also emphasize that the overvaluation of reparative pedagogies could eventually be unproductive, if they relied too much on the cognitive content of a story and ignored the complex affective implications of stories of suffering. We would further highlight the importance of acknowledging the affective infrastructure of everyday oppression, injustice and human rights violations, that is, the need to historicize violence, oppression, and social injustice and articulate *in practice* the affective connections of one's life to another. Reparative pedagogies move the ego into the space of an other person and his or her traumatic experiences to "make meaning from senselessly shattered sociality and social relations" (Tarc, 2011, p. 355), without idealizing or sentimentalizing those experiences or relations. This is precisely why Tarc's analysis of reparation "is situated on the jagged edge of psychical and social existence, of self and other" (ibid., p. 356). Making reparation is fundamentally a *psychosocial practice* rather than merely a critical mode and this is what reparative pedagogies should aim for, that is, inspiring actions and activism that find even minor ways of 'repairing' shattered sociality and social relations.

Therefore, an essential element of pedagogies of reparation in CHRE is engaging students in political action that enables them not only to examine how seemingly 'noble' ideas human rights are or how they might unwillingly constitute forms of cruel optimism in a culture of political oppression, but also to take action—in their micro-political world of school and community—to 'respond' pragmatically to the brokenness of people and the social injustice. Engaging students in acts of reparation that are grounded in action extending beyond classroom walls infuses reparative pedagogies with the materiality of larger political projects of social justice (e.g. see Butler, 2004, 2009). Butler's work on grievability and common vulnerability with others, for example, instils reparative pedagogies a political efficacy or activist slant that offers an action-orientation. This combination invites new opportunities to engage ethically and politically with traumatic representations of curriculum and grievable lives in both (psychically) reparative and (socially) provocative ways (Farley, 2014; Zembylas, 2014).

Conclusion

This chapter has argued that there is an urgent need to engage with a deeper analysis of the contemporary culture of political depression and its affective implications in human rights education. An attempt was made to articulate some of the content and strategies of pedagogies of reparation and their significance in what is being formulated as critical human rights education. Reparative pedagogies in CHRE invite in the classroom the challenge of how students can learn from unimaginable traumatic histories, while acknowledging the affective politics of histories of violence, oppression, and social injustice so as to better explain the tensions and failures of the human rights paradigm.

The arguments developed here could apply beyond the particular case of HRE to include the development of reparative pedagogies as critical pedagogies in other areas or fields such as peace education, intercultural education or citizenship education. Through such pedagogies, we can practice seeing ourselves and others differently, more compassionately (Kelly, 2004), yet without pity or sentimentality (Zembylas, 2013). As Tarc (2011) writes, a reparative curriculum "offers students and scholars a pedagogical mourning space, a space of collective work where we might grieve violence-stricken thinking, knowledge, and human history" (p. 369). Our analysis in this chapter has emphasized that reparative pedagogies have a lot to by reminding us that a depressive position is not the end of the story, but rather the point of departure for responding productively to cruel optimism. What we can best learn from such pedagogical practices is, perhaps, that human rights violations might find some repair and rest—not at the distant, macro-level, but rather at the everyday, ordinary micro-level of the justice-seeking pedagogies that neither avoid suffering nor fetishise it.

References

Abrams, K. (2011). Emotions in the mobilization of rights. *Harvard Civil Rights-Civil Liberties Law Review, 46*, 551–589.

Adami, R. (2014). Re-thinking relations in human rights education: The politics of narratives. *Journal of Philosophy of Education, 48*(2), 293–307.

Ahmed, S. (2000). *Strange encounters: Embodied others in post-coloniality*. London: Routledge.

Ahmed, S. (2004). *The cultural political of emotion*. Edinburgh, UK: Edinburgh University Press.

Ahmed, S. (2010). *The promise of happiness*. Durham, NC: Duke University Press.

Al-Daraweesh, F. (2013). Human rights and human rights education: Beyond the conventional approach. *In Factis Pax, 7*(1), 38–58.

Al-Daraweesh, F., & Snauwaert, D. (2013). Towards a hermeneutical theory of international human rights education. *Educational Theory, 63*(4), 389–411.

Amsler, S. (2011). From 'therapeutic' to political education: The centrality of affective sensibility in critical pedagogy. *Critical Studies in Education, 52*(1), 47–63.

Arendt, H. (1994). *Eichmann in Jerusalem: A report on the banality of evil*. New York: Penguin Books.

Athanasiou, A., Hantzaroula, P., & Yannakopoulos, K. (2008). Towards a new epistemology: The 'affective turn'. *Historein, 8*, 5–16.

Baxi, U. (2002). *The future of human rights*. New Delhi, India: Oxford University Press.

Baxi, U. (2007). *Human rights in a posthuman world*. New Delhi, India: Oxford University Press.

Bekerman, Z., & Zembylas, M. (2012). *Teaching contested narratives: Identity, memory and reconciliation in peace education and beyond*. Cambridge, UK: Cambridge University Press.

Berlant, L. (Ed.). (2004). *Compassion: The culture and politics of an emotion*. New York/London: Routledge.

Berlant, L. (2008). *The female complaint: The unfinished business of sentimentality in American culture*. Durham, NC: Duke University Press.

Berlant, L. (2011). *Cruel optimism*. Durham, NC: Duke University Press.

Boler, M. (1999). *Feeling power: Emotions and education*. London: Routledge.

Britzman, D. P. (2000). If the story cannot end: Deferred action, ambivalence and difficult knowledge. In R. I. Simon, S. Rosenberg, & C. Eppert (Eds.), *Between hope and despair: Pedagogy and the representation of historical trauma* (pp. 27–58). Lanham, MD: Rowman & Littlefield.

Butler, J. (2004). *Precarious life: The powers of mourning and violence*. London: Verso.

Butler, J. (2009). *Frames of war: When life is grievable*. London: Verso.

Clough, P. (2007). Introduction. In P. Clough & J. Halley (Eds.), *The affective turn: Theorizing the social* (pp. 1–33). Durham, NC: Duke University Press.

Council of Europe. (2009a). *Compasito: Manual on human rights education for children*. Strasburg, France: Council of Europe Publishing.

Council of Europe. (2009b). *Human rights education in the school systems of Europe, Central Asia and North America: A compendium of good practice*. Strasburg, France: Council of Europe Publishing.

Coysh, J. (2014). The dominant discourse of human rights education: A critique. *Journal of Human Rights Practice, 6*(1), 89–114.

Cvetkovich, A. (2003). *An archive of feelings: Trauma, sexuality, and lesbian public cultures*. Durham, NC: Duke University Press.

Cvetkovich, C. (2012). *Depression: A public feeling*. Durham, NC: Duke University Press.

Da Costa, D. (2014). Cruel optimism and waiting for belonging: Towards a global political of affect. *Cultural Studies, 30*(1), 1–23. https://doi.org/10.1080/09502386.2014.899607

Donnelly, J. (2003). *Universal human rights in theory and practice* (2nd ed.). Ithaca, NY: Cornell University Press.

Douzinas, C. (2000). *The end of human rights: Critical legal thought at the turn of the century*. Oxford, UK: Hart Publishing.

Douzinas, C. (2007). *Human rights and empire: The political philosophy of cosmopolitanism*. Oxford/New York, UK: Routledge-Cavendish.

Douzinas, C. (2013). *Philosophy and resistance in the crisis*. Cambridge, UK: Polity Press.

Eng, D., & Kazanjian, D. (2003). *Loss: The politics of mourning*. Berkeley, CA: University of California Press.

Farley, L. (2014). Psychoanalytic notes on the status of depression in curriculum affected by histories of loss. *Pedagogy, Culture & Society, 22*(1), 117–136.

Flatley, J. (2008). *Affective mapping: Melancholia and the politics of modernism*. Cambridge, MA: Harvard University Press.

Hoover, J. (2013). Towards a politics of human rights: Ambiguous humanity and democratizing rights. *Philosophy & Social Criticism, 39*(9), 935–961.

Horowitz, A., & Wakefield, J. (2007). *The loss of sadness: How psychiatry transformed normal sorrow into depressive disorder*. Oxford, UK: Oxford University Press.

Kaplan, A. (2005). *Trauma culture: The politics of terror and loss in media and literature*. New Brunswick, NJ: Rutgers University Press.

Keet, A. (2009). Reflections on the colloquium within a human rights discourse. In M. Nkomo & S. Vandeyar (Eds.), *Thinking diversity, building cohesion: A transnational dialogue on education* (pp. 211–220). Amsterdam, The Netherlands: Rozenberg Publishers.

Keet, A. (2010). *Human rights education: A conceptual analysis*. Saarbrücken, Germany: Lambert Academic Publishing.

Keet, A. (2012). Discourse, betrayal, critique: The renewal of human rights education. In C. Roux (Ed.), *Safe spaces: Human rights education in diverse contexts* (pp. 7–27). Rotterdam, The Netherlands: Sense Publishers.

Kelly, U. A. (2004). The place of reparation: Love, loss, ambivalence and teaching. In D. Liston & J. Garrison (Eds.), *Teaching, learning, and loving: Reclaiming passion in educational practice* (pp. 153–167). New York: RoutledgeFalmer.

Klein, M. (1984). Love, guilt and reparation. In M. Klein (Ed.), *Love, guilt, and reparation, and other works, 1921–1945* (pp. 306–343). New York: The Free Press. (Original work published 1937).

Kristeva, J. (2001). *Melanie Klein* (R. Guberman, Trans.). New York: Columbia University Press.

Lohrenscheit, C. (2002). International approaches in human rights education. *International Review of Education, 48*(3–4), 173–185.

Lorde, A. (1984). *Sister outside: Essays and speeches by Audre Lorde*. Freedom, CA: Crossing Press.

Malabou, C. (2008). *What should we do with our brains?* New York: Fordham University Press.

Moyn, S. (2014). A powerless companion: Human rights in the age of neoliberalism. *Law and Contemporary Problems, 77*(4), 147–169.

Pedwell, C., & Whitehead, A. (2012). Affecting feminism: Questions of feeling in feminist theory. *Feminist Theory, 13*(2), 115–129.

Rand, E. (2015). Bad feelings in public: Rhetoric, affect, and emotion. *Rhetoric & Public Affairs, 18*(1), 161–176.

Rice, J. (2008). The new "new": Making a case for critical affect studies. *Quarterly Journal of Speech, 94*(2), 200–212.

Sedgwick, E. (2003). *Touching feeling: Affect, pedagogy, performativity*. Durham, NC: Duke University Press.

Simon, R. I. (2005). *The touch of the past: Remembrance, learning, ethics*. New York: Palgrave.

Sliwinski, S. (2005). Thinking without banisters: Toward a compassionate inquiry into human rights education. *Educational Theory, 55*(2), 219–230.

Tarc, A. M. (2011). Reparative curriculum. *Curriculum Inquiry, 41*(3), 350–372.

Taubman, P. (2009). *Teaching by numbers: Deconstructing the discourse of standards and accountability in education*. New York: Routledge.

Todd, S. (2003). *Learning from the other: Levinas, psychoanalysis and ethical possibilities in education*. Albany, NY: State University of New York Press.

Young, I. M. (1990). *Justice and the politics of difference*. Princeton, NJ: Princeton University Press.

Zembylas, M. (2013). The 'crisis of pity' and the radicalization of solidarity: Towards critical pedagogies of compassion. *Educational Studies: A Journal of the American Educational Studies Association, 49*, 504–521.

Zembylas, M. (2014). The teaching of patriotism and human rights: An uneasy entanglement and the contribution of critical pedagogy. *Educational Philosophy and Theory, 46*(10), 1143–1159.

Zembylas, M. (2016). Towards a critical-sentimental orientation in human rights education. *Educational Philosophy and Theory, 48*(11), 1151–1167.

Chapter 7
Plasticity, Critical Hope and the Regeneration of Human Rights Education

Introduction

In the previous chapter we considered how disavowal of the link between the political sphere and affect could lead to cheap sentimentalism in HRE. Specifically, we suggested that the notion of political depression offered an alternative understanding of depression beyond the individual and the pathologised that this might also produce new forms of hope. The present chapter offers a plastic reading of 'critical hope' as a 'left over' form of a radical and transformative HRE that has not yet materialised. The premise of our argument, as has been built up in previous chapters, is that generally HRE has, despite its "explosive reserves" Malabou (2011, p. 85), developed into an unproductive and declarationist pedagogy that works against the 'critical.' Using Malabou's concept of 'plasticity' which follows, in our logic, from Derrida's deconstruction, a case is made that the regeneration of HRE can best be conceived of on the level of 'left over' forms. This line of reasoning advances from an engagement with the concepts of 'plasticity' and 'deconstruction,' linked to a critique of HRE. It provides the basis to argue that 'critical hope' is both a 'left over' form of current conceptions of HRE and is constitutive of its radicalisation.

As seen from previous chapters, HRE is currently one of the most dominant pedagogical formations within the cluster of peace, democracy and citizenship education. This dominance is derived from the ascendancy of the human rights language within the global geo-political discourse of the United Nations and the ensuing human rights standards. The massive injection of resources that has gone into the explosion of HRE over the past 30 years (Suarez, 2006; Suarez & Ramirez, 2004) argues with reference to *the* analyses of Mouffe, Brown, Butler, Ranciere, Derrida and others, to the "deadening effects of rights-centred constitutionalism on spontaneous political action" (Honig, 2006, p. 170). Honig (2006) argues for a kind of rights that continuously agitates against even the very laws within which *they* are

M. Zembylas, A. Keet, *Critical Human Rights Education*, Contemporary Philosophies and Theories in Education 13,
https://doi.org/10.1007/978-3-030-27198-5_7

inscribed. This agitation should have been a function of a radical HRE within which political action could take rational form. *The* absence of such radicalism is a consequence of the deadening effects of which Honig speaks, constituted, in part, by an unproductive and uncritical HRE. Human rights education needs regeneration and such regeneration, to our minds, can best be conceptualised within the scheme of 'plasticity.'

Critical hope is encrypted into the aspirational logic of human rights that permeates HRE (Andreopoulous & Claude, 1997; Bajaj, 2011; Flowers, 2004; Lynch, Modgil, & Modgil, 1992). Therefore, in this instance, it has to protrude as that which is 'left over' from a demand for a radical HRE that did not materialise over the past 20 years (Keet, 2010, 2012). Non-materialisation of this kind takes shape against the backdrop of massive social pathologies as the canvas on which 'hopelessness' adopts a variety of meanings. One of these relates to a growing acknowledgement that current forms of HRE do not match up to the hope on which the dominance of the human rights discourse is found.

Drawing from previous chapters, a CHRE constructs a relationship of 'questioning' between itself and the human rights universals that it is tasked to legitimate. Such questioning will uncover *the* 'explosive reserves' of HRE to resist and rebel against the domination of power in pursuit of social justice. This is the radicalised version of HRE that has not *yet* materialised. This conception of the critical and critique gives meaning to the critical in 'critical hope' as an 'educated hope' (Giroux, 2009). As will be discussed later, we conceive of critical hope as the "straining forward movement" toward the 'event,' as Derrida (1999, p. 248) would have it, or toward the "immanent possibilities in a given situation" as Delanty (2011) argues. These potentialities are dependent on the 'regenerative' which can, in turn, best be rethought on the level of the left over. That is, regeneration requires a de-layering movement that can excavate what is left over from the promising inscription of 'critical hope' into HRE. From this plane, a transformative reconstitution of HRE can be launched which both perpetually regenerates itself and continually renews critical hope within its own inscription. These are the 'explosive reserves' that Malabou (2011) may have in mind for HRE. That is, to 'repair' or to 'recover,' are most productive on the level of the left over as a transformative dialectic *steered* by plastic reading.

The left over is given shape by the notion of plasticity which can only become intelligible in conversation with deconstruction, which in turn has *logocentrism* as its main focus of critique according to Mikics's (2009) intellectual biography of Derrida. Human rights *were* not spared this critique. Thus, even though deconstruction's battle with *logocentrism* as a 'metaphysics of presence' is not the main focus of this chapter, its critique of human rights invites plasticity as a conceptual frame for, at least, considering the future pedagogical viabilities of a critical hope as the left-over form of a radical HRE that *never* came into being.

Plasticity, Malabou (2010, p. 52) argues, is the "shape or form of that which remains or survives in *the* wake of deconstruction." In the case of HRE, critical hope, we suggest, is inscribed in these left-over shapes. Stated differently, it was there already as a *kernel.* Likewise, associated pedagogical formations such as democracy and citizenship education (see Chap. 9 where we discuss the entanglements of HRE with these types of education) are simultaneously fashioned on critical hope on the one hand, and driven by explicit aspirational standards and hopeful content on the other. No doubt, scholars of Dewey and Freire will argue that these connections are historically common within critical pedagogies. The point here is that these relatively new pedagogical formations owe their very architectures to a certain 'idea of hope' that is converted into and reduced to human rights standards.

In most instances critical hope is perceived as having disappeared ironically under the weight of the standards which aim to express it, while there is a dominant view that HRE potentially is the most productive pedagogical formation in relation to critical hope. This is underscored by the adoption of the United Nations Declaration on Human Rights Education and Training (UNDHRET) on 19 December 2011 (resolution 66/137), a landmark moment in the history of HRE (see Chap. 2). The attraction of HRE in relation to critical hope lies in it being able to conceive of critical hope in an integrated and relational genre, cutting across the various foci of and approaches to HRE, and straddling moral, legal, social and political conceptions (Roux, 2012). Herein rests the potential productivity of HRE in developing holistic notions of critical hope as pedagogical principles that can respond to the overwhelming pessimistic élan of despair.

Plasticity and the 'Left Over' Forms of Human Rights Education

> Human rights education and training comprises all educational, training, information, awareness-raising and learning activities aimed at promoting universal respect for and observance of all human rights and fundamental freedoms and thus contributing, inter alia, to the prevention of human rights violations and abuses by providing persons with knowledge, skills and understanding and developing their attitudes and behaviours, to empower them to contribute to the building and promotion of a universal culture of human rights (Article 2, UNDHRET).

Following this definition of HRE, article four of UNDHRET provides that HRE should *be* based on the "principles of the Universal Declaration of Human Rights (UDHR) and relevant treaties and instruments" (GA 66/137). This refers to more than 200 human rights instruments. Official United Nations documents describe human rights as rights inherent to all human beings as expressed in "treaties and other sources of law at the national regional and international levels" which go under the collective term of "international human rights instruments (treaties, declarations, principles, recommendations, guidelines, etc.)" (UN NGLS, 2008, p. v).

Given the massive expansion of rights standards over the past 60 year, we are, without doubt, in an age of rights (Baxi, 2008), paradoxically as the inverted hope against the human suffering that is endemic to the world. The conventional version of HRE which we are consistently arguing against in this book, has allowed for 'naïve hope' to undercut the transformative potential of what should be one of the most powerful pedagogical endeavours in contemporary times. The perceived legitimacy of human rights universals constructed HRE free from the demand of *pedagogical justification.* Consequently, because it could not set up and maintain the necessary critical distance between rights and its educational form, HRE became the legitimating extension of human rights itself. It thus aided in what Slaughter (2007, p. 2) describes as human rights that have reached rhetorical, juridical and political hegemony. This makes critical deconstructive analyses of HRE toilsome, partly because a morally and diplomatically legitimated set of human rights standards have layered the possible *kernels* of the *radical form* of HRE to such an extent that careful 'excavations' are required. Nevertheless, such analyses have been and are important because they may just be *the* most productive movement in the reconstitution of HRE, especially in exploring the conditions that allowed such layering to materialise in the first place. It is to this possibility that we now turn our argument by risking a discussion on deconstruction and plasticity in relation to the *regenerative* options available to HRE.

Derrida (1998, p. 27) argues that deconstruction "undeniably obeys an *analytic* exigency, at once critical and analytic" and always steering towards "*undoing, desedimenting, decomposing, deconstituting* sediments, *artefacta,* presuppositions, institutions [...]." This unbinding insists on the "irreducibility of difference" and the possibility and desire to recapture "the originary."

> Very schematically: an opposition of metaphysical concepts (for example, speech/writing, presence/absence, etc.) is never the face-to-face of two terms, but a hierarchy and an order of subordination. Deconstruction cannot limit itself or proceed immediately to a neutralisation: it must, by means of a double gesture, a double science, a double writing, practice an overturning of the classical opposition and a general displacement of the system [...] Deconstruction does not consist in passing from one concept to another, but in overturning and displacing a conceptual order, as well as the non-conceptual order with which the conceptual order is articulated. (Derrida, 1982, p. 329)

In an intricate series of studies by Derrida (Mikics, 2009), deconstruction has the metaphysics of presence and logocentrism as its target. The overturning and displacement of this system invokes its de-constitution. From this basis, deconstruction's movement of decomposing structures and practices establishes the referral to difference and otherness as an "asystematic reserve, a non-present remainder or heterogeneous other which exceeds all structures and systems even while making them possible [...]. Deconstruction affirms an inappropriable difference, or the repressed other [...]" (Wortham, 2009, p. 38). The asystematic reserve, though repressed, constitutes in part, the privileged centre of meaning. Thus, Taylor (2004) writing for the *New York Times,* suggests that the "guiding insight of deconstruction is that every structure [...] that organises our experience is constituted and maintained through acts of exclusion."

Applying this reading to HRE will inevitably lead to questioning the privileged centre of meaning-making that is based on "an epistemology of diplomatic consensus" (Keet, 2007; see also Chap. 1). That is, the truth indices of rights reside in the trade-offs of the diplomatic processes of the United Nations in Geneva and New York. Moreover, HRE uncritically imports 'diplomatic truths' to frame the real-life experiences of individuals and groups in the image of such truths. But, such authority of truth can be over turned. For instance, refugee rights, instead of a *humanitarian* reading, may be interpreted as attempts at justifying the governance of the 'foreign' body within the logic of the nation state. For this reason, Soguk's (1999) *States and Strangers: Refugees and Displacements of Statecraft* offers a great example of a deconstructive reading in the field of human rights. The international construction of *refugee rights* can thus be shown to disclose the asystematic reserves of the inappropriable differences that it represses, and the violence that it allows, theoretically and materially. Privileging and repression, in this sense, serve the purposes of a discursive regime such as law and human rights to "constitute and regulate, imagine and test, kinds of subjects, subjectivities and social formations" (Slaughter, 2007, p. 8). Similarly, Brown (2002, p. 459) argues that human rights "produce and regulate the subjects to whom they are assigned." In this scheme, HRE is the major conduit through which the strategies of regulation are legitimised. Even in this troubling example of refugee rights, there are left over forms after deconstruction. Other examples may also be offered.

Tie (2009), in response to the dislocations of human rights ensuing from deconstructive and 'postmodern' readings, suggests that such movements may close the possibility of the political commitments that accompany human rights. Taking issue with Ignatieff's (2004) and Tie (2009) argument that human rights allow for "the betrayal of liberty in the name of its defence" and Douzinas's (2000) and Tie (2009) "analysis of the complicity of human rights in the centralisation of political power," Tie (2009, p. 89) argues that human rights may incite political contest with the "express purpose of giving effect to the materiality of the representations through which observing subjects encounter violations of human rights." How such materiality is uncovered is, of course, not this straightforward; neither is the claim that human rights can give effect to a materiality that is suffocated by standards. However, the possibility of the claim resides in plasticity, *after* the de-layering of standards. That is, the 'left over' forms of the political commitments of human rights may be re-activated by deconstructive readings and regenerated by a plastic reading.

What would be regarded as the substantive shifts between deconstruction and plasticity? We will limit our argument here to 'form,' a concept which seems to signify one of the major movements from Derrida's deconstruction to Malabou's plasticity. The metaphysics, against which Derrida battles, refers, in his under standing, to "the search for an essence behind or above sensible appearances" (Mikics, 2009, p. 1). The task of a deconstructive reading is to show that such essences do not exist as privileged centres of meaning-making. Form, for Derrida, has such an intonation of 'essence.' He thus opts for 'trace' and argues that trace dissociates itself from form. The key to tracing the 'trace' resides in Derrida's treatment of the 'sign' in writing:

> If every sign acquires its value only on the strength of its difference from other signs, nevertheless other signs leave their trace in the sense that they are constitutive of the difference that maintains the sign's identity. Every sign bears the traces of the others from which it differs, but to which it also deters in order to receive its value as a (differential) sign. The trace is thus not reducible to the sign, nor can it be turned into a sign. (Wortham, 2009, pp. 229–230)

The trace does not present itself as an essence or an originating kernel of meaning, because it can be substituted by other concepts such as *différance* or *supplement*. It appears as 'presence' with the traces of others that are 'absent' and thus escapes the metaphysical binary of presence/absence. However, the location of trace outside of metaphysics also places it outside of 'metamorphosis,' outside of 'transformation.' Therefore, deconstruction may limit the transformation it aspires to, given the rejection of form. "Inconvertible," is how Malabou (2010, p. 47) describes the trace's relationship to form: the trace cannot be converted to form since "the graphic element (of otherwise than Being) – namely the trace – definitely dissociates itself from the plastic element (of Being) – namely form." But one "must be in good shape to welcome the trace" argues Malabou (2010, p. 49), and thus she does not "believe in the absence of form or in a possible beyond of form [...] Form is the metamorphisable but immovable barrier of thought." The shift from deconstruction to plasticity now emerges as plasticity retains the transformable form that deconstruction rejects as metaphysical, even though the trace, as Malabou has showed, requires a 'shape' to welcome it. This explains plasticity's focus on the 'left over forms and shapes' in the wake of deconstruction. It is thus possible, and it is towards this possibility that we are now directing our attention, to argue that these forms are productive elements of and the necessary requirements for metamorphosis, transformation, change and regeneration.

Malabou's (2005) *The Future of Hegel* re-introduces the concept of plasticity to mean "the capacity to receive form and the capacity to produce form" (p. 9). Plasticity also refers to a philosophical attitude that Hegel described as a "sense of receptivity and understanding on the part of the listener" (p. 10) which Malabou (2005) paraphrased as the reader and interlocutor being "receptive to the form, but they in their turn are led to construct and form what they hear and read." She interprets Hegel's dialectic as a process of plasticity, "a movement where formation and dissolution, novelty and anticipation, are in continual inter play" (During, 2000, p. 191). Hegel's dialectic does not lead, as generally inter prated, to a closure, but to a future that is open (p. 192). Steering away from 'transcendentalist' readings of Hegel, Malabou (2011, p. 65) insists that plasticity is "not an empty, transcendental instance." Rather, plastic reading is a "new, transformed type of structural approach" that "moves beyond what might appear to be the decisive limitations" of the deconstructive readings inaugurated by her teacher, Derrida (James, 2012, p. 84). In essence, plasticity is the "shape or form of that which remains or survives in the wake of deconstruction," a "movement or passage between the formation and dissolution of form" (James, 2012, p. 84).

The dialectic is regenerated as a forward movement because of its plasticity (Crockett, 2011, p. xii) and therefore 'plasticity' might "power social, economic, political and personal transformation" (Shread, 2010, p. xxx). On the *regenerative* inscription of transformation into dialectic, Malabou (2011, p. 88) suggests that "regenerative plasticity [does] … speak to us of [...] regeneration without sublation," without (Hegelian) *Aufhebung*. In this instance, Malabou writes about plasticity in relation to the neurobiological sciences via the plasticity of the brain; the insights from regenerative medicines; and the biological capacities for regeneration in, for instance, the salamander (Malabou, 2011). Thus, in terms of analytical productivity, 'regenerative plasticity' without total negation or sublation surpasses the analytical movement of the 'deconstruction of form'. Here, human rights and HRE are provided with *a way out.* It may reconstitute, transform and regenerate itself around the left-over shapes in a plastic movement *after* deconstruction.

How may HRE go about these non-normative movements as located within a plastic reading where HRE has to live the deconstruction of human rights, and thus its own? It must be open to deconstructive analyses to excavate its radical potential which has been suffocated by the massive off-load of human rights standards onto the principle of rights. Baudrillard (1999, pp. 273–274) would have argued that these standards have expelled human rights from its own principle. There is a case to be made for a strangled or expelled principle (Baxi, 2008, 2009) if the dominant moral, political, juridical and rhetorical language of our time itself dissolves into the social pathologies it has to address. This, we contend, seems to be *the* case with human rights, and HRE. Nevertheless, plasticity would suggest that the left-over form of the principle of rights can *be* regenerated so as to result in a metamorphosis of human rights itself.

Douzinas's (2006, p. 626) critique has shown that the collapse of human rights into legal rights resulted in human rights forfeiting the critical distance necessary for "dissent, resistance, and rebellion against the domination of power, the oppression of wealth and the injustice of law." Human rights were thus already conscripted into serving the domination of power. Douzinas's deconstructive reading follows from Derrida's *Force of Law* (1992) in which his "primary concern in relation to justice is to distinguish between law and justice," to "insist right away on reserving *the* possibility of a justice, indeed of a law that not only exceeds or contradicts 'law' *(droit)* but also, perhaps, has no relation to law, or maintains such a strange relation to it that it may just as well command the *'droit'* that excludes it" (Briggs, 2001, pp. 257–258; Derrida, 1992, pp. 5–6). Again, here, there is a law by the name of 'justice' that exceeds law (*droit)* as dependent on enforceability and, as such, is located beyond the limits of law itself (Borradori, 2003, p. 164). This justice may mandate the very law that excludes it. The implications for HRE should be shattering-transformative. Collapsing human rights into legal rights combines them into *droit* with the possibility of placing *justice* outside the operational horizons of human rights itself. Human rights education is therefore pre-determined by the institution of human rights as *droit* and suffers law's resistance towards deconstructive analysis which renders a 'plastic transformative' reading challenging.

Critical Hope and the Regeneration of Human Rights Education

As a professional field with its associated discourses, a conscious movement towards deconstructive readings seems to us a viable option to regenerate HRE. Nothing, in this context, would be closer to inertia and self-annihilation if our field does not respond to this challenge. This would simply be a first step to allow plastic readings. Following Malabou, there will be a 'left over' form of HRE after deconstruction which we chose to name 'critical hope' as that what which we regard to be an originary inscription into HRE. In what follows, we link critical hope to the 'political' to remain consistent with Malabou's materiality of form, the materiality of plasticity and her aversion to a 'transcendental' interpretation and a *beyond* of form.

Benhabib (2011), in *Dignity in Adversity: Human Rights in Troubled Times,* engages with the complexities of a human rights disclosed by deconstruction where her brand of cosmopolitanism does not denote "a privileged attitude but rather, a field of unresolved contrasts" (p. 2). We see here again the kind of sensibility apparent in Arendt's focus on aporia (see Chap. 4). This kind of cosmopolitanism is required because our times are "inhospitable to the practice of critique – especially self critique; … [the] resignation to the contracting space of possibilities" (Kompridis 2006, p. 247) is palpable. With the dissolution of these possibilities, the future "may no longer to be open to us, no longer welcoming" (Kompridis, 2006, p. 247). This confirms our earlier analyses of human rights and HRE in previous chapters of this book, especially those analyses that cover the period of the last two decades. That is, it is a symptom of total scepticism and despair to have an overload of human rights standards in the midst of unproductive social action, or inaction, against the human rights violations that are littering our social landscape. To counter this, Benhabib (2011, p. 192), following Bloch (1986), calls for the "revitalisation of a utopian tradition for without hope alternative politics becomes impossible."

In Zournazi's (2002) *Hope: New Philosophies of Change,* Mouffe and Laclau tie hope to "the passions that make up our everyday reflections on the world, and to our political activities" (p. 122). The short supply of hope, for Rorty (1999), is linked to the positioning of the philosophy of language and the foci on 'identity' and 'difference' which seem to "result in a loss of hope" or an "inability to construct a plausible narrative of progress" (p. 232). Hope, in the context of a Deweyan social democracy, is for Rorty (1999) located in a utopia in which the "moral identity of every human being is constituted in large part [...] by his or her sense of participation in a democratic society" (p. 238). A critical formulation of HRE may contribute to such a sense as is already assumed in curriculum formulations in various parts of the world. We are, limitedly so, uneasy with the concept of hope as linked to *utopia,* that is so say, "that which can never be real" (Cheah & Guerlac, 2009, p. 23). Derrida (Cheah & Guerlac, 2009) argues that utopia "can too easily be associated with dreams" whilst the 'impossible' is a "movement to desire, action, and decision: it is the figure of the very real. It has its hardness, closeness, and urgency" (p. 23).

In his engagement with Marxism, via *Spectres of Marx* (1994) and *Ghostly Demarcations* (1999), Derrida also frames the messianic as referring to "the coming of *the* eminently real, concrete event [...] [a] straining forward toward the event" which makes it "inseparable from a promise and an injunction that call for commitment without delay" (Derrida, 1999, pp. 248–249). Here, Derrida's formulations of 'impossibility' and the 'messianic' are associated with the political conception of 'critical hope' which takes on a 'material dimension' through plastic reading.

We align ourselves with conceptions of critical hope that are tied to Derrida's 'straining forward toward an event' works within Benhabib's cosmopolitanism; are rooted in Mouffe and Laclau's understanding of hope as located in the political; aims at developing Rorty's plausible narrative of progress; and which is inseparable from Derrida's insistence on a commitment without delay. This framing of 'critical hope' can seamlessly transfer to the critical pedagogies of Freire (1995, 2007) and McLaren (2000). Freire is an obvious candidate for a conceptual rooting of 'critical hope' and, as Burawoy and Von Holdt (2012, p. 111) argue, he "is much more optimistic than Bourdieu, for he sees within the psyche two selves, the humanistic individual and the oppressor; the true self and the false self." Freire thus substitutes Bourdieu's socio analysis with a "heavy dose of psychoanalysis" (Burawoy & Von Holdt, 2012, p. 111). It is the 'humanism' of Freire, which anchors his 'pedagogy of hope' (1995). Further, Freire's later collaborator, Giroux (2009, p. 3), thinks of 'educated hope' in an instructive and productive manner:

> Hope,[...], is the precondition for individual and social struggle, the ongoing practice of critical education in a wide variety of sites [...] But hope is also a referent for civic courage and its ability to mediate the memory of loss and the experience of injustice as part of a broader attempt to open up new locations of struggle.

Giroux's educated hope has to be integrated with the moral imperatives of hope within Rorty's analyses, and the Derridean ethical commitment towards the other without delay, which is a 'straining forward movement'. A HRE that has this kind of hope inscribed in its make-up will be transformative. Critical hope, as argued, is, in the case of HRE, the name given to the left-over form *after* deconstruction. A HRE that lives the deconstruction of human rights can regenerate itself around the left-over form in a plastic movement of a dialectic that is infinitely transformative and affirmative. Douzinas (2006) may then see HRE as that which pedagogically develops the activist and social justice qualities of human rights *per se*. The dissent, resistance, and rebellion against the "domination of power, the oppression of wealth and the injustice of law" (Douzinas, 2006, p. 626) may well turn out to be *the* new thickness around the left-over form and *kernel* of HRE. Plasticity suggests that this thickness will continually be the subject of a transformative dialectic.

Conclusion

The social theoretical argument that we pursue in this chapter has a simple aim and attempts a modest contribution. The following claims are made. First, HRE is constituted by and constitutes the élan of despair that has paralyzed its potential as a radical pedagogical form. Second, HRE has evolved into a conservative educational form with an uncritical relationship with human rights universals and law. Third, HRE is meant to be radical simply in terms of the purpose historically assigned to human rights as the counterpoint of the domination of power. Fourth, HRE pedagogically failed to nurture the radical possibilities of human rights and has contributed to its sterility and that of its own. Fifth, the massive project of human rights standards generation provided HRE with a legitimacy that had the consequence of layering imprisonment. That is, HRE became the pedagogical arm of human rights in a relationship of reciprocal legitimisation, with negative consequences for its self-radicalisation. Sixth, HRE must live its own deconstruction and that of human rights to disclose its own 'left over' form that goes by the name of 'critical hope,' and which was originally etched into its logic and purpose. Seventh, plasticity enters *after* deconstruction to provide HRE with the conceptual architecture to regenerate and re-constitute itself around the left-over form of 'critical hope' as a process of radicalisation to be infinitely moderated by a plastic reading of transformative dialectics. Eighth, HRE has to recover the hospitality of critique whose absence is precisely one of the symptoms of the loss of critical hope.' That is, the very critical distance between HRE and the universals that it is mandated to teach is an additional space for encrypting critical hope that makes 'resistance' and activism possible.

References

Andreopoulous, G. J., & Claude, R. P. (Eds.). (1997). *Human rights education for the twenty-first century*. Philadelphia: University of Pennsylvania Press.

Bajaj, M. (2011). Human rights education: Ideology, location, and approaches. *Human Rights Quarterly, 33*, 481–508.

Baudrillard, J. (1999). The perfect crime. In O. Savic (Ed.), *The politics of human rights* (pp. 273–280). London: Verso.

Baxi, U. (2008). *The future of human rights* (3rd ed.). New Delhi, India: Oxford University Press.

Baxi, U. (2009). *Human rights in a posthuman world*. New Delhi, India: Oxford University Press.

Benhabib, S. (2011). *Dignity in adversity: Human rights in troubled times*. Cambridge, UK: Polity Press.

Bloch, E. (1986). *The principle of hope*. Cambridge, MA: MIT Press.

Borradori, G. (2003). *Philosophy in a time of terror*. Chicago: University of Chicago Press.

Briggs, R. (2001). Just traditions? Deconstruction, critical legal studies, and analytic jurisprudence. *Social Semiotics, 11*, 257–274.

Brown, W. (2002). Suffering the paradoxes of rights. In W. Brown & J. E. Halley (Eds.), *Left legalism/left critique* (pp. 418–432). Durham, NC: Duke University Press.

Burawoy, M., & Von Holdt, K. (2012). *Conversations with Bourdieu*. Johannesburg, South Africa: Wits University Press.

Cheah, P., & Guerlac, S. (2009). *Derrida and the time of the political*. Durham, NC: Duke University Press.

Crockett, C. (2011). Foreword. In C. Malabou (Ed.), *Plasticity at the dusk of writing* (pp.?). New York: Columbia University Press.

Delancy, G. (2011). 'Varieties of critique in sociological theory' and their methodological implications for social research. *Irish Journal of Sociology, 19*, 68–92.

Derrida, J. (1982). Signature event context. In *Margins of philosophy* (page numbers) (A. Bass, Trans.). Chicago: University of Chicago Press.

Derrida, J. (1992). Force of law: 'The mystical foundation of authority'. In D. Cornell, M. Rosenfeld, & D. G. Carlson (Eds.), *Deconstruction and the possibility of justice* (pp. 3–67). New York: Routledge.

Derrida, J. (1994). *Specters of Marx*. London: Routledge.

Derrida, J. (1998). *Resistances of psychoanalysis*. Stanford, CA: Stanford University Press.

Derrida, J. (1999). Marx & sons. In M. Sprinker (Ed.), *Ghostly demarcations* (pp. 213–269). London: Verso.
Douzinas, C. (2000). *The end of human rights: Critical legal theory at the turn of the century*. Oxford, UK: Hart Publishing.
Douzinas, C. (2006). 'Left or rights?' In T. Campbell (Ed.), *Review of rights: A critical introduction, Journal of Law & Society*.
During, L. (2000). The future of Hegel: Plasticity, temporality, dialectic. *Hypatia, 15*, 196–220.
Flowers, N. (2004). How to define human rights education? A complex answer to a simple question. In B. B. Georgi & M. Seberich (Eds.), *International perspectives in human rights education*. Gütersloh, Germany: Bertelsmann Foundation Publishers.
Freire, P. (1995). *Pedagogy of hope*. New York: Continuum.
Freire, P. (2007). *Pedagogy of the oppressed*. New York: Continuum.
Giroux, H. (2009). *The audacity of educated hope*. Retrieved from http://www.counterpunch.org/2009/01/23/the-audacity-of-educated-hope/
Honig, B. (2006). Dead rights, live futures. In L. Thomassen (Ed.), *The DerridaHabermas reader*. Chicago: University of Chicago Press.
Ignatieff, M. (2004). *The lesser evil: Political ethics in an age of terror*. Edinburgh, UK: Edinburgh University Press.
James, I. (2012). *The new French philosophy*. Cambridge, UK: Polity Press.
Keet, A. (2007). Human rights education or human rights in education: A conceptual analysis. *Doctoral dissertation, retrieved from Dissertation Abstract International Section A: Humanities and Social Sciences, 68*(8-A), 32–64.
Keet, A. (2010). *Human rights education: A conceptual analysis*. Saarbrücken, Germany: Lambert Academic Publishing.
Keet, A. (2012). Discourse, betrayal, critique. In C. Roux (Ed.), *Safe spaces: Human rights education in diverse contexts* (pp. 7–28). Rotterdam, The Netherlands: Sense Publishers.
Kompridis, N. (2006). *Critique and disclosure*. Cambridge, MA: MIT Press.
Lynch, J., Modgil, C., & Modgil, S. (Eds.). (1992). *Human rights, education and global responsibilities*. London: Falmer Press.
Malabou, C. (2005). *The future of Hegel: Plasticity, temporality and dialectic*. London: Routledge.
Malabou, C. (2010). *Plasticity at the dusk of writing*. New York: Columbia University Press.
Malabou, C. (2011). *Changing difference*. Cambridge, UK: Polity Press.
McLaren, P. (2000). *Che Guevara, Paulo Freire and the pedagogy of revolution*. Lanham, MD: Rowman & Littlefield.
Mikics, D. (2009). *Who was Jacques Derrida?* New Haven, CT: Yale University Press.
Rorty, R. (1999). *Philosophy and social hope*. London: Penguin Books.
Roux, C. (Ed.). (2012). *Safe spaces: Human rights education in diverse contexts*. Rotterdam, The Netherlands: Sense Publishers.
Shread, C. (2010). Translator's note. In C. Malabou (Ed.), *Plasticity at the dusk of writing* (pp. xxvii–xxxxx). New York: Columbia University Press.
Slaughter, J. R. (2007). *Human rights, inc.: The world novel, narrative form and international law*. New York: Fordham University Press.
Soguk, N. (1999). *States and strangers: Refugees and displacements of statecraft*. Minneapolis, MN: University of Press.
Suarez, D. (2006). *Creating global citizens? Human rights in Latin America and the Caribbean*. Stanford, CA: Stanford University.
Suarez, D., & Ramirez, F. (2004). *Human rights and citizenship: The emergence of human rights education*. In working papers, number 12, Centre on Democracy, Development, and the Rule of Law, Stanford Institute for International Studies.
Taylor, M. C. (2004, October 14). The real meaning of deconstruction. *The New York Times*. Retrieved from http://www.nytimes.com/2004/10/14/opinion/l4iht-edtaylor.html?pagewanted=all&_r=O
Tie, W. (2009). Beyond the dislocation(s) of human rights. *Social and Legal Studies, 18*, 71–91.

United Nations Non-Governmental Liaison Service [NGLS]. (2008). *The United Nations human rights system: How to make it work for you*. Geneva, Switzerland: United Nations.
Wortham, S. M. (2009). *The Derrida dictionary*. New York: Continuum.
Zournazi, M. (2002). *Hope: New philosophies for change*. Annandale, Australia: Pluto Press.

Chapter 8
Affect and Counter-Conduct: Cultivating Action for Social Change

Introduction

In Chap. 6 we discussed how HRE approaches often treat human rights violations in 'cheap sentimental' terms rather than within a framework that inspires activism and action for social change (Zembylas, 2016). The key feature of this concern, along with critiques of declarationist HRE (see Chaps. 2, 3, and 4) is that dominant approaches of HRE do not promote enough criticality and action, but rather settle within a liberal framework that emphasizes human rights as universal values for all, while failing to inspire in children and youth critical feelings and actions to struggle against 'everyday' human rights violations. As a consequence, HRE approaches often appear divorced from the specificity of local struggles (Adami, 2012; Coysh, 2014), resulting in superficial and sentimentalized responses toward human rights violations that reify human rights as an abstract, juridical category (Zembylas, 2016). Thus, our discussion here advances the focus on the 'ordinary' everyday aspects of the experience of human rights violations that are often lost in the reification of human rights as an abstract and universal category—a thread throughout this book.

In particular, this chapter builds on the theme of affect introduced in Chap. 6 and partly extended in Chap. 7, and explores the entanglement between two partially connected concerns that offer the potential to animate current discussions on human rights teaching and learning: 'affect' and 'counter-conduct'. Both of these terms, we argue, are at the heart of renewing HRE approaches that aim at cultivating resistance in children and youth so that they respond in critically affective and action-oriented ways to human rights violations and social injustices in 'the everyday'. The first term—affect—pays attention to the dynamics of affective life as *practice* (Wetherell, 2012) and highlights the ethical and political implications for human rights teaching and learning (Zembylas, 2016). From this work, we learn that HRE needs to move away from cheap sentimentalized approaches, towards critical hope, for instance, as

M. Zembylas, A. Keet, *Critical Human Rights Education*, Contemporary Philosophies and Theories in Education 13,
https://doi.org/10.1007/978-3-030-27198-5_8

we argued in the previous chapter, if human rights teaching and learning are going to promote solidarity and action-oriented empathy with human rights struggles in everyday life. The second term—Foucault's (2009) notion of 'counter-conduct'—names the struggles and forms of resistance against "the processes implemented for conducting others" (p. 201). By turning to this concept, this chapter acknowledges the important theoretical insights advanced by those approaches to human rights and HRE that recognize not only the governing effects of rights—through various processes of legal, political, pedagogical, and ethical subjectification of children and youth—but also the destabilisations of conduct, which struggles through rights can bring about (Odysseos, 2016). This chapter examines how critical enactments of HRE enable ways of "escaping, subverting and evading" (ibid., p. 181) processes of normalisation that obscure the agency of children and youth. Calling for greater attention to 'counter-conduct', we argue, shows how human rights teaching and learning may enable forms of resistance that interrupt juridical conceptions of human rights and forge in children and youth action-oriented and critically affective understandings and practices of human rights. Our key argument is to highlight how a critical formulation of HRE needs to move towards a more *performative* understanding of human rights, that is, seeing human rights as a practice or "way of doing things" (Foucault, 2008, p. 318) in 'the everyday', rather than as an application of a moral ideology or a universal set of standards.

Counter-Conduct

The notion of 'counter-conduct' was examined in the *Security, Territory, Population* lecture course in 1977–1978 (Foucault, 2009) and in a lecture Foucault gave in May 1978 entitled "What is Critique?" (Foucault, 2007). Surprisingly, it is a concept that has, until recently, received scant attention within the social sciences (Odysseos, Death & Malmvig, 2016), yet it is a key concept that contains a conceptual 'hinge', allowing us to link together the ethical and political dimensions of Foucault's thought (Davidson, 2011). As Davidson explains, this concept has been rather undervalued due to the main legacy of Foucault's course giving rise to the so-called 'governmentality studies'. Indeed, in the field of education, Foucault's work has been extensively used to theorise power, the subject and governmentality (e.g. see Ball, 1990; Peters & Besley, 2007; Popkewitz & Brenna, 1998). Yet, as Davidson (2011) reminds us, "one should not overlook the fact that pastoral power and governmentality are historically and philosophically contiguous in that they take as the object of their techniques and practices the *conduct* of human beings" (p. 26).

Foucault (2009) locates the emergence of counter-conduct practices within the history of Christian pastorate; 'counter-conducts' denote dissent against a variety of pastoral 'governing' practices aiming to regulate religious conduct. In other words, counter-conduct refers to forms of resistance or refusal whose aim was to invoke new practices that escape normalized practices of conduct. For example, in the Christian Church of the Middle Ages, Foucault identified such counter-conductive practices in movements of asceticism, mysticism and Reformation efforts. However, as Odysseos (2016) observes, counter-conducts did not always take the form of rejection or refusal of conduct, but rather they were manifested "as a questioning, reworking and elaboration of pastoral power, which at times eroded but also at other times reinforced, redirected or improved the mechanisms… of conducting power" (pp. 183–84). This idea highlights the "immediate and founding correlation between conduct and counter-conduct" (Foucault, 2009, p. 196), that is, how the issue of government is inextricably linked to the issue of how *not* to be governed (Odysseos et al., 2016). As Foucault clarified in his lecture 'What is Critique?':

> I do not mean by that that governmentalization would be opposed in a kind of face-off by the opposite affirmation, "we do not want to be governed, and we do not want to be governed *at all*." I mean that, in this great preoccupation about the way to govern and the search for the ways to govern, we identify a perpetual question which could be: "how not be governed *like that*, by that, in the name of those principles, with such and such an objective in mind and by means of such procedures, not like that, not for that, not by them". (2007, p. 44)

Foucault's invention of the term counter-conduct, which he admits is a "badly constructed word" (2009, p. 201), indicates not only his dissatisfaction with traditional vocabularies such as revolt, dissent, disobedience, and others, but also his meticulous attempt "to conceptualize the multiple dimensions and inter-relationalities of both practices of resistance and practices of governance" (Rossdale & Stierl, 2016, p. 159). In other words, Foucault's concern is the *practices*—rather than the ideologies—through which counter-conducts are variably expressed. For him, Rossdale and Stierl point out, the process of conducting oneself differently necessitates concrete enactments, that is, specific tactics rendered in 'the everyday' (Demetriou, 2016). Conceptualizing resistance through counter-conduct shifts the focus from abstract idea(l)s "towards practical materializations and thereby also helps dispense with the heroification of the resisting subject" (Rossdale & Stierl, 2016, p. 162).

It is precisely this movement towards practice that makes Davidson (2011, p. 28) suggest that "the notion of counter-conduct adds an explicitly ethical component to the notion of resistance […] [and] allows one to move easily between the ethical and the political, letting us see their many points of contact and intersection." For Davidson, counter-conduct forms the key concept that binds together "the political and ethical axes of Foucault's thought" (ibid., p. 26), namely, his earlier work on power relations and his later explorations of the 'care for the self.' While never fully free from power relations and governmentality, counter-conduct practices point to the possibilities for the subject to become otherwise, conduct his or herself differently, and formulate counter-narratives. The ethical dimension of counter-conduct, therefore, is clearly present in the constitution of oneself as a moral subject and the related notions of 'practices of the self' and 'modes of subjectivation':

> There is no specific moral action that does not refer to a unified moral conduct; no moral conduct that does not call for the forming of oneself as an ethical subject; and no forming of the ethical subject without 'modes of subjectivation' and an 'ascetics' or 'practices of the self' that support them. (Foucault, 1990b, p. 28)

Foucault's proposition to understand counter-conduct in ethical and political terms draws attention to the specific practices with which governed subjects challenge, evade, transform and possibly subvert pastoral governing in everyday life (Odysseos, 2016). It is for this reason that counter-conduct is a productive concept, argues Demetriou (2016), precisely because it highlights the acts that are situated in the everyday and they are not confined merely to resistance, but rather they can take various manifestations.

The entanglement of the ethical and the political becomes clearer in the connection that Foucault (2007) draws between counter-conduct and what he calls the 'critical attitude.' Foucault defines the critical attitude "as the movement by which the subject gives himself the right to question truth and power,…the art of voluntary insubordination" (ibid., p. 47). As Lemke (2011) explains: "The activity of problematization, the art of voluntary insubordination and the audacity to expose oneself as a subject…are the three elements that define critical activity according to Foucault" (p. 24). Furthermore, for Davidson (2011), the critical attitude is a political and ethical attitude that is characterized by a critique of the way in which our conduct is governed. This critical attitude is not something abstract, as pointed out earlier, but rather an intellectual and ethical practice of subject formation that is crucial to the different selves we seek to become (Odysseos et al., 2016).

For example, as Cadman (2010) points out, rights can be seen as political practices with "an active and performative role … [that] is achieved through another understanding: 'the *right* to question' governmental regimes of truth" (p. 541). As Cadman explains further, 'the right to question' helps us view counter-conducts as practices that enable governed subjects to experience and possibly transfigure a given field of power relations by questioning the regime of truth through which individuals are governed. Yet, it is important to clarify that this questioning may take different manifestations that "challenge, redirect or modify techniques of power that govern our conduct, without the requirement of intention rejection or explicitly political expression" (Odysseos, 2016, p. 189). According to these terms, it can be argued that human rights are not grounded on metaphysical values but initiated as practices of counter-conduct and 'the right to question.' The next part of the chapter takes a step further and discusses the important role of affect in these practices, before exploring the implications of the entanglement of affect and counter-conduct in HRE.

Affect

In line with the argument that counter-conducts are ethical and political practices, our analysis here adopts the perspective suggesting that the concept of 'practice' offers a productive way of theorizing 'affect' too (Burkitt, 2014; Gammerl, 2012; Reckwitz, 2012; Scheer, 2012; Wetherell, 2012, 2013; Wetherell et al. 2015). Practice theory, which has had a significant impact on social sciences in recent years, has also begun to provide a framework for thinking about affect (Scheer, 2012).

Generally speaking, practice refers to a "nexus of doings and sayings" (Schatzki, 1996, p. 89). According to Schiatzki's formulation of practice theory, acts range from ephemeral doings to long-term habits; thus, one of the main advantages of practice thinking is that it highlights social action as constantly in motion, while also recognizing that the past constraints the present and the future.

Following Schartzki, Reckwitz (2012) argues that every social practice has affective dimensions; in other words, practices are always affective regardless of whether an act is habituated or learned and culturally specific. In her recent contributions to affect as activity, Wetherell (2012, 2013) and Wetherell et al. (2015) focuses on what she calls the 'affective-discursive practice', namely, the patterned forms of activity that articulate, mobilize and organize affect and discourse as a central part of practice. This aspect of practical activity is particularly important because it highlights the micro-political level or the micro-physics of power relations involved in 'the everyday'. The significance of all of this, is that it allows us not only to situate affect within the everyday, but also to establish the connection between (counter-) conduct practices and affect; this connection is often missed in HRE approaches or it is viewed rather superficially. However, this connection gives us a good cause to reconsider the task of rendering everyday acts as a tool for reconceptualizing practices of critical affect and counter-conduct in human rights teaching and learning (more on this in the last part of the chapter).

The social practice approach, then, focuses on the entanglements of affect and discourse evident in the everyday, and considers the patterning of the affective-discursive as the main route for the social analysis of affect and emotion. As Burkitt (2014) argues, emotions are not things in themselves, or abstractions or quantities inside us, as basic emotions research assumes. Emotions are relational patterns, and as such, they are distributed and located across the psychosocial field (Wetherell, 2012). As Wetherell further explains,

> From an affective practices standpoint, specifying the exact relationship between affect and discourse is less interesting than investigating the range and entire patterning of affective assemblages operating in important scenes in everyday life along with their social consequences and entailments. Affect and discourse intertwine in these patterns to varying extents and in varying ways. (2012, p. 52)

Therefore, the main concern of the social practice approach is to identify what Wetherell et al. (2015) call the 'affective-discursive canon' found, for example, in texts, curricula or pedagogies about human rights. "By 'affective-discursive canon'," write Wetherell et al., "we mean the established, immediately familiar and orthodox procedures for emoting and making sense" (ibid., p. 60) found in different manifestations of social practice. For instance, analyzing the affective life of a HRE approach or curriculum means focusing on the assembling of affective-discursive orthodoxies about human rights and exploring the construction of children and youth as emotional subjects within a particular psychosocial context in which human rights are understood and practiced.

A specific example of a psychosocial context is the flow of emotions within the nation-state, creating what Kenway and Fahey (2011) call 'the emotional archive of the nation state'. This archive stores emotions associated with important historical and social events of the nation-state that are 'written' in its consciousness (e.g. important human rights violations). In highlighting the entanglement between the micro- and macro-levels, Kenway and Fahey find Hochschild's (1983) notion of 'feeling rules' to be valuable, because it emphasizes how certain rules and codes at the national level are manifested at the micro-level of individuals, navigating certain emotional behaviours. The ideas of the emotional archive of the nation-state and the feeling rules are helpful, for example, in that they draw analytic attention to the affective features of particular educational policies or pedagogies about human rights and show how these features could potentially drive children and youth's affective life toward particular directions (e.g. the sentimentalization of certain historical events in which the nation-state has been a 'victim' of gross human rights violations).

Particularly in relation to the entanglement of emotions and human rights, it has been argued that emotions constitute key players in the experiences of those who perceive, mobilize or claim human rights (Abrams, 2011). Abrams identifies five different ways that show how emotions are involved in the processes of rights assertion and recognition. The first way is responding to a moral shock; rights assertion often begins with the recognition of an injury. Understanding that one has sustained an injury is entwined with a range of emotions from grief or shock to fear, anger and shame. The second way is coalescing with others; the recognition that one has sustained an injury may transform one's life circumstances and may cause people to reach out to others. This outreach helps people regain their affective balance or strategize about possible ways of responding. The third way is ascribing responsibility; the process of ascribing responsibility for a particular injury is often strongly mediated by emotions. These emotions may influence the assignment of responsibility as well as the mobilization to claim the rights in response to the injury. The fourth way is mobilising rights; the ability to mobilise a claim framed in the language of rights requires certain emotions. For example, the mobilization of rights through protest and social movement activity demands an appeal to particular affective tendencies or emotion cultures among the participants or the creation of new emotion cultures that support particular forms of response. Finally, the fifth way refers to the emotional effects of mobilization; that is, the mobilization of rights is informed and infused by varied forms of affect and it produces certain emotional consequences.

The power and tenacity with which emotions and rights are related are particularly evident in human rights discourses expressed in terms of *suffering*. As Barreto explains:

> One is obliged to face nakedly the fact of suffering. For the victims, the violation of their rights does not mean first of all the breaching of constitutions or international treaties, nor the negation of political ideas or ethical principles. For the victims, violence has material consequences in the body and mind, and is cause of immediate distress and physical or psychological pain. (2013, p. 110)

Human rights discourse and practice, then, is inevitably entwined with suffering and the emotions implicated, because it is the language of emotions that enables the injured to express their suffering. As Barreto further asserts, it is possible to speak about the victims of mass killings in the language of statistics or in terms of a political discourse of injustice, but the introduction of the language of suffering "is the immediate and sometimes the only speech or meaningful utterance available to those tormented by the torturers, to the mother facing the disappearance of her son, to the child who knows his father has been killed" (ibid., 111).

Consequently, it is important for human rights educators to turn their attention to affects and emotions and reconsider their role in HRE practices. In fact, some scholars argue that a theorisation of/about human rights which fails to recognize the affective implications of suffering, oppression and human rights violations is unable to explain many tensions and failures in human rights discourses and practices (Cvetkovich, 2012; Zembylas, 2016). The issue of course is not simply to recognise that affective investments constitute a starting point for new insights into human rights struggles, but rather to develop pedagogical practices that enact these investments in critical ways.

The Entanglement of Affect and Counter-Conduct in Critical Human Rights Education

In the last part of the chapter, we ground the above observations in an attempt to suggest new openings in CHRE that take into consideration two potential avenues: first, how to promote forms of counter-conduct that are empathetic and action-oriented in response to human rights violations, oppressions and social injustices; and second, how these counter-conductive practices escape, subvert and evade uncritical sentimentalism by invoking critical affect. We will consider both of these potential avenues below.

Concerning the first potential avenue, critical forms of HRE need to pay attention to the 'ordinariness' of suffering, oppression and social injustices in 'the everyday', rather than getting lost into the abstract and intangible concepts of universal human rights (Coysh, 2014). This conceptualisation of HRE historicises and politicises human rights violations through a turn to counteracting the everyday manifestations of these violations. Encouraging children and youth to engage in everyday counter-conductive practices against human rights violations recalibrates the human rights orientation away from an overwhelming focus on legalistic and declarational perspectives towards the mobilisation of human rights to engender "inventive, self-transfiguring practices" (Odysseos, 2016, p. 182) against normalization processes.

Importantly, Foucault's notion of counter-conduct compels human rights educators to reconsider 'the everyday' (e.g. everyday sufferings, oppressions, and human rights violations) not only as an important source of how human rights are manifest as a governing legalistic technology in schools and the society at large, but also as a point of departure to engage children and youth in the cultivation of critical attitudes toward normalized ways of being. As Foucault (1990a) reminds us: "It is not that life has been totally integrated into techniques that govern and administer it; it constantly escapes them" (p. 143). This idea implies an exploration of the ways in which human rights discourses and practices in schools enable new subjectivities that make it possible for children and youth to assume more activist roles for social change in their community.

Here we begin to raise a whole new set of questions to guide the development of critical HRE practices in the everyday and which we suggest should be fundamental to an approach that takes into consideration theoretical insights from Foucault's notion of counter-conduct: How do certain responses against human rights violations in schools encourage or discourage counter-conduct in children and youth? Which forms of human rights teaching and learning facilitate the practice of solidarity and action-oriented empathy? What new practices of self-conduct are produced through various expressions of counter-conduct such as protest, dissent or disobedience? The aim of critical forms of HRE is essentially the ethical and political resubjectivisation of children and youth so that they enact ways of "not being like that".

Concerning the second potential avenue, a critical formulation of HRE needs to advance a social justice-oriented human rights pedagogical practice that encourages critically affective responses to human rights violations. This implies developing affective –discursive practices that do not sentimentalise issues of power, justice, struggle, and inequality. This point also highlights that to formulate both critically affective and action-oriented responses to human rights violations, human rights educators need to examine how dominant HRE approaches may inevitably be embedded within particular affective politics; for example, this affective politics may fail to uncover the tensions and failures of the human rights paradigm and may pathologise negative affects expressed about the political failure of human rights around the world. An HRE that is truly 'critical' and goes beyond a liberal and sentimental approach towards human rights needs to critique the cultural, social, political and affective conditions that make possible the perpetuation of human rights violations.

A critical issue that is highlighted by recent studies in the social sciences and humanities regarding the role of affects and emotions is how psychic elements of relationality as responses to suffering, violence and trauma are entangled with historical, cultural, social and political norms and conventions (Zembylas, 2014). Affects and emotions shape and are shaped by "the political contours of our social imaginaries" (Rice, 2008, p. 206). This means that we are enabled to theorise affects and emotions—and thus 'suffering' as a key concept in HRE—as intersections of language, desire, power, bodies, social structures, subjectivity, materiality and trauma. The turn to affects and emotions, then, points to a dynamism that recognizes bodily matters and their interrelations with political economies; this idea has profound implications in our attempts to teach about human rights without neglecting the concept of suffering and its implications, especially in relation to sentimentality (Zembylas, 2016).

A theory of human rights and HRE which acknowledges the role of emotions and suffering within the context of historical and political structures of power can give a powerful voice to human suffering. Yet, to go *beyond* a sentimental HRE, the first step that is needed for human right educators and learners is their ability to trace the process of sentimentalization of narratives of suffering and how this process can end up being fixed into self-centred accounts of others' suffering in our globalized world. One of us has argued in the past (Zembylas, 2016) that *critical sentimental education* can approach stories of human rights abuse with *both* criticality *and* affective engagement, highlighting the importance of critical consciousness around issues of power relations and various types of injustices and inspiring transformative action to dismantle these injustices. In this chapter we want to build on these contributions and go a step further by focusing on how counter-conduct expands the potential for critical interventions as human rights educators by enabling children and youth "to redirect, transform and occasionally subvert historically contingent mechanisms of conduct that seek to constitute them" (Odysseos, 2016, p. 194) as normalised subjects who simply buy into cheap sentimentality.

To do this, we need to raise a whole new set of questions that would create openings for counter-conduct practices in the everyday, while also addressing the dangers of cheap sentimentalism. For example: How are children and youth's affects governed through declarational approaches? How are affects such as solidarity mobilised through and become part of HRE pedagogies? What modes of selfhood and what processes of reflection and action do counter-conduct practices make possible for children and youth? Which pedagogical practices enable teachers and students to respond critically and productively to stories of suffering, trauma and human rights violations without idealising or sentimentalising these stories? These questions can help reveal the often neglected reversibility and fragility of declarational approaches, thus allowing human rights educators to write the agency of the governed children and youth back into account.

Theorising counter-conduct in conjunction with affect in HRE enables us to pay more thorough attention into how human rights and HRE create modes of subjectification that counter processes of conduct in schools "with alternative forces, energies, visions, aspirations and desires" (Odysseos, 2016, p. 197) that go beyond sentimental and declarational accounts. For example, students are enabled to establish and maintain critical attentiveness and self-empowerment, when they begin to interrogate and challenge both discourses and day to day practices based on ontological binaries such as us/them, citizen/foreigner, friends/enemies, and good/evil. A critical orientation to HRE offers an alternative vision of agency and solidarity for children and youth, by engaging them in pragmatic everyday actions that practically question these binaries and lay the seeds for systemic and structural change. It is more likely that children and youth will begin to overcome the dangers of cheap sentimentality, not only when they understand critically the conditions (structural inequalities, poverty, globalization etc.) that give rise to suffering and acknowledge the affective connections between themselves and others, but also when they 'translate' this understanding into day to day practices of different sorts.

Conclusion

In this chapter, we used the concepts of affect and counter-conduct to explore two issues: first, how to encourage children and youth to enact forms of counter-conduct that are critical in/for human rights struggles, rather than responses which are sedimented through the governing technologies of declarational approaches of HRE; and second, how these counter-conduct practices may constitute ethical and political practices that critique liberal and sentimental forms of affect about human rights violations. Our claim is that theoretical insights that pay attention to counter-conduct and affect offer possibilities for reconsidering some of the normalised ideas in HRE. The stake in this claim is for a repositioning of the two concepts in theorising HRE approaches so that more criticality is instilled as both an ethical and political orientation.

Highlighting affect and counter-conducts in HRE draws attention to the embodied practices and performances of assuming critical attitudes; practices that seek to be transformative of the ways in which children and youth can become otherwise. It is argued that the rethinking that these two concepts can be brought to bear on our understandings and pedagogies of HRE helps us to grasp them more fully as valuable to our abilities, as human rights educators, to challenge and displace declarational and sentimental approaches of human rights teaching and learning. These efforts are inevitably troubling and unsettling compared to the dominant HRE approaches yet such a reworking of ethical and political commitments contests mainstream perspectives on HRE, eschewing both sentimentalised responses toward human rights violations and reifications of human rights as abstract, juridical categories. Bringing theoretical insights from recent theories of affect, as we have tried to do in the last three chapters, we hope to have shown that more engagement with the 'everyday' material implications of these insights could offer valuable recalibrations of current HRE practices.

References

Abrams, K. (2011). Emotions in the mobilization of rights. *Harvard Civil Rights-Civil Liberties Law Review, 46*, 551–589.

Adami, R. (2012). Reconciling universality and particularity through a cosmopolitan outlook on human rights. *Cosmopolitan Civil Societies Journal, 4*(2), 22–37.

Ball, S. (Ed.). (1990). *Foucault and education: Disciplines and knowledge*. London/New York: Routledge.

Barreto, J. M. (2013). Human rights and emotions from the perspective of the colonized: Anthropofagi, legal surrealism and subaltern studies. *Revista de Estudos Constitucionais, Hermeneutica e Teoria do Direito, 5*(2), 106–115.

Burkitt, I. (2014). *Emotions and social relations*. London: Sage.

Cadman, L. (2010). How (not) to be governed: Foucault, critique and the political. *Environment and Planning D: Society and Space, 28*, 539–556.

Coysh, J. (2014). The dominant discourse of human rights education: A critique. *Journal of Human Rights Practice, 6*(1), 89–114.

Cvetkovich, C. (2012). *Depression: A public feeling*. Durham, NC: Duke University Press.
Davidson, A. (2011). In praise of counter-conduct. *History of the Human Sciences, 24*(4), 25–41.
Demetriou, O. (2016). Counter-conduct and the everyday: Anthropological engagements with philosophy. *Global Society, 30*(2), 218–237.
Foucault, M. (1990a). *The history of sexuality (Vol. 1): An introduction*. London: Penguin.
Foucault, M. (1990b). *The history of sexuality (Vol. 2): The use of pleasure*. New York: Vintage.
Foucault, M. (2007). *The politics of truth*. Los Angeles: Semiotext(e).
Foucault, M. (2008). *The birth of biopolitics: Lectures at the Collége de France 1978–1979* (M. Senellart, Ed.). New York: Picador.
Foucault, M. (2009). *Security, territory, population: Lectures at the Collége de France 1977–1978* (Vol. 4). New York: Macmillan.
Gammerl, B. (2012). Emotional styles – Concepts and challenges. *Rethinking History, 16*(2), 161–175.
Hochschild, A. R. (1983). *The managed heart: Commercialization of human feeling*. Berkeley, CA: University of California Press.
Kenway, J., & Fahey, J. (2011). Getting emotional about 'brain mobility'. *Emotion, Space and Society, 4*(3), 187–194.
Lemke, T. (2011). *Foucault, governmentality, and critique: Cultural politics and the promise of democracy*. Boulder, CO: Paradigm.
Odysseos, L. (2016). Human rights, self-formation and resistance against disposability: Grounding Foucault's 'theorizing practice' of counter-conduct in Bhopal. *Global Society, 30*(2), 179–200.
Odysseos, L., Death, C., & Malmvig, H. (2016). Interrogating Michel Foucault's counter-conduct: Theorizing the subjects and practices of resistance in global politics. *Global Society, 30*(2), 151–156.
Peters, M. A., & Besley, T. (Eds.). (2007). *Why Foucault? New directions in educational research*. New York: Peter Lang.
Popkewitz, T. S., & Brenna, M. (Eds.). (1998). *Foucault's challenge: Discourse, knowledge, and power in education*. New York: Teachers College Press.
Reckwitz, A. (2012). Affective spaces: A praxeological outlook. *Rethinking History, 16*(2), 241–258.
Rice, J. (2008). The new "new": Making a case for critical affect studies. *The Quarterly Journal of Speech, 94*(2), 200–212.
Rossdale, C., & Stierl, M. (2016). Everything is dangerous: Conduct and counter-conduct in the occupy movement. *Global Society, 30*(2), 157–178.
Schatzki, T. R. (1996). *Social practices: A Wittgensteinian approach to human activity and the social*. New York: Cambridge University Press.
Scheer, M. (2012). Are emotions a kind of practice (and is that what makes them have a history)? A Bourdieuian approach to understanding emotion. *History and Theory, 51*, 193–220.
Wetherell, M. (2012). *Affect and emotion: A new social science understanding*. London: Sage.
Wetherell, M. (2013). Affect and discourse – What's the problem? From affect as excess to affective/discursive practice. *Subjectivity, 6*(4), 349–368.
Wetherell, M., McCreanor, T., McConville, A., & Moewaka Barnes, H. (2015). Settling space and covering the nation: Some conceptual considerations in analyzing affect and discourse. *Emotion, Space and Society, 16*, 58–64.
Zembylas, M. (2014). Theorizing 'difficult knowledge' in the aftermath of the 'affective turn': Implications for curriculum and pedagogy in handling traumatic representations. *Curriculum Inquiry, 44*(3), 390–412.
Zembylas, M. (2016). Toward a critical-sentimental orientation in human rights education. *Educational Philosophy and Theory, 48*(11), 1151–1167.

Chapter 9
Crisis and Critique: Critical Theories and the Renewal of Citizenship-, Democracy-, and Human Rights Education

Introduction

So far, in previous chapters we have discussed how social, political, economic, and environmental challenges are accompanied by a general mistrust in democratic institutions (Brown, 2016; Cruz & Brown, 2016; Dean, 2009; Klein, 2008; Krastev, 2014); the neoliberal attrition of human rights; and the way these are knitted together with the status, quality, and agency of citizenship (Brown, 2005; Dean, 2005, 2009; Deutscher & Lafont, 2017; Keet, 2015). These, inevitably, have implications for human rights education (HRE). This chapter argues that such implications can become more intelligible by engaging, through critique, with the crises of our times. The interplay between crisis and critique, so this chapter argues, will open up new possibilities for emancipatory praxes within HRE that are better rooted within social reality. An enhancement of the social justice potential of HRE is also anticipated. Treating crisis and critique as analytically and historically central to the program of critical theory, this chapter further suggests that the major shifts in critical theory provide productive pathways for the renewal of HRE.

In this chapter, we discuss not only HRE, but it's entanglements with citizenship education and democracy education, together Citizenship, Democracy and Human Rights Education (CDHRE). The theorization of the entanglement among citizenship-, democracy-, and human rights education within a broader frame so late in the book is, of course, purposive. Through discussing this entanglement we wish to highlight that citizenship-, democracy-, and human rights education are co-constitutive in everyday life, hence it is more strategic to really treat them as relational than to compartmentalize them for academic purposes. Although our focus in this book has been HRE, we do not want to give up the idea that the entanglement among citizenship-, democracy-, and human rights education is crucial in the formulation of more 'criticality' in HRE. Thus, we apply the theoretical possibilities of thinking through crisis and critique broadly to CDHRE, rather than narrowly to HRE.

M. Zembylas, A. Keet, *Critical Human Rights Education*, Contemporary Philosophies and Theories in Education 13,
https://doi.org/10.1007/978-3-030-27198-5_9

Citizenship-, Democracy-, and Human Rights Education

Citizenship education (CE), democracy education (DE), and human rights education (HRE) co-constitute one another. That is, their organising themes and aims are, to a large extent, related, with only slight differences in foci and emphasis. Thus, their program content substantively overlaps. The literature confirms such co-constitution and overlaps (Arthur, Davies, & Hahn, 2008; Heater, 2004; Kerr, 2013; Laker, 2016; Toots, De Groof, & Kavadias, 2012). The clustering of CE,[1] DE, and HRE (CDHRE) has become more pronounced and intelligible through the work of the Council of Europe (Kerr, 2013). So, in the sense of associating it with CE and HRE, it is probably more productive to frame DE, for the purposes of this chapter, as education for democratic citizenship (EDC).[2] As a 'family' of educations, CDHRE, to be loyal to its purposes and aims, has to engage the crises haunting the everyday existences of the majority of the world's inhabitants.

The world is precarious, as the realities that authored the United Nations Sustainable Development Goals (SDGs)[3] so clearly disclose: massive socioeconomic inequalities, hunger, poverty, wars, conflicts, systemic discrimination of all sorts, environmental degradation, and so on; rooted in existing global economic arrangements and practices. And, as Butler (2010, p. 3) so powerfully argues, such precarity is differentially and disproportionately distributed according to 'specific ontologies of the subject'; ontologies co-constructed by contemporary citizenship, democracy, and rights discourses. Those to whom the SDGs speak as 'victims' and 'unfortunates' carry the bulk of exposure to 'injury, violence and death' (Butler, 2010, p. 3).

Against the backdrop of these realities, it, from time to time, strikes one as surprising and even incredulous to see an array of 'social justice educations' disentangled from one another in the absence of an integrated education and political program while at their core they share more or less the same objectives. Its junctures are readily conceded as is the case in a thoughtful and considered piece by Tibbitts and Kirchschlaeger (2010) on *Perspectives of Research on Human Rights Education:*

> These efforts (HRE), which has gained momentum since the early 1990s, has spawned a growing body of educational theory, practice and research that often intersects with activities in other fields of educational study, such as citizenship education, peace education,

[1] CE is defined by UNESCO as educating children, from early childhood, to become clear-thinking and enlightened citizens who participate in decisions concerning society (UNESCO, 1998a).

[2] 'Education for democratic citizenship' means education, training, dissemination, information, practices and activities which aim, by equipping learners with knowledge, skills and understanding and moulding their attitudes and behaviour, to empower them to exercise and defend their democratic rights and responsibilities in society, and to value diversity and to play an active part in democratic life, with a view to the promotion and protection of democracy and the rule of law (Kerr, 2013).

[3] These are no poverty; no hunger; good health; quality education; gender equality; clean water and sanitation; renewable energy; good jobs and economic growth; innovation and infrastructure; reduced inequalities; sustainable cities and communities; responsible consumption; climate actions; life below water; life on land; peace and justice; and partnerships for the goals. See the full document at https://unstats.un.org/sdgs/report/2016/

> anti-racism education, Holocaust/genocide education, education for sustainable development and education for intercultural understanding. (p. 8)

Somewhere else Keet (2010) attempted a *Conceptual Typology of Human Rights Education and Associated Pedagogical Forms*. In this analysis, he probed the way in which HRE scholars and practitioners such as Lenhart and Savolainen (2002, p. 146) present HRE as an ‘emerging global educational philosophy’ that ‘unite and subsumes these other disciplines [which we refer to as educations]’ (Flowers, 2004, p. 118). This follows Tarrow’s (1992) proposition that suggests that HRE is central to and entangled with multicultural, antiracist, civic, global, development, peace, environmental, and moral education. The recent reflections on Betty Reardon’s life (Reardon & Snauwaert, 2015), as a key figure in these educations, confirm their interwovenness; not only as fields of praxes but also as practitioner-identities and subjectivities. Nevertheless, there remains a subtext of distinctiveness between these educations (Keet, 2010; Lynch, 1992; Tarrow, 1992). Moreover, a global, desegregated program between these educations with a rational political orientation in the context of the world crises is yet to be conceived.

The justifications for sustaining superficial boundaries and margins between these educations are yet to be explored. Yet, there have been various forms of ‘integrations’ over the past two decades (Huddleston, 2016; Smith, 2015; UNESCO, 1998b) that have not been upscaled, conceptually and practically. One may argue that this weakness makes it almost impossible for these educations to respond to the global, regional, and local challenges it purports to tackle. A useful starting point, building on the massive work already done within the scope of critical pedagogies, is to work toward an educational orientation and formation that views CE, DE, and HRE as co-constituting each other. This inevitably and suitably will bring CDHRE in closer conversation with the various interpretive schemes of critical social theories; and the postcolonial and decolonial critiques embedded within it.

For one, CDHRE will have to shed its façade of virtue as an instinctive, automatic public good. By doing so, it will reveal to itself its complicity in the crises of our times through critiques of its own assumptions and practices. Key to such endeavour is to explore the connections between the crises of the world and the general disillusionment with democratic institutions and the human rights project within which CDHRE is implicated. Such enquiry, for now, can best be undertaken using the tools available within the historical program of crisis and critique of critical theories.

Crisis and Critique

Critical Theory in Critical Times (2017), a compilation of essays edited by Penelope Deutscher and Cristina Lafont, is an industrious exercise in the self-criticism of critical theory’s foundational assumptions, as Charles W. Mills (2017) observes, despite his reservations on the whiteness of critical theory. Critical theory’s roots in

Left Hegelian Marxism has, in varieties of ways, been dedicated to Marx's injunction of a '*ruthless criticism of everything existing'* (Marx in Tucker, 1978, p. 13) (emphasis in original); a criticism that 'must not be afraid of its own conclusion, or of conflict with the powers that be' (ibid. 1978, p. 13). This is a now well-known reference to Marx. What is seldom cited is Marx's refusal to set up 'any dogmatic flag' (ibid. 1978, p. 13) in the sentence immediately following the one on 'ruthless criticism.' Criticism is an opening up; to clarify in any critical program the 'meaning of its own struggle and its own desires' (ibid. 1978, p. 15). The program of critique that Marx had in mind refers to the agenda of the journal *Deutsch–Französische Jahrbücher* (German–French Annals) that he was setting up with Arnold Ruge at that time. However, only one edition was published.

Almost a century after Marx and Ruge, Walter Benjamin and Bertolt Brecht planned to launch a journal named *Krisis und Kritik* that reestablished the ancient etymological roots of these two concepts (Olaison, Pedersen, & Sørensen, 2009). This was a response to the political crisis in the form of fascism, a theme that would feature strongly in the Critical Theory (CT) of the Frankfurt School. This journal project was aborted, and critique became one of the first casualties of fascism (Olaison et al., 2009). In 2014, more than 80 years later, Agon Hamza became the editor-in-chief of a new journal titled *Crisis and Critique*; a Marxist journal of philosophy (Bjerre & Hamza, 2014) aiming at 'reinventing the idea of radical emancipation.'

Elsewhere Keet (2014) has explored crisis and critique as a combination of concepts with a rich history in critical social theory. At the heart of critique, so he argues, is renewal: 'The transformation of our cultural traditions, institutions, knowledges and practices in a world in which current social, political, cultural and economic arrangements only further serve to structurally anchor inequalities, discrimination and exclusion' (p. 135). We are aligned with Holloway's (2012, p. 515) definition of critique as 'the opening of categories that are closed, to reveal the antagonism within them, to reveal the crisis that they conceal.' Holloway continues, 'When we criticise the categories, we criticise the social relations that give rise to those categories. We open both' (Holloway, 2012, pp. 515–516). Thus, critique 'aspires to find emancipatory alternatives to the conditions that block free human existence and damage social relations'; it can be viewed as a praxis (Cordero, 2014). The key point here is that from Marx to Habermas, Honneth, Dean, Brown, Forst, and Fraser, to name some of the key contemporary critical theorists, crisis and critique has been central to critical theory's analytical categories and key to its major shifts.

Why would reflections on crisis and critique in the mould of critical theory be important for CDHRE? The answer is straightforward. They constitute the location of *the critical*: that place from which we can cut through surface appearances; disrupt our receivable categories and interpretive schemes; and go behind that which we produce as truths. Simply put, *the critical* is the source of our disrupted self as CDHRE practitioners. From this vantage point, it may be possible to disclose, to ourselves, that the pragmatic and real-life expressions of liberal democracy and human rights with its associated conceptions of citizenship have masked and deepened societal crises, thus paving the way for *neoliberalism's stealth revolution*, as Brown (2015) argues. Our dilemma then is the emergence of democracy and human rights as the 'primary signifier[s] of the potential of emancipatory political struggle' (Dean, 2005, p. 154) that, as ensnared and detained within neoliberalism, may 'indicate a diminishment in political dreams, the loss, perhaps, of hopes for equity and social justice' (Dean, 2005, p. 154). A CDHRE that does not respond to these realities can do nothing other than reproduce the status quo. To work against such possibility would require CDHRE practitioners to foreground the analytical categories of crisis *and* critique. Stated differently, CDHRE should embed itself in critical theories of society.

Critical Theories

All theories of society that subject its object to critical examination can be regarded as critical theory (Honneth, 2007). This chapter does not refer to this all-encompassing notion of critical theory. We are aligned with Nancy Fraser's (1985, p. 97) observation that no one as yet, has improved on Marx's 1843 definition of critical theory as 'the self-clarification of the struggles and wishes of the age' within which an emancipatory intent is inscribed. We are also in agreement with Allen's (2016) distinction between a narrow and too broad conception of critical theory.[4] The narrow conception refers to the German tradition of social theory associated with the Frankfurt School and its inheritors. The two broad conceptions denote any theory and practice with emancipatory intent and includes work under the 'banner of feminist theory, queer theory, critical race theory, and post- and decolonial theory' (Allen, 2016, p. xi); *and* the French theories associated with 'poststructuralism.'

In slight deviation from Allen (2016), we are not categorising post- and decolonial theory under the broad notion of critical theory. The targeted, yet wide-ranging scholarship under their banners dictates that they be treated separately. We are also adding a further distinction that merges African Studies and African American Studies into Africana Critical Theory (Rabaka, 2009) with its focus, among other things, on the political economy of race and gender, decolonisation, critical race

[4] Allen, 2016, pp. xi–xii. 'In its most narrow usage, "critical theory" refers to the German tradition of interdisciplinary social theory, inaugurated in Frankfurt in the 1930s, and carried forward today in Germany by such thinkers as Jürgen Habermas, Axel Honneth, and Rainer Forst and in the United States by theorists, such as Thomas McCarthy, Nancy Fraser, and Seyla Benhabib. In a more capacious usage, "critical theory" refers to any politically inflected form of cultural, social, or political theory that has critical, progressive, or emancipatory aims. Understood in this way, critical theory encompasses much, if not all, of the work that is done under the banner of feminist theory, queer theory, critical race theory, and post- and decolonial theory. A distinct but related capacious usage of the term refers to the body of theory that is mobilised in literary and cultural studies, otherwise known simply as "theory." Here critical theory refers mainly to a body of French theory spanning from poststructuralism to psychoanalysis, and including such thinkers as Michel Foucault, Jacques Derrida, Gilles Deleuze, and Jacques Lacan.

theory, and the critical philosophy of race. To make references to these distinctions more manageable in the text, we are denoting them as follows throughout this chapter. First, 'critical theory' (CT) refers to the Frankfurt School and its inheritors. Second, Allen's two broad conceptions of critical theory, excluding post- and decolonial theory, is referred to as 'critical theory.' Third, postcolonial and decolonial theory are designated as such. Fourth, Africana Critical Theory is denoted as ACT. Fifth, we regard crucial works such as *Southern Theory* (Connell, 2007) and *Theory from the South* (Comaroff & Comaroff, 2012) as a strand of critical theory associated with both post- and decolonial theory. The five strands are collectively signified as 'critical theories.'

Shifts in Critical Theories and Implications of CDHRE

An analysis of the major shifts in critical theories with all its complexities is, to say the least, an ambitious undertaking. Fortunately, these are already well- captured in the writings of the 'founders' of the Frankfurt School and others (Bronner & Kellner, 1989; Connerton, 1976; Habermas, 1985; Held, 1980; Honneth, 2007, 2012; Horkheimer, 1972; Horkheimer & Adorno, 1972). However, our aim here is to provide a summary of these shifts within critical theories broadly speaking and consider its implications for CDHRE.

The shifts in critical theories are commonly linked to critiques; irrespective of whether these critiques are internal, external, Africana, postcolonial, or decolonial. From within, CT has been critiqued, revised, and challenged with alternative propositions for its project. This mainly includes shifts from Horkheimer and Adorno and their circles' Marxist functionalism that presented 'a closed theoretical sphere of capitalist domination and cultural manipulation' (Honneth, 2007, p. 65), to Habermas's (1985) theory of communication, to Honneth's (2007, 2012) theory of recognition. In other words, first a shift from class and social labour to social interaction and communication as analytical categories within which to locate the critique of social domination and concomitant emancipatory potentials. And second, a shift from justice petitions rooted in distorted communication to demands for recognitive justice within which to situate a program of emancipation. For Habermas, deliberations that challenge distorted communication, generate, through the democratic procedure, valid and legal norms that capture the petitions for justice (Renault, 2005). Honneth, on the other hand, suggests a form of recognitive justice rooted in social recognitions constituted by the triad of love, respect, and esteem (Pilapil, 2011); or love, rights and solidarity.

Critiquing Habermas's assumption that distorted communication is the primary resource for identifying injustice, from which the emancipatory impulse of CT stems, Honneth (2007, 2012) suggests that recognitive justice and not communicative justice should form the basis for understanding the emancipatory drive of social agents. His recognition version of CT is particularly disapproving of the legal, procedural conceptions of social justice.

> Nothing has been more fatal to the formulation of a concept of social justice than the recent tendency to dissolve all social relations into legal relationships, in order to make it all the easier to regulate these relationships through formal rules. (Honneth, 2014, p. 67)

But, for Honneth, in *The Struggle for Recognition* (1995) and his later work (2007, 2012, 2014), 'rights' remain central to a theory of justice. Though presenting a more pluralistic conception of justice through the three levels of recognition, Honneth is yet to explore the already dominant configuration of legal proceduralism embedded in rights and democracy that advances existing capitalist democracies, reproduces socioeconomic inequalities, and generates varieties of human rights violations.

Typically, for CDHRE practitioners the notions of citizenship, democracy, and human rights as formulated within CT are treated as integral to the idealist idea of human and social progress. The citizen situated in democratic aspirations is a rights bearer where 'democracy and human rights express a common aspiration for human autonomy, dignity, equality and freedom' (Schaffer, 2015, p. 96). The Habermasian thesis of the co-originality of democracy and human rights as set out in *Between Facts and Norms* (Habermas, 1996) is based on the assumptions of his theory of communicative action (Habermas, 1996). From here we derive the idea of deliberative democracy and its procedural conceptions. Thus rights, though intersubjectively rooted, can discursively be elaborated into a comprehensive system folded into democracy (Flynn, 2003); a theme that generally governs approaches to CDHRE.

CT has not shied away from rooting its program in broad normative claims against which injustices are identified. It has thus been accused of being married to one or other form of metadiscourse. Thus, externally, the critique of CT is, in large part, derived from the 'postmodernist' and 'poststructuralist' schools of thought. For the 'postmodernist,' especially arguing against the Frankfurt School, CT's appeal to 'some grand narrative' (Lyotard, 1999, p. xxiv) is misplaced. That is, its adherence to modernist conceptions of for instance progress, democracy, human rights, and so on is misdirected.

The general argument levelled against CT, in this case, is precisely its uncritical adherence to these classical notions. Instructive for CDHRE has been the critique of CT's modernist assumption of the already-constituted human rights and democratic citizen. Likewise, the poststructuralist critique decentres the human rights subject and the foundationalism of democracy and rights and displaces the absolute meanings of democracy and rights. Thus, the productive option available to CDHRE is to see its understandings of the concepts of citizenship, democracy, and rights as an interplay of the critiques within CT and critical theory. That is, critical theory, in its broad sense, alerts us to how rights, because it adheres to an idea of a finished human rights subject, are both implicated in capitalist and neoliberal domination *and* in its failure to perpetually steer law toward an 'impossible commitment to an unconditional justice' (Douzinas & Gearty, 2014, p. 2). In a sense, rights desire a foundation in truth, as we note from its codification in human rights instruments and law, but 'needs to fail to have one in order to maintain its hegemonic power as the progressive ideal of the post-political age' (Douzinas & Gearty, 2014, p. 2). It follows then that the emancipatory potential of CDHRE resides in working with these kinds of paradoxes of rights, citizenship, and democracy (Birmingham & Yeatman, 2014; Douzinas & Gearty, 2014). That is, to converse with professionals and communities with whom we work in authentic ways, placing on the table the impossible promises and absurdities that profoundly impact our shared everyday lives, but, which nonetheless, are skimmed over in our practices.

The critique of CT from a postcolonial perspective argues that the Frankfurt School, 'despite its seminal insights into the relationships between domination, modern society, and the opportunities for redemption through art as critique, is stunningly silent on racist theory, anti-imperialist resistance, and oppositional practice in the empire' (Said, 1994, p. 278). For Said (1994), it was only Fanon that converted his Marxist, Freudian, and other heritages into an 'anti-authoritarian' service. At the heart of the postcolonial critique of CT is its adherence to the dominant, Eurocentric narratives of progress. Postcolonial approaches work to challenge these narratives 'and to reconfigure them to provide more adequate categories of analysis, where adequacy is measured in terms of increasing inclusivity and is oriented "backwards" as well as "forwards"' (Bhambra, 2007, p. 15). The implications for CDHRE are obvious. If the dominant narratives constructed the 'human' of human rights in limiting terms, it is incapable of imagining forms of social life outside of its own interpretive horizon. Using Allen's (2016) insights, we argue that because CDHRE employs conceptions of citizenship, democracy, and human rights as incorporated into the notion of progress as formulated within the sphere of European modernity, it fails to explore that its practical expression as education 'has served and continues to serve the ideological function of rationalising and legitimising contemporary forms of informal imperialism, neocolonialism, and racism' (Allen, 2016, p. 19). An uncritical CDHRE may also be implicated in epistemological essentialism since, given the phase-development within which it is located, it may assume to know on what basis it claims to know how 'advances' in citizenship, democracy, and human rights counts as progress (Allen, 2016).

CT's obedience to an idea of progress that draws its resources from a phased-development, Eurocentric logic, has been the subject of criticism from a decolonial perspective as well (Quijano, 2000). We devote Chap. 10 to this decolonial criticism and its potential implications for HRE, but for now, suffice to say that, for some, the postcolonial critique is not sufficient. For instance, Grosfoguel (2011) argues for decolonising postcolonial studies itself, given its roots in French poststructuralism and calls for epistemic frameworks from the Global South to contribute 'to a radical decolonial critical theory' (Grosfoguel, 2011, p. 2). In essence, the postcolonial and post-modern critique is, for Grosfoguel (2011), a Eurocentric critique of Eurocentrism. A decolonial critique, however, is a critique of Eurocentrism from 'subalternised and silenced knowledges' (Grosfoguel, 2011, p. 3). The propositions for CDHRE are disrupting. Not only are its organising concepts taken to task for being imprisoned by Eurocentric conceptions of progress and social evolution, it now also has to excavate subalternised understandings of rights, citizenship, and democracy (Mignolo, 2014) to be of any critical pedagogical and emancipatory value in the Global South. CDHRE practitioners who argue that the understandings of rights, citizenship, and democracy are, in any case, contextualised as a decolonial movement within its praxes, have always missed the point that 'contextualisation', in this instance, is an act of epistemic invasion and of colonisation.

Nevertheless, a radical decolonial critical theory, as Grosfoguel (2011) would have it, should, we think, engage with both a Eurocentric *and* Subalternised critique of Eurocentrism. Zeleza (2009) and Gikandi (2002) make more or less similar points in their critique of the way in which Africa Studies and postcolonial studies remain locked in Eurocentric frames in which Africa is written by analogy, subjected to reference points authored somewhere else.

In the same way as Grosfoguel (2011) is setting the scene for exploring a radical decolonial critical theory, Rabaka (2009) is arguing for an ACT that situates critical theory within the interpretive schemes provided by Du Bois, James, Fanon, Cabral, and the like and the 'developments in philosophy of race, sociology of race, psychology of race, anthropology of race, history of race, and critical race theory; Pan-Africanism, anti-colonialism, decolonisation theory, and critical postcolonial theory; black Marxism, black nationalism,' and so forth (Rabaka, 2009, p. ix). Rabaka (2009) argues for a critical theory to be more attuned to the lived experiences of black people, and the black radicalism that emanates from such experiences. It is worthwhile here to quote him at length (2009).

> Deeply indebted to Mills work, Africana critical theory advocates a *conjunctive* approach to critical theory; an approach which places race *and* gender *and* class *and* sexuality at the centre of, not only critical analyses of contemporary society, but of the creation and reconstruction of the radical theories and revolutionary praxes aimed at transforming contemporary society. Africana critical theory, therefore, does not argue that race and racism are the most pressing social and political problems confronting the critical theorists of the twenty-first century, and it does not claim that class should be replaced with race or gender as the central problematic of critical theory. However, it does audaciously assert that critical theory stands in need of radical reconstruction, and that critical race theory, philosophy of race, sociology of race, feminism, womanism, and postcolonialism, among other theoretical perspectives, should be critically utilised to *supplement* conventional critical theory's critiques of capitalist class struggle and political economy. The main idea here is to correct the methodological omissions and strengthen the epistemic weaknesses of classical and contemporary critical theory, not prescribe yet another intellectually insular and myopic methodology. (p. 302)

Allen's (2016) charge that CT has been all too silent on the problem of imperialism ties in with Rabaka's observation. But, whereas Allen marshals Adorno's and Foucault's insights for a decolonial CT, Rabaka has a renewal of critical theory via 'black,' 'race,' and feminist studies in mind. Charles W. Mills, (2017) on the other hand, argues for both the decolonisation and deracialisation of CT as ways of retrieving it, because CT, in decentring race, has been blinded to its own whiteness (Mills, 2017).

> As a consequence, it has been handicapped in achieving that self-critical and 'estranging' illumination of 'the social institutions and practices, patterns of cultural meaning and subject formation, and normative commitments that have made us who we are,' which has been an epistemic and ethical goal from the beginnings of Western philosophy. (Mills 2017, p. 264)

The critique of Allen (2016), Rabaka (2009), and Mills (2017) extends to one of citizenship, democracy, and human rights as key to both the constitution of the idea of progress within Eurocentrism as taken up by CT and critical theory, together with the legitimisation of whiteness in the way these concepts find practical expression in our social institutions and practices, including how they are furthered by CDHRE. What brings Allen, Rabaka, and Mills together is their belief that CT should not be discarded but regenerated, and with them, we can launch the program for the renewal of CDHRE.

This chapter is punctuated with tentative ideas on how such renewal may take shape. To summarise, such renewal will entail a complex set of movements in the direction of critical and decolonial pedagogies and critical social theories in general; this includes careful consideration of the shifts in critical theories. As argued earlier, the analytical categories of crisis and critique themselves is the location of the *critical*; the vantage point from which to disrupt ourselves as CDHRE practitioners. A *critical* CDHRE would know that the focus on capitalist domination and cultural manipulation through Marxist interpretive schemes seem to be more pertinent today than ever before. But, it will also know how to integrate such analysis with the analysis of social interaction and communicative action that Habermas's has in mind. Further, it will be attuned to the limitations of the legalistic notions of citizenship, democracy, and human rights, and models itself on pluralistic conceptions of justice. In short, a *critical* CDHRE will know that the notions of citizenship, democracy, and human rights are both affirmed and critiqued by shifts in CT and critical theories and will view such paradoxes as productive.

A *critical* CDHRE will assume responsibility for its adherence to modernist conceptions of citizenship, democracy, human rights, and progress that permeate the United Nations (UN) instruments with which we work. And then question it through incessant critique. It will undertake the task of engaging, against its grain, with unfinished, nonhuman rights subjects, and interrogate democracy and rights as grand narratives. Absolute meanings of citizenship, democracy, and human rights will be dislocated, and their absurdities and aporias, as suggested in Chap. 4, will be key to the content and approach of *critical* CDHRE. Further, the critique of the notion of progress will bring *critical* CDHRE in conversation with critical decolonial theory and ACT. However, when all is said and done, the project of formulating these into a pragmatic education project should be the responsibility of the collective of CDHRE practitioners across the globe.

Conclusion

If we accept that the renewal of our social practices is dependent on our capacity and commitment to be attuned to the crises generated within and outside our modes of thinking and doing, an unending critique of our praxes would be a permanent orientation. This critique would also have its gaze on the normalised legitimacy of the concepts we work with: citizenship, democracy, and human rights and its inversion and deployment in the local and global processes of domination. For all its shortcomings, CT and critical theories have been central in providing productive interpretive schemes to guide the tools we work with in the directions of social justice.

However, as we have seen from the forgoing arguments, critical theories have to engage with the erosion of citizenship, democracy, and human rights under the annihilating influence of neoliberalism's stealth revolution (Brown, 2015); combat its own Eurocentric inheritance; struggle with its silences on global racism and others forms of discriminations; and take more seriously the post- and decolonial critiques levelled against it. In a sense, the critiques of and among critical theories extend to CDHRE. Incriminated in the global crises we are facing, CDHRE should be articulated as incessant critiques of its organising categories (citizenship, democracy, human rights) and its pragmatic manifestation in a world soaked with human rights violations. Its responsibility is to work against the growing mistrust in democratic and human rights institutions by adopting the critical pedagogical posture. A posture that will demonstrate to those with whom we work that the differential distribution of precarity can be countered by a *critical* CDHRE.

References

Allen, A. (2016). *The end of progress: Decolonising the normative foundations of critical theory*. New York: Columbia University Press.

Arthur, J., Davies, I., & Hahn, C. (Eds.). (2008). *SAGE handbook of education for citizenship and democracy*. Los Angeles: SAGE Publications Ltd.

Bhambra, G. (2007). *Rethinking modernity: Postcolonialism and the sociological imagination*. New York: Springer.

Birmingham, P., & Yeatman, A. (Eds.). (2014). *The aporia of rights: Explorations in citizenship in the era of human rights*. New York: Bloomsbury Publishing.

Bjerre, H. A., & Hamza, A. (2014). Editorial Note. *Crisis and Critique, 1*(1), 1–3.

Bronner, S. E., & Kellner, D. (Eds.). (1989). *Critical theory and society*. New York: Routledge.

Brown, W. (2005). *Edgework: Critical essays on knowledge and politics*. Princeton, NJ: Princeton University Press.

Brown, W. (2015). *Undoing the demos: Neoliberalism's stealth revolution*. Cambridge, MA: Zone Books, MIT Press.

Brown, W. (2016). Sacrificial citizenship: Neoliberalism, human capital, and austerity politics. *Constellations, 23*(1), 3–14.

Butler, J. (2010). *Frames of war: When is life grieveable?* London: Verso.

Comaroff, J., & Comaroff, J. L. (2012). Theory from the south: Or, how Euro-America is evolving toward Africa. *Anthropological Forum, 22*(2), 113–131.

Connell, R. (2007). *Southern theory: The global dynamics of knowledge in social science*. Crows Nest, Australia: Allen & Unwin.

Connerton, P. (1976). *Critical theory*. Harmondsworth, UK: Penguin.

Cordero, R. (2014). Crisis and critique in Jürgen Habermas's social theory. *European Journal of Social Theory, 17*(4), 497–515.

Cruz, K., & Brown, W. (2016). Feminism, law, and neoliberalism: An interview and discussion with Wendy Brown. *Feminist Legal Studies, 24*, 69–89.

Dean, J. (2005). Zizek against democracy. *Law, Culture and the Humanities, 1*(2), 154–177.

Dean, J. (2009). *Democracy and other neoliberal fantasies: Communicative capitalism and left politics*. Durham, NC: Duke University Press.
Deutscher, P., & Lafont, C. (Eds.). (2017). *Critical theory in critical times: Transforming the global political and economic order*. New York: Columbia University Press.
Douzinas, C., & Gearty, C. (Eds.). (2014). *The meanings of rights: The philosophy and social theory of human rights*. Cambridge, UK: Cambridge University Press.
Flowers, N. (2004). How to define human rights education? A complex answer to a simple question. In V. B. Georgi & M. Seberich (Eds.), *International perspectives in human rights education* (pp. 105–127). Gütersloh, Germany: Bertelsmen Foundation Publishing.
Flynn, J. (2003). Habermas on human rights: Law, morality, and intercultural dialogue. *Social Theory and Practice, 29*(3), 431–457.
Fraser, N. (1985). What's critical about critical theory? The case of Habermas and gender. *New German Critique, 35*, 97–131.
Gikandi, S. (2002). Globalisation and the claims of postcoloniality. *The South Atlantic Quarterly, 100*(3), 627–658.
Grosfoguel, R. (2011). Decolonising post-colonial studies and paradigms of political-economy: Transmodernity, decolonial thinking, and global coloniality. *Transmodernity: Journal of Peripheral Cultural Production of the Luso-Hispanic World, 1*(1), n.p.
Habermas, J. (1985). *The theory of communicative action (Vol. 2). Lifeworld and system: A critique of functionalist reason*. Boston: Beacon Press.
Habermas, J. (1996). *Between facts and norms: Contributions to a discourse theory of law and democracy*. Cambridge, MA: MIT Press.
Heater, D. (2004). *A history of education for citizenship*. London: RoutledgeFalmer, Taylor & Francis.
Held, D. (1980). *Introduction to critical theory: Horkheimer to Habermas*. Berkeley, CA: University of California Press.
Holloway, J. (2012). Crisis and critique. *Capital & Class, 36*(3), 515–519.
Honneth, A. (1995). *The struggle for recognition: The moral grammar of social conflicts*. Cambridge, MA: MIT Press.
Honneth, A. (2007). Recognition as ideology. In B. van den Brink & D. Owen (Eds.), *Recognition and power: Axel Honneth and the tradition of critical social theory* (pp. 323–347). Cambridge, UK: Cambridge University Press.
Honneth, A. (2012). *The i in we: Studies in the theory of recognition*. Cambridge, UK: Polity Press.
Honneth, A. (2014). *Freedom's right: The social foundations of democratic life*. Cambridge, UK: Polity Press.
Horkheimer, M. (1972). *Critical theory: Selected essays* (Vol. 1). London: A&C Black.
Horkheimer, M., & Adorno, T. W. (1972). *Dialectic of enlightenment: Max Horkheimer and Theodor W. Adorno*. New York: Seabury Press.
Huddleston, R. E. (2016). *A report on education for democratic citizenship and human rights education policy and practice in six eastern partnership countries*. Strasbourg, France: Council of Europe.
Keet, A. (2010). A conceptual typology of human rights education and associated pedagogical forms. *Journal of Human Rights Education, 3*, 30–41.
Keet, A. (2014). Spectacle and spectators: Higher education and the 'disappearance' of democracy (Part 1): Exploration of the critical relationship between higher education and the development of democracy in South Africa. *South African Journal of Higher Education, 28*(3), 849–865.
Keet, A. (2015). It is time: Critical human rights education in an age of counter-hegemonic distrust. *Education as Change, 19*(3), 46–64.
Kerr, D. (2013, December). *The council of Europe charter on education for democratic citizenship and human rights education (EDC/HRE): And its implementation*. Retrieved from https://ec.europa.eu/jrc/sites/jrcsh/files/cce2013rome_s2_the-council-of-europe-charter-on-edc-and-hre.pdf

Klein, N. (2008). Wall St. crisis should be for neoliberalism what fall of Berlin Wall was for communism [Interview]. *Democracy Now*. Page numbers? Or website?
Krastev, I. (2014). *Democracy disrupted: The politics of global protest*. Philadelphia: University of Pennsylvania Press.
Laker, J. (Ed.). (2016). *Palgrave studies in global citizenship education and democracy*. London: Palgrave Macmillan.
Lenhart, V., & Savolainen, K. (Eds.). (2002). Human rights education as a field of practice and of theoretical reflection. *International Review of Education (Special Issue on Education and Human Rights), 48*(3–4), 145–158.
Lynch, J. (1992). *Education for citizenship in a multicultural society*. London: Cassell.
Lyotard, J. F. (1999). *The postmodern condition*. Minneapolis, MN: University of Minnesota Press.
Mignolo, W. D. (2014). From 'human rights' to 'life rights'. In C. Douzinas & C. Gearty (Eds.), *The meanings of rights: The philosophy and social theory of human rights* (pp. 161–180). Cambridge, UK: Cambridge University Press.
Mills, C. W. (2017). Criticising critical theory. In P. Deutscher & C. Lafont (Eds.), *Critical theory in critical times: Transforming the global political and economic order* (pp. 233–250). New York: Columbia University Press.
Olaison, L., Pedersen, M., & Sørensen, B. M. (2009). 'No we can't.' Crisis as chance. *Ephemera: Theory and Politics in Organisation, 9*(1), 1–8.
Pilapil, R. (2011). Psychologisation of injustice? On Axel Honneth's theory of recognitive justice. *Ethical Perspectives, 18*(1), 79–106. Retrieved from. https://doi.org/10.2143/EP.18.1.2066214
Quijano, A. (2000). Coloniality of power and Eurocentrism in Latin America. *International Sociology, 15*(2), 215–232.
Rabaka, R. (2009). *Africana critical theory: Reconstructing the black radical tradition, from W.E.B. Du Bois and C.L.R. James to Frantz Fanon and Amilcar Cabral*. Lanham, MD: Lexington Books.
Reardon, B., & Snauwaert, D. (2015). *Betty A. Reardon: A pioneer in education for peace and human rights*. New York: Springer.
Renault, E. (2005). Radical democracy and an abolitionist concept of justice. A critique of Habermas. *Critical Horizons, 6*(1), 137–153.
Said, E. W. (1994). *Culture and imperialism*. New York: Vintage.
Schaffer, J. K. (2015). The co-originality of human rights and democracy in an international order. *International Theory, 7*(1), 96–124.
Smith, M. (2015). *Lessons from integrating peace, human rights, and civic education into social studies curricula and textbooks*. Paris: International Institute for Educational Planning.
Tarrow, N. (1992). Human rights education: Alternative conceptions. In J. Lynch, C. Modgil, & S. Modgil (Eds.), *Human rights, education and global responsibilities* (pp. 21–34). London: Falmer Press.
Tibbitts, F., & Kirchschlaeger, P. G. (2010). Perspectives of research on human rights education. *Journal of Human Rights Education, 3*, 8–29.
Toots, A., De Groof, S., & Kavadias, D. (2012). Comparative studies of civic and citizenship education. *Journal of Social Science Education, 11*(1), 3–6.
Tucker, R. C. (Ed.). (1978). *The Marx-Engels reader*. New York/London: Norton and Company.
UNESCO. (1998a). *Citizenship education for the 21st century*. Retrieved from http://www.unesco.org/education/tlsf/mods/theme_b/interact/mod07task03/appendix.htm
UNESCO. (1998b). *Learning to live together in peace and harmony. Values education for peace, human rights, democracy and sustainable development for the Asia-Pacific region*. Bangkok, Thailand: UNESCO.
Zeleza, P. (2009). African studies and universities since independence: The challenges of epistemic and institutional decolonisation. *Transition, 101*, 110–135.

Chapter 10
Decolonial Strategies and Pedagogical/Curricular Possibilities

Introduction

It has been pointed out throughout this book that human rights are full of contradictions and Human Rights Education (henceforth HRE) has not only failed to address these contradictions, but it has also legitimated a narrow and uncritical type of human rights discourse in education. One of the most blatant contradictions pointed out is how everyone is supposed to have human rights, yet the reality is very different, as most people do not. While the United Nations guarantees human rights and countries are supposed to protect them, many countries around the world are actually violating them. The roots of these contradictions, as Yang emphasizes, "lie in the modern condition, which is a *colonial* condition" (2015, p. 226, added emphasis). Therefore, it is argued that the human rights field needs decolonial strategies for the project of decolonising human rights to be advanced (Barreto, 2012) and HRE, in turn, will also need to become 'decolonising' (Tuck & Yang, 2012). We opened this conversation in the previous chapter, and touched on it in Chap. 5, this chapter focuses entirely on this process of decolonisation.

Generally speaking, colonialism denotes the exploitation of human beings and non-human worlds in order to build the wealth and the privilege of the colonizers (Mignolo, 2003). Colonisation of the land, argues Mignolo, goes hand in hand with geo-politics of knowledge, and specifically the domination of Eurocentric thought that classifies regions and people around the world as underdeveloped economically and mentally. Decolonisation refers to the interrogation of how Eurocentric thought, knowledge and power structures dominate present societies, and how that thought and knowledge has consistently undermined the exploitation of colonised people and their losses (Brayboy, 2006). The decolonising project, then, disrupts Western epistemology as part of the larger colonial project, introducing multiplicity and 'pluriversality', namely, turning the process of knowledge production open to epistemic diversity (Mignolo, 2006).

M. Zembylas, A. Keet, *Critical Human Rights Education*, Contemporary Philosophies and Theories in Education 13,
https://doi.org/10.1007/978-3-030-27198-5_10

The purpose of this chapter is to explore what *decolonising*—as both a verb and an adjective—HRE might imply and how this "intellectual and political enterprise" (Barreto, 2012, p. 2) could make a contribution to a self-renewing and critical orientation towards human rights and HRE. Our point of departure is Tuck and Yang's (2012, p. 2) provocative observation that, "Decolonisation, which we assert as a distinct project from other civil and human rights-based social justice projects, is far too often subsumed into the directives of these projects, with no regard for how decolonisation wants something different than those forms of justice." While this critique emphasizes, rightly so, what is incommensurable between decolonising projects and other social justice projects, the decolonising project also highlights a radical position that is necessary for 'transformative' (Bajaj, Coslaghi, & Mackie, 2016) forms of HRE that take into consideration social justice issues: it interrogates the very nature of the epistemological and ontological grounding inherent both in the human rights discourse and in HRE, namely, the colonial condition and the liberal notions of the 'human' and 'rights' in European Enlightenment. There is much to be gained, both politically and intellectually, from moving away from a competition over how decolonising and other social justice projects—which are not always commensurable—are nevertheless co-implicated. In this chapter, then, we want to offer an analysis of the human rights (education) regime that illuminates both the distinctness of decolonisation *and* the ways in which it is linked with other social justice projects.

As we have pointed out at the beginning of this book, the human rights regime is embedded within a specific cultural and historical framework involving the foregrounding of Western colonial knowledges (Baxi, 2007; Mutua, 2002; Spivak, 2004). As we have argued, HRE has also been shaped within this colonial condition that delimits its own space, both theoretically and practically (see also, Osler, 2015; Yang, 2015). For HRE to be decolonising, then, there has to be serious strategic work that challenges Eurocentric thinking and recontextualises HRE theory and pedagogical practice in the historical horizon of coloniality. In order for HRE to become more 'critical' and 'transformative', it needs to go beyond the epistemological and ontological grounding inherent in the dominant human rights regime. For this to happen, we need to develop HRE theory and practice that go beyond critical pedagogies which highlight the human as the unit of liberation (Yang, 2015); we need decolonising pedagogies and curricula that problematise the very premises of human rights and HRE. In emphasizing decolonial perspectives that enable human rights educators to reposition the theoretical frame of mainstream HRE, this chapter provides a set of strategies and ideas for enacting a decolonisation approach in HRE curriculum and pedagogy. We end with a discussion of decolonisation because, to some degree, it serves as a critique of much of the theoretical work in the rest of the book, which has largely explored the possibilities of CHRE through Western theoretical traditions. This chapter thus serves to take another important step in the long journey of *inventing* a CHRE.

The Eurocentric Horizon of Understanding Human Rights and Its Critiques

As noted in Chap. 2, human rights have gained their modern existence within a particular political order and historical events that incrementally developed a set of concepts we now recognize as 'human rights'. Their history indicates that human rights are a Western concept grounded in liberal views of Modernity and the Enlightenment and specifically humanist notions of 'the human' as an autonomous, rational, and sovereign 'individual' (Donnelly, 2003; Douzinas, 2000; Mutua, 2002). As post/de/colonial scholars argue, the very constitution of 'human' in human rights discourses is predicated upon Eurocentric assumptions within which only particular kinds of subjects are recognizable as 'human' (Brown, 2004; Mignolo, 2006); all else is constituted as 'Other' through practices of racialisation, sexualisation and naturalisation (Braidotti, 2013; Wynter, 2003). Pointing to the Eurocentric character of the corpus of today's conceptualisations of human rights reveals their epistemological and ontological grounding, "as it comprises the unveiling of a genealogical link between knowledge and history" (Barreto, 2012, p. 3). Inasmuch as such a connection is made, argues Barreto, it becomes evident that the hegemonic theory of human rights "is the offspring of a particular perspective grounded in a historical and geographical context" (ibid.). Human rights discourse, then, has colonising and orientalising functions for those who have been, and still are, systematically excluded from its imaginary (Khoja-Moolji, 2017; Yeğenoğlu, 1998).

For instance, Khoja-Moolji (2017) analyses the well-known case of Malala Yousafzai and her attack by the Taliban as an example of the making of humans and their others in and through human rights advocacy. Western media and public discourses have systematically reinscribed Malala as perennially vulnerable to brown, Muslim, male violence and viewed her empowerment as individualised action against repressive local cultures and communities. Malala's work is assumed to advance women's rights as signs of modernity, enlightenment and progress. Any critique of Malala "is read as regressive, backward, premodern, and against the principles of human rights" (Khoja-Moolji, 2017, p. 377). The acquisition of more rights by individuals is assumed to be the only way to secure development and emancipation, explains Khoja-Moolji, while alternative conceptions of what it means to be human to lead a meaningful life—e.g. humanity in relational terms; the inclusion of nonhumans in systems of living—are either undermined and ridiculed or utterly discarded. When living that is experienced in such complex ways is reduced to a list of rights or to legal and state-defined definitions, it can be read as a form of violence and coloniality (ibid., p. 378). The production of Malala's case as a particular kind of vulnerable, suffering and empowered subject in and through the language of human rights "has the effect of (re)installing the white Anglophone male as representing full humanity" (ibid., p. 380).

One of the major critiques (see Chap. 9) raised over the years, then, is that Eurocentric theory of human rights presents itself as objective and universal, assuming exclusive authority and legitimacy, while other conceptions and histories (e.g. Third World approaches or perspectives from the South) are silenced. A Third Word approach to human rights theory, for example, encompasses a different interpretation of the history of rights in the context of colonisation, bringing into consciousness "five hundred years of utopian mobilisation of natural rights, the Rights of Man and human rights to resist imperialism" (Barreto, 2012, p. 4). Non-Western perspectives are often delegitimated as backward because they do not express moral concerns in a framework of Eurocentric thought, yet they nonetheless address them in some other epistemic framework (Al-Daraweesh & Snauwaert, 2013). As Al-Daraweesh and Snauwaert emphasize, non-Western communities have moral concerns that are 'isomorphic equivalents' of human rights, namely, traditions, social practices or moral systems (e.g. Confucianism, Buddhism) that conceptualize what it means to be human, how one might live with dignity and in which ways individuals within social groups may realize their full potential.

One may easily identify the existing imperialist traces of Eurocentrism in how human rights have become over the years essentialized in universal norms often expressed in juridical terms (e.g. international law). As Barreto poignantly observes:

> By framing human rights in conceptions of history based exclusively in European milestones, the theory of rights remains within a Eurocentric horizon of understanding. Having been born out of the experiences of bourgeois revolution, European theories deal mainly with relations between state and society, or between governments and individuals, putting aside the problematic interactions between empires and colonies. (2012, p. 4)

It is not surprising, then, that some of the most powerful critiques of human rights over the years point out that the human rights regime serves the interests of Western powers (e.g. Mutua, 2002) acting in neo-colonial terms (Baxi, 2007; Spivak, 2004). By assuming that European perspectives create a rule of law and of human rights, the hegemonic discourse of human rights is founded on an interpretation of modern history that fails to acknowledge the problematic entanglement between Europe and former European colonies (Gonçalves & Costa, 2016).

In particular, there are concerns whether Eurocentric approaches to human rights eventually correct dominant power structures that are responsible for human suffering in the first place or whether they in fact perpetuate colonial thinking and practices. In a rather polemic tone, Mutua (2002) argues that interpretations of human rights are not neutral but very much embedded in cultural and political assumptions, and writes that "The grand narrative of human rights contains a subtext which depicts an epochal contest pitting savages, on the one hand, against victims and saviours, on the other" (2002, p. 10). Human rights discourses, then, function as a subtle form of neo-colonialist crusade, where 'civilised' nations must teach 'primitive savages' the proper way of living and behaving. Mutua's main assertion is that: "Constructed primarily as the moral guardian of global capitalism and liberal internationalism, the human rights corpus is simply unable to confront structurally and in a meaningful way the deep-seated imbalances of power and privilege which bedevil our world" (ibid., p. 157).

Furthermore, post/de/colonial theorists like Bhabha (1999), Chakrabarty (2000), Spivak (2004), and Baxi (2007) highlight the influence of colonial thinking and practices on human rights and argue that Eurocentric thinking entails the danger of perpetuating colonial power relations (see Zembylas & Bozalek [2014] for a detailed discussion). In particular, Bhabha's (1999) work acknowledges how rights and obligations constitute modernist myths that perpetuate colonial power relations. He questions whether the global human rights discourse, framed in legal terms, can be a tool with which colonialism can be overcome. Similarly, Chakrabarty (2000) analyzes how Western political concepts such as 'human rights' are neither stable nor singular in their meaning—contrary to how they are often presented by ideological discourses of modernity. Also, Spivak (2004) argues that a critical historical analysis of human rights in the last hundred and 50 years reveals how human rights are articulated within the language frame of the hegemonic culture. As she writes: "The idea of human rights, in other words, may carry within itself the agenda of a kind of social Darwinism—the fittest must shoulder the burden of righting the wrongs of the unfit—and the possibility of an alibi" (ibid., p. 524). For Spivak, the only chance to correct this structural injustice of human rights is to appeal to responsibility; that is, to develop social responsibility through learning from the subaltern. Likewise, Baxi (2007) suggests that the modern conception of human rights was based on mechanisms of exclusion and thus a major task of human rights narratology is to give language to histories of human pain and suffering.

All in all, the critiques of Eurocentrism and the questioning of its hegemony rejects the identification of essential or universal traits of the 'human' or 'rights', seeing them as culturally and historically constructed within a European narrative. As Sen (2009) comments on the perceived universalism of human rights and the critiques raised:

> There is something very appealing in the idea that every person anywhere in the world, irrespective of citizenship, residence, race, class, caste or community, has the same basic rights which others should respect. The big moral appeal of human rights has been used for a variety of purposes, from resisting torture, arbitrary incarceration and racial discrimination to demanding an end to hunger and starvation, and to medical neglect across the globe. At the same time, the basic idea of human rights, which people are supposed to have simply because they are human, is seen by critics as entirely without any kind of reasoned foundation. (p. 355)

These critiques which have been discussed in previous chapters—e.g. the ideological functions of human rights, human rights idolatry, the moral dominance of the human rights discourse and expectations associated with human rights founded in Western epistemology—show how hegemonic discourses of human rights grounded in a universalist epistemology of the West have advanced and sustained imperialism "by selecting the holders of truth, dictating the colonisation of culture and propelling the West to world hegemony" (Barreto, 2012, p. 6). Resisting the entanglement of modernity and coloniality in the field of human rights has to dismantle first the link between Eurocentric theory of rights and the historical event of coloniality.

Therefore, what these critiques emphasize is the need to adopt a different viewpoint, and, as a consequence, to be able to think of human rights from an alternative standpoint such as that of the South. A critical approach towards juridical, universalist and Eurocentric forms of human rights opens up spaces for their productive reconstruction and integration into struggles for social justice (Keet, 2010). Calls for the reconstruction of human rights in ways that bring into critical consciousness the entanglement of modernity and coloniality extend the space of understanding human rights beyond the borders of Europe and the perceived 'universal' conception of rights (Barreto, 2012). One of the central arguments of this chapter, as advanced throughout the book, is that a decolonising approach is an emerging necessity for repositioning and renewing HRE, because Eurocentric theories of human rights provide fertile grounds for a declarationist and conservative strand of HRE to become dominant.

The Global Discourse of HRE and the Struggles for Decolonisation

As we pointed out in earlier chapters, mainstream HRE projects in schools, universities, non-governmental organisations and communities seldom question the epistemological and ontological underpinnings of the Eurocentric theory of human rights. It is not surprising, then, that although different models of practice exist in HRE, the theoretical underpinnings of HRE either remain underdeveloped or simply perpetuate an uncritical advancement of human rights universals as an uncontested social good. Building on the argument about the 'imprisonment' of human rights into colonial and neoliberal arrangements, we suggested in Chap. 2 that the legalistic framework of human rights has also limited the promise of HRE within a normative form that is often grounded in a 'declarationist' approach.

In particular, the construction of a global HRE discourse has relied upon the subjugation of particular types of knowledge, according to Coysh (2014). This process of subjugation occurred in two ways: first, by institutionalization and formalization of HRE so that historical knowledges are masked; and second, by subjugating a whole range of different forms of knowledge that were discounted as naive or inferior. The colonial condition, then, has been very much embedded in the subjugation of alternative conceptions of human rights. What is remarkable is not so much the institutionalization and formalization processes themselves through United Nations agencies but the speed at which this construction achieved hegemonic status. The way that the language of international human rights norms and standards are prioritized in many models of HRE practice is evidence of this, says Coysh (2014). As a consequence, "rather than widening the scope for social transformation, the dominant discourse of human rights education has in fact narrowed the opportunities for this to take place" (ibid., 108).

All in all, the aforementioned calls for reconfiguring, repositioning or renewing HRE so that it becomes 'critical' and 'transformative' are well aligned with recent arguments for decolonising HRE (Yang, 2015). Importantly though, as Tuck and Yang (2012) warn us, we need to be careful with the adoption of decolonising discourse as its superficial and uncritical use will turn decolonisation into a metaphor rather than a strategy, a politics, and a practice that exposes and dismantles coloniality. Oppression and colonisation are not the same, as Tuck and Yang explain and add:

> Calling different groups 'colonized' without describing their relationship to settler colonialism is an equivocation [...]. In particular, describing all struggles against imperialism as 'decolonising' creates a convenient ambiguity between decolonisation and social justice work [...]. 'We are all colonized' may be a true statement but is deceptively embracive and vague, its reference: 'None of us are settlers.' Equivocation, or calling everything by the same name, is a move towards innocence that is especially vogue in coalition politics among people of colour. (p. 17)

While Tuck and Yang are right in that there are parts of the decolonisation project that are not easily absorbed by human rights based approaches, it would be politically unwise, in our view, to allow this assumption stand in the way of important political alliances with other minoritised groups. This is by no means to suggest that the set of evasions or 'settler moves to innocence', as Tuck and Yang call them, are underestimated or overlooked in the name of a vague call for alliances. But if decolonisation is going to truly become more than a metaphor—namely, a practice, a strategy, an alternative framing of human rights and HRE in praxis—then it will require all the solidarity that is needed from differently colonized groups. This claim neither sanctions equivocation nor forecloses new potential alliances and solidarities among different colonised groups.[1]

In addition, Yang (2015) points out that if HRE is going to be truly decolonising, it has to dismantle first the concept of 'Human' as it continues "to mean a settler and a property owner whose 'Rights' to land, life, and liberty are actually entitlements enforced by settler nation-states" (226). It has already been mentioned earlier that a 'critical' form of HRE has to denaturalise the categories of 'human' and 'rights' grounded in Eurocentric theories of human rights. On the one hand, there are important commonalities in the political project of a 'critical' and a 'decolonising' HRE that ought to be kept in mind; on the other hand, to acknowledge Tuck and Yang's (2012) warning, critical theory and pedagogy may not be always appropriate for making sense of the colonial condition and for transforming those who carry the burden of Eurocentric knowledge of human rights. In the next part of the chapter, we will discuss some decolonial strategies that could reposition human rights and HRE, while the last part will become more specific in suggesting how a decolonising pedagogy and curriculum in CHRE might look like.

[1] Sylvia Wynter's (2003) work offers a profound way of linking various forms of violence (e.g. colonialism, slavery, capitalist exploitation), while remaining attentive to their particularities (see also Wynter in Mignolo 2015). Her point is that while there are important distinctions among various social justice projects, the political struggles that seek to redress these violences have to critique the dominant version of the human she calls "Man" (i.e. a Western bourgeois conception of the human).

Decolonial Strategies for Human Rights and HRE

According to Barreto (2012), the quest to decolonize human rights can be summed up in two statements made by Walter Mignolo: "the future demands thinking beyond the Greeks and Eurocentrism" (2003, p. 85), and "a radical reconceptualisation of the human rights paradigm" (2000, p. 739). According to Mignolo (2009), the concepts of 'human' and 'rights' were inventions of European humanists during Enlightenment to challenge the power of the Church and highlight the autonomy and rationality of each individual. The liberal reforms and revolutions in the seventeenth and eighteenth centuries consolidated a secular notion of humanity which was recognized in The Declaration on the Rights of Man and Citizen after the French Revolution (Mignolo, 2009). In the Universal Declaration of Human Rights of 1948, the notions of the 'human' and 'rights' inherited the liberal ontological and epistemological premises of the West, legitimating Eurocentric thinking while excluding other sites of knowledge (Mignolo, 2011).

Mignolo (2009, 2011) suggests that there are two options in responding to the notions of the 'human' and 'rights' as inventions of Western imperial knowledge: first, to accept what 'human' and 'rights' are according to the Western framework of knowledge; and, second, to engage in 'epistemic disobedience' by denouncing the unilateralism of the universal, and by affirming that being human is not being Christian and rights are not framed in liberal legality. Mignolo argues for the latter option, the decolonial option, because it does not attempt to replace the old Eurocentric truth with a new truth but rather to keep the definition of what it means to be human open. He uses the term 'pluriversality' to denote the notion of universal knowledge for humanity, yet one which embraces openness to dialogue among different epistemic traditions (Mignolo, 2006). As Acuña (2013) notes, the decolonial option strongly criticises liberal legality and the epistemological and ontological foundations of Western modernity/coloniality. But more importantly, what the decolonial option does for human rights is to de-link them from Western epistemologies and ontologies and enact an alternative approach.

For example, Khoja-Moolji (2017) discusses a series of human rights summer camps she organized for adolescent girls in Pakistan to show the implications of alternative epistemic traditions in the discussion about human rights. Participants in this HRE program, says Khoja-Moolji, often saw themselves as linked with the welfare of their families and communities, with each having a particular set of responsibilities embedded in a relational system of living, human as well as nonhuman. "Such a conceptualization of the body," explains Khoja-Moolji, "poses a challenge to human rights discourses that abstract the body in its experiences of vulnerability and empowerment" (p. 394). Thus, for instance, when some male members of the girls' households died or fell ill, many girls decided to stay back from school and help with the responsibilities of their families for waged labour. In this context, assertions of education as a right could not deter these girls from prioritising household responsibilities over school. Rights-based approaches would have failed to recognize the complexities of life, in effect silencing the 'messiness' of the everyday lives of these people and their social systems. This example shows not only the multiple axes along which humans experience their humanity (Khoja-Moolji, 2017), often as a response (with tremendous dignity) to the painful legacy of colonial practices that have led to extreme poverty and marginalization. It also shows how rights-based discourses may often become a very effective rhetorical device that implicitly transfers the blame to the 'vulnerable' victims of various oppressions: they, as individuals, supposedly have to stand up against these oppressions and claim their 'rights', yet in reality their ontological conceptions of being and living may be quite different from Western individualism (Santos, 2013).

The project of decolonising human rights or decolonising HRE, then, is inevitably part of the wider task of decolonising education and knowledge. We will present, then, a number of strategies that have already advanced the project of decolonising human rights (see Barreto, 2012), claiming that they can also support HRE to become decolonising. Here we focus on three such strategies—which are further 'translated' into decolonising pedagogy and curriculum of HRE in the last part of the paper: first, the re-contextualisation of human rights and HRE so that there is inclusion of different traditions of human rights and a critical relationship with human rights universals in HRE theory and practice; second, the critique of critical theory and pedagogy and its enrichment with decolonial thinking and praxis; and, finally, the adoption of an ethics of emotions as an ethics of human rights and HRE. Each of these strategies is briefly discussed below.

The first decolonial strategy is what Barreto (2012) calls the 're-contextualisation' of human rights which includes the necessity of extending the history and context of human rights beyond the borders of Europe. As he writes: "The re-contextualisation and contextualisation of the hegemonic theory of human rights in the material conditions of modern/colonial geography and history paves the way for re-drawing and re-writing the geography and history of human rights" (ibid., p. 6). Furthermore, Barreto explains, the standard way of presenting human rights is often situated in no context at all, highlighting the 'universal' conception of rights. Imperialism has been advanced and sustained because 'the truth' (i.e. Western epistemology) has colonized other cultures (Mignolo, 2011). Therefore, resisting colonisation in the field of human rights implies dismantling the hegemony of Western epistemology by recognizing the historical setting within which different traditions of human rights have emerged outside the borders of Europe—among colonised people in the South or in the Third World (Barreto, 2012).

In the field of HRE, the above idea implies both the inclusion of different traditions of human rights and a critical relationship with human rights universals. A critical and hermeneutic approach to HRE, argue Al-Daraweesh and Snauwaert (2013), includes local cultural conceptualisations of human rights, that is, different conceptions of human rights altogether that express the moral concerns of different (non-Western) cultures and match the values of the Western conceptualisation of human rights. Human rights cannot be based anymore in a priori universal principles detached from the historical and cultural context—the traditional framework of human rights theory and history (Barreto, 2012). As we have emphasized in our proposal for CHRE throughout this book, an important aspect for HRE to be 'critical' is to stand in a critical relationship with human rights universals. Therefore, a critical dialogue is needed between local notions of human rights and international legal documents and declarations. Decolonisation of HRE means recognizing the contributions made by Southern and Third World cultures. Most importantly, though, it means acknowledging that the global discourse of human rights and HRE has emerged in the background of the history of modern colonisation of the world and the struggle against imperial violence. As Barreto writes,

> we can speak of the 'colonial origins of human rights'. [...] The foundational stages of human rights theory and history in modern times are to be found not only in the Enlightenment, but even before that, in the resistance to the display of the capacity for destruction of imperialism—the dark side of the other constitutive pillar of modernity. Modernity cannot be identified exclusively with emancipation; plunder and genocide were prior realities of its formation. (2012, p. 17)

A CHRE, therefore, needs to offer a counter-narrative of human rights that shows the struggles of indigenous people against slavery, racial domination and the colonial enterprise. To become truly critical and transformative, a recontextualised HRE needs to acknowledge the barbarism of European civilization, long before the Enlightenment and the Holocaust, and how the tradition of human rights emerged in the context of colonialism.

The second decolonial strategy is the critique of critical theory (Barreto, 2012; Broeck, 2013) and critical pedagogy (Tuck & Yang, 2012; Yang, 2015), as we have discussed in the previous chapter. Broeck (2013) argues that critical theory needs to be modified to account for the violence generated by imperialism. As it stands at the moment, says Broeck, critical theory highlights humanism as the epitome of modernity, while it fails to recognize how capitalism, imperialism and colonialism were also made possible in modern Europe and led to slave trading and colonialist practices. Therefore, Broeck suggests that critical theory needs to adopt a *longue durée* historical approach that widens its field of study to recognise the entanglement of modernity with coloniality and to read history from the point of view of the colonized or the slave. For human rights, this implies re-writing their history, as Barreto (2012) says, that is, expanding the standard accounts of the trajectory of rights in modern times.

Along similar lines, yet focusing on critical pedagogy, Tuck and Yang (2012) emphasize that it is important to acknowledge that there are significant differences between critical pedagogy and decolonising projects. For example, argue Tuck and Yang, Freire situates the work of liberation in the minds of the oppressed, as a humanist self-critique, whereas decolonising projects (e.g. Fanon) always position the work of liberation in the particularities of colonisation and the structures of the colonisation process. Tuck and Yang push for a much sharper distinction between critical pedagogy and decolonising work, suggesting that decolonising pedagogy is an alternative to critical pedagogy precisely because the latter remains deeply humanist when it comes to liberation, whereas for HRE to be decolonising, it has to dismantle the category of human (see also Yang, 2015).

Finally, the third decolonial strategy suggested here is the adoption of an ethics of emotions as an ethics of human rights and HRE. As pointed out in Chaps. 6, 7, and 8, the affective turn in the social sciences and the humanities has offered various insights towards establishing a link between colonialism, human rights, and emotions, especially in relation to how human suffering is entangled with colonialism and elicits rights-talk (Barreto, 2012). These issues push the boundaries of thinking about what human rights can *do* in the context of multiple temporalities and historical changes in local and global power relations, (post)colonial processes, (post) national discourses and biopolitical arrangements (Athanasiou, Hantzaroula & Yannakopoulos, 2008).

The affective turn raises new important questions about human rights and their transformative possibilities in HRE: How can explorations of human rights activism become strategic sites of ethical and political transformation that pay attention to different manifestations of social injustice? How can human rights create possibilities to resignify emotional and social injury in ways that continuously rework and unsettle affective attachments to particular bodies, discourses and practices such as the mythology of national belonging? How do biopolitics emerge as a crucial feature of human rights in the making of modern individuals and communities imagined through the normativity of emotional bonds and solidified through the emotional power and performative force of identity work? (Zembylas 2014, 2016) All in all, the decolonisation of human rights in HRE needs to offer possibilities of approaching human rights from a critical emotional orientation.

Decolonising Pedagogy and Curriculum in CHRE

In the last part of this chapter, we further elaborate on the aforementioned decolonial strategies by attempting to 'translate' those into 'decolonising pedagogy' and 'decolonising curriculum' in CHRE. In particular, we underscore the need for HRE to draw upon theoretical and conceptual tools that will facilitate this endeavour. In this respect, we draw upon the concepts of 'decolonising pedagogy' (Tejeda & Gutierrez, 2005; Tejeda, Espinoza & Gutierrez, 2003) and 'decolonising curriculum' (Grande, 2004; Subedi, 2013) to argue for the importance of developing 'critical' and 'transformative' forms of HRE "that take into consideration the distinct social locations and forms of marginalization faced by different groups" (Bajaj et al., 2016, p. 15).

First of all, decolonising pedagogy aims at interrupting Eurocentric knowledge at the level of the classroom with the hope that these interventions help undermine historical distributions of power structures. According to Tejeda et al. (2003), "there is a direct and material relation between the political processes and social structures of colonialism on the one hand, and Western regimes of knowledge and representation on the other" (p. 24). Decolonising pedagogy in HRE, for example, challenges the dominant thinking and meanings attached to human rights as those have been integral to colonial conditions across the world. The decolonising pedagogy proposed by Tejeda et al.

> must be guided by a conceptually dynamic worldview and a set of values that make it anticapitalist, antiracist, antisexist, and antihomophobic. It is informed by a theoretical heteroglossia that strategically utilizes theorizations and understandings from various fields and conceptual frameworks to unmask the logics, workings, and effects of […] colonial domination, oppression, and exploitation in our contemporary contexts. (p. 21)

A decolonising pedagogy in HRE, then, draws theoretically from various conceptual frameworks (e.g. postcolonial studies, spatial theory, critical pedagogy, critical race theory, Black feminist theory) so that human rights educators and learners are offered the tools to re-contextualize human rights. To achieve this goal, educators and learners need to take a critical stance toward human rights as they are conceptualized/interpreted in the material conditions of coloniality and its persisting effects. We contend that developing a critical consciousness of neocolonial conditions by showing the connections between Eurocentric epistemology of human rights and colonial domination is fundamental for a decolonising pedagogy in HRE.

However, the cultivation of critical consciousness in decolonising pedagogy is entangled with educators' and learners' emotional investments (Zembylas 2013a, 2014, 2016). A fundamental challenge, then is: How does an educator deal pedagogically with the learner who resists or rejects critical perspectives and who openly expresses racist, colonialist or nationalist views because his or her privileges are being threatened or lost; or the learner who is so traumatized from racism, colonialism or nationalism that he or she feels that nothing can be done to rectify the situation? As Jansen (2009) maintains, critical theory and critical pedagogy receives and constructs the world as divided (e.g. black/white, oppressors/oppressed) and then takes sides to free the oppressed. However, the rhetoric of critical pedagogy as we know it might prove inadequate, because it remains too firmly grounded in such binary pairings as oppressor/oppressed, master/slave, and power/freedom (Albrecht-Crane, 2005; Worsham, 2001; Yoon, 2005).

Consequently, decolonising pedagogy in HRE has to move beyond critical pedagogy not only because critical pedagogy highlights the human as the unit of liberation whereas decolonising pedagogy has to denaturalize the category of the Human (Yang, 2015), but also because the difficult knowledge emerging from counter-narratives of human rights has to be foregrounded rather than backgrounded (Zembylas, 2014). Working from the assumption that decolonising pedagogy in HRE must engage this terrain of difficult emotional knowledge in ways that have not been sufficiently addressed by critical pedagogy so far, decolonising pedagogy needs to pay attention to difficult knowledge of human rights as a source of fruitful and critical sentimental rather naive sentimental ways (Zembylas, 2016). To do so, a nuanced understanding of decolonising pedagogy in HRE needs to pay attention to two important insights.

First, decolonising pedagogy in HRE needs to recognize that global discourses of human rights formulate pedagogies of emotion in society and in schools, exerting a powerful impact on the affective struggle for empowerment and resistance (cf. Worsham, 2001). Therefore, human rights pedagogues who wish to develop a decolonising approach need to be critically aware of the emotional consequences when they categorise individuals into 'oppressors' and 'oppressed'; failing to understand how learners' emotional attachments are strongly entangled with traumatic historical circumstances of human rights violations and material conditions will undermine human rights educators' pedagogical interventions. Second, as Worsham (2001) further states, there are many emotional manifestations of disempowerment and lack of resistance such as boredom, apathy, resentment, hatred, anger, nostalgia, sorrow, loss, shame, guilt and humiliation, and generally the ways those emotions are organized and practiced across differences of race, class, and gender (Zembylas, 2013a). A form of decolonising pedagogy that does not apprehend its own limitations of the complex discourses and practices of emotion that are embedded in particular local contexts is less likely to acknowledge emotion as a crucial aspect of political struggle for change and solidarity. Thus the desire for empowerment and resistance cannot be taken for granted as a 'natural resource' for any sort of critical pedagogies (Amsler, 2011); rather, the affective tensions around issues of empowerment and resistance must be placed at the heart of decolonising pedagogy in HRE.

Finally, in relation to decolonisation and the curriculum, to 'decolonise curriculum' means to critically examine dominant structures of knowledge and their relationship to power—as they operate and are reproduced in and through the curricular content and design—recentering knowledge in the intellectual histories of colonized people (Grande, 2004). Decolonising HRE curriculum, for example, entails the inclusion of the histories and experiences of colonized people, thus constructing "a genealogy for human rights that differs from the usual one" (Gilroy, 2010, p. 57). As Gilroy writes further, this genealogy

> should begin with the history of conquest and expansion, and must be able to encompass the debates about how colonies and slave plantations were to be administered. [...] The counter-narrative of human rights we require is evident in opposition to racial orders, in the struggles of indigenous peoples and in the post- and anti-colonial pursuit of liberation from imperial domination. (ibid., pp. 71–72)

Decolonisation of the HRE curriculum, therefore, means to offer accounts of human rights that would force European thinking and knowledge to confront its barbarism and coloniality. To achieve this, the decolonising approach needs to embrace three critical curriculum approaches: antiessentialism, contrapuntal readings, and ethical solidarity (Subedi, 2013).

As noted throughout the book, there are often essentialist and universalist notions of human rights promoted in mainstream HRE, therefore, an antiessentialist approach critiques the monolithic portrayal (i.e. Eurocentric) of human rights, while emphasizing the value of recognizing not only the link between Western epistemology and modernity/coloniality but also the contributions made by Third-World countries and cultures. The antiessentialist HRE curriculum, then, draws strength from the idea of multiple perspectives on human rights, rather than universalizing human rights as a Western achievement. Second, the decolonising curriculum values contrapuntal readings (Subedi, 2013), meaning that it explicitly focuses on questions of colonisation and imperialism. For example, Eurocentric theories of human rights deal mainly with relations between state and society, or between governments and individuals, putting aside the problematic of the entanglements with empires and colonies (Barreto, 2012). The decolonising curriculum in HRE encompasses a different philosophy of the history in which human rights interpretations are based on, giving birth to a new paradigm of HRE that historicizes notions of human rights in the colonial condition and their entanglements with power structures. Finally, the decolonising curriculum is attentive to how questions of solidarity have been conceptualized, and it emphasizes the need to mobilize collective struggles across differences (Subedi, 2013). For example, in relation to HRE, as discussed in Chap. 8, this strategy implies that to promote action-oriented empathy and solidarity, there has to be a systematic investigation of the different ways in which feelings of empathy are evoked in the classroom and have differential implications for those who suffer (Zembylas, 2013b). To interrogate the trappings of sentimentality and especially narratives of pity, human rights educators and learners need to challenge the emotional investments and emotion-informed ideologies that underlie their responses toward suffering and seek to promote sympathy and solidarity that make a concrete difference in sufferers' lives (Zembylas, 2016).

Conclusion

In this chapter, we have argued that a decolonising approach in HRE examines human rights issues through a critical lens that interrogates the Eurocentric grounding of human rights universals and advances the project of re-contextualizing human rights in the historical horizon of modernity/coloniality. This alternative configuration of HRE as 'critical' and 'transformative' offers pedagogical and curricular possibilities that go beyond conventional forms of HRE and create openings for pedagogical praxis along social justice lines. The quest to create these openings and possibilities is a fundamental element for decolonising the theory and pedagogical practices of human rights. As Gorski (2008) has pointed out more than a decade ago about decolonising intercultural education, we also argue that attaining a decolonising HRE requires not only subtle shifts in pedagogical practice, but also important shifts of consciousness that prepare us to see the political and theoretical moves that are necessary and influence HRE theory and practice. Needless to say, any decolonisation project is messy, because conventional HRE practices are often implicated in the legacy of colonialism (Smith, 1999). Yet, the move to create spaces for decolonising pedagogy and curriculum in HRE can take HRE theory and practice to a less Eurocentric outlook and thus a more multiperspectival understanding of human rights—one that recognizes the histories of coloniality, the entanglements with human rights and the consequences for social justice projects.

References

Acuña, R. (2013). Critical human rights and liberal legality: Struggling for 'the rights to have communal rights'. *Philosophy Study, 3*(2), 246–261.
Albrecht-Crane, C. (2005). Pedagogy as friendship: Identity and affect in the conservative classroom. *Cultural Studies, 19*(4), 491–514.
Al-Daraweesh, F., & Snauwaert, D. (2013). Toward a hermeneutical theory of international human rights education. *Educational Theory, 63*(4), 389–411.
Amsler, S. (2011). From 'therapeutic' to political education: The centrality of affective sensibility in critical pedagogy. *Critical Studies in Education, 52*(1), 47–63.
Athanasiou, A., Hantzaroula, P., & Yannakopoulos, K. (2008). Towards a new epistemology: The 'affective turn'. *Historein, 8*, 5–16.
Bajaj, M., Cislaghi, B., & Mackie, G. (2016). *Advancing transformative human rights education: Appendix D to the report of the global citizenship commission*. Cambridge, UK: Open Book Publishers.
Barreto, J.-M. (2012). Decolonial strategies and dialogue in the human rights field: A manifesto. *Transnational Legal Theory, 3*(1), 1–29.
Baxi, U. (2007). *Human rights in a posthuman world*. New Delhi, India: Oxford University Press.
Bhabha, H. (1999). The postcolonial and the postmodern: The question of agency. In S. During (Ed.), *The cultural studies reader* (pp. 189–208). London: Routledge.
Braidotti, R. (2013). *The posthuman*. Cambridge, UK: Polity.
Brayboy, B. M. J. (2006). Toward a tribal critical race theory in education. *The Urban Review, 37*(5), 425–446.
Broeck, S. (2013). The legacy of slavery: White humanities and its subject. In J. M. Barreto (Ed.), *Human rights from a third world perspective: Critique, history and international law* (pp. 102–116). Cambridge, UK: Cambridge Scholars Publishing.
Brown, W. (2004). "The most we can hope for": Human rights and the politics of fatalism. *The South Atlantic Quarterly, 103*(2/3), 451–463.
Chakrabarty, D. (2000). *Provincializing Europe: Postcolonial thought and historical difference*. Princeton, NJ: Princeton University Press.
Coysh, J. (2014). The dominant discourse of human rights education: A critique. *Journal of Human Rights Practice, 6*(1), 89–114.
Donnelly, J. (2003). *Universal human rights in theory and practice* (2nd ed.). Ithaca, NY: Cornell University Press.
Douzinas, C. (2000). *The end of human rights: Critical legal thought at the turn of the century*. Oxford, UK: Hart Publishing.
Gilroy, P. (2010). *Darker than blue: On the moral economies of black Atlantic culture*. Cambridge, MA: Harvard University Press.
Gonçalves, G. L., & Costa, S. (2016). The global constitutionalization of human rights: Overcoming contemporary injustices of justifying old asymmetries? *Current Sociology Monograph, 64*(2), 311–331.
Gorski, P. (2008). Good intentions are not enough: A decolonising intercultural education. *Intercultural Education, 19*(6), 515–525.
Grande, S. (2004). *Red pedagogy: Native American social and political thought*. Boulder, CO: Rowman & Littlefield.
Jansen, J. (2009). *Knowledge in the blood: Confronting race and the apartheid past*. Stanford, CA: Stanford University Press.
Keet, A. (2010). *Human rights education: A conceptual analysis*. Saarbrücken, Germany: Lambert Academic Publishing.
Khoja-Moolji, S. (2017). The making of humans and their others in and through transnational human rights advocacy: Exploring the cases of Mukhtar Mai and Malala Yousafzai. *Signs: Journal of Women in Culture and Society, 42*(2), 377–402.

Mignolo, W. (2000). The many faces of cosmo-polis: Border thinking and critical cosmopolitanism. *Public Culture, 12*(3), 721–748.

Mignolo, W. (2003). Philosophy and the colonial difference. In E. Mendieta (Ed.), *Latin American philosophy* (pp. 80–88). Bloomington, IN: Indiana University Press.

Mignolo, W. (2006). Citizenship, knowledges, and the limits of humanity. *American Literary History, 18*(2), 312–331.

Mignolo, W. (2009). Who speaks for the 'human' in human rights? Human rights in Latin American and Iberian cultures. *Hispanic Issues, 5*(1), 7–24.

Mignolo, W. (2011). *The darker side of Western modernity: Global futures, decolonial options*. Durham, NC: Duke University Press.

Mignolo, W. (2015). Sylvia Wynter: What does it mean to be human? In K. McKittrick (Ed.), *Sylvia Wynter: On being human as praxis* (pp. 106–123). Durham, NC: Duke University Press Books.

Mutua, M. (2002). *Human rights: A political and cultural critique*. Philadelphia: University of Pennsylvania Press.

Osler, A. (2015). Human rights education, postcolonial scholarship, and action for social justice. *Theory & Research in Social Education, 43*, 244–274.

Santos, B. (2013). Human rights: A fragile hegemony. In F. Crèpeau & C. Sheppard (Eds.), *Human rights in diverse societies: Challenges and possibilities* (pp. 17–25). Newcastle, UK: Cambridge Scholars.

Sen, A. (2009). *The idea of justice*. London: Penguin Books.

Smith, L. (1999). *Decolonising methodologies: Research and indigenous peoples*. London: Zed Books.

Spivak, G. (2004). Righting wrongs. *The South Atlantic Quarterly, 103*(2/3), 523–581.

Subedi, B. (2013). Decolonising the curriculum from global perspectives. *Educational Theory, 63*(6), 621–638.

Tejeda, C., Espinoza, M., & Gutierrez, K. (2003). Toward a decolonising pedagogy: Social justice reconsidered. In P. Trifonas (Ed.), *Pedagogies of difference: Rethinking education for social justice* (pp. 10–40). New York: RoutledgeFalmer.

Tejeda, C., & Gutierrez, K. (2005). Fighting the backlash: Decolonising perspectives and pedagogies in neo-colonial times. In P. Pedraza & M. Rivera (Eds.), *Latino education: An agenda for community action* (pp. 261–294). Mahwah, NJ: Lawrence Erlbaum Associates.

Tuck, E., & Yang, K. W. (2012). Decolonisation is not a metaphor. *Decolonisation: Indigeneity, Education & Society, 1*(1), 1–40.

Worsham, L. (2001). Going postal: Pedagogic violence and the schooling of emotion. In H. Giroux & K. Myrisides (Eds.), *Beyond the corporate university* (pp. 229–265). New York: Rowman & Littlefield.

Wynter, S. (2003). Unsettling the coloniality of being/power/truth/freedom: Towards the human, after man, its overrepresentation—An argument. *CR: The New Centennial Review, 3*(3), 257–337.

Yang, K. W. (2015). Afterword: Will human rights education be decolonising? In S. R. Katz & A. McEvoy Spero (Eds.), *Bringing human rights education to US classrooms: Exemplary models from elementary grades to university* (pp. 225–235). New York: Palgrave Macmillan.

Yeğenoğlu, M. (1998). *Colonial fantasies: Towards a feminist reading of orientalism*. Cambridge, UK: Cambridge University Press.

Yoon, K. H. (2005). Affecting the transformative intellectual: Questioning "noble" sentiments in critical pedagogy and composition. *JAC: A Journal of Rhetoric, Culture & Politics, 25*(4), 717–759.

Zembylas, M. (2013a). Critical pedagogy and emotion: Working through troubled knowledge in posttraumatic societies. *Critical Studies in Education, 54*(2), 176–189.

Zembylas, M. (2013b). The 'crisis of pity' and the radicalization of solidarity: Towards critical pedagogies of compassion. *Educational Studies: A Journal of the American Educational Studies Association, 49*, 504–521.

Zembylas, M. (2014). Theorizing 'difficult knowledge' in the aftermath of the 'affective turn': Implications for curriculum and pedagogy in handling traumatic representations. *Curriculum Inquiry, 44*(3), 390–412.
Zembylas, M. (2016). Toward a critical-sentimental orientation in human rights education. *Educational Philosophy and Theory, 48*(11), 1151–1167.
Zembylas, M., & Bozalek, V. (2014). A critical engagement with the social and political consequences of human rights: The contribution of the affective turn and posthumanism. *Acta Academica, 46*(4), 30–48.

Chapter 11
Conclusion: An Unfinished Project

We began this book by engaging with several critiques raised about human rights and Human Rights Education (hereafter HRE), interrogating the Western, colonial, and neoliberal foundations of HRE that advance human rights as universal and uncontested global norms. We have argued that these critiques point to the need for more theoretical and pedagogical work towards recognising the entanglement of coloniality/neoliberalism and human rights/HRE and we have taken up various theoretical ideas in the chapters that followed to 'pluriversalise' (Mignolo, 2006) human rights and HRE—namely, to turn the process of knowledge production in human rights and HRE open to epistemic diversity in order to increase possibilities for *criticality* and *transformation*. Informed by various concepts grounded in decolonial, critical, and social justice theories, our analysis has highlighted that the struggle for social justice can be enriched by creating spaces of Critical Human Rights Education (hereafter CHRE). Therefore, to promote social justice we also need to begin interrogating the ways that HRE and other education interventions are complicit in the construction of everyday injustices. The present book builds on the work we have both done over the years to develop a more nuanced understanding of the impact of modernity, neoliberalism and coloniality on the dominant discourses and practices of HRE. Hence, in choosing various ideas that inspired us as theoretical lenses, our intention has been to show different possibilities for criticality, decoloniality and pluriversality that recognise the profound consequences of modernity, neoliberalism and coloniality in the formation of dominant discourses and practices of HRE. Through this book, then, we hope to have made a contribution to the efforts that view the pluriversalisation of HRE as inextricable part of the wider task of decolonising knowledge and education and struggling for social justice praxes.

To distance ourselves from modernist, neoliberal and colonial thinking in human rights and HRE, we have emphasised from the very beginning that we first need to acknowledge the historical use of human rights for regulation and domination, namely, how and why we have arrived at the "conventional understanding of human rights" (Santos, 2015, p. 7) which includes the following: human rights are

M. Zembylas, A. Keet, *Critical Human Rights Education*, Contemporary Philosophies and Theories in Education 13,
https://doi.org/10.1007/978-3-030-27198-5_11

universally valid irrespective of the social, political and cultural context in which they operate and of the different human rights regimes existing in different regions of the world; they are premised upon a conception of human nature as individual, self-sustaining and qualitatively different from the non-human nature; what counts as violation of human rights is defined by universal declarations, multilateral institutions (courts and commissions) and established, global (mostly North-based) non-governmental organisations; the recurrent phenomenon of double standards in evaluating compliance with human rights in no way compromises the universal validity of human rights; the respect for human rights is much more problematic in the global South than in the global North.

Our critique of HRE in this book has not been targeted only at the epistemological grounding of this conventional understanding of human rights, but also at its political consequences—such as, for example, the questions of 'for whom', 'what for' and 'from where'—that highlight a critical self-reflection of the historical framework in which human rights and HRE are enunciated. These critical, hermeneutical, and historicised reflections urged by various theorists whose ideas we have taken up in this book, create new possibilities to think of human rights and HRE from different standpoints such as those of the South (Connell, 2007). Such approaches to human rights and HRE arise from a different geopolitical space and a different historical horizon of understanding human rights and HRE, therefore, they have the potential to develop new discourses and perspectives of human rights and HRE.

The capacity for the renewal and reimagination of human rights as a critical project, therefore, is depended on an ongoing dialogue between different conceptions of rights and HRE. To enable a renewal of human rights and HRE discourses, we need to abandon their claim to universality and replace that by a pluriversal understanding of rights. To put this differently, using the term suggested by decolonial scholar Walter Mignolo (2006), we need to 'pluriversalise' human rights, namely, to recognise that there are plural principles of human rights across all cultures rather than only the Western ones. That Western epistemology appears universalistic compared to epistemologies of the South is because Western conceptions of human rights are part of the imperial and colonial project (Mignolo, 2009, 2011).

To pluriversalise human rights, firstly human rights need to be interpreted within their historical horizon, that is, the history of rights has to extend to other geographies and historical thinkers who approach rights from perspectives beyond Europe (i.e. Third World, South, indigenous). A different mapping of the sources of notions of human rights, argues Barreto (2012, 2013), makes it clear that human rights discourse has also developed in locations outside the borders of Europe—among colonised peoples or in the Third World. Understanding the historical and political effects of this thinking about human rights will create opportunities for a different mapping of human rights altogether—one that embraces the diversity of knowledges "not just at the clean centres of cosmopolitan power, but at the messier margins of provincial suffering" too (Woessner, 2013, p. 68). A new genealogy of rights can be outlined, then, "following the trail of suffering left by the history of modern imperialism and the resistance to it" without countering such move any more "as incorrect and unsuitable to the very nature of rights" (Barreto, 2014, p. 407).

This new genealogy of human rights can in itself function as a decolonial strategy that also needs to preface the African, black experience; "since the birth of racial subject – and therefore of Blackness – is linked to [a] history of capitalism" (Mbembe, 2017, p. 179) that is in part served by human rights. Since Blackness became equated with the nonhuman in order to uphold forms of oppression, Mbembe (2017) argues that this equation came to serve as the template for all new forms of exclusion. In a sense, the human rights discourse has to engage with 'Black Reason'; "the consciousness of the inescapable experiences that have shaped all black people in one way of another, which is that every black man and woman alive today have all to some extent been products of slavery or colonialism or apartheid" (Apata, 2017, p. 4). We had this encounter in mind when we, in Chap. 9, for instance, set out ways of classifying 'critical theories' broadly speaking, so as to locate, from a human rights perspective, a decolonised Africana Critical Theory as formulated by Bassey (2007) and Rabaka (2009), and maybe, a Black Critical and Cultural Theory as proposed by DeCristo (2017).

We have also insisted from the beginning of this book that as long as human rights remain Eurocentric, capitalist and colonialist, they will be part of globalisation from above, a process in which understandings of rights from Europe become global, leaving no space for alternative conceptions of human rights. However, a theoretical reworking of human rights is necessary to ensure that rights remain globally meaningful while acquiring local legitimacy, if a counter-hegemonic politics and praxis of human rights is going to be imagined (Barreto 2014). For this to happen, it is necessary that the Western understanding of human rights drops the universality that characterises it, namely, the claim of Eurocentric framing as universally valid, the idea of a universal human nature apprehended by reason, and the need to protect individual autonomy to the detriment of notions of duty in relation to the community and the world (Santos 2014, 2015). The different theoretical ideas we have discussed in previous chapters highlight that the multiplicity and richness of human rights conceptions can contribute to an ongoing agonistic process of cultivating criticality and transformation.

A renewal of the framing of human rights has obvious theoretical and pedagogical implications for rethinking HRE too. The concepts outlined in earlier chapters from the work of various theorists open possibilities for pluriversalising HRE, because HRE scholars, educators and activists are enabled to reimagine human rights and HRE; that is, HRE scholars, educators and activists can imagine themselves as critical educators who engage their students in interpretations of human rights across different settings, and redesign curricula and practices to enact the pluriversality of knowledges about human rights. In particular, understanding the historical trajectories of human rights as concepts that do not reside exclusively in the West (embedded in the context of colonialism), but include numerous standpoints from the South, can help HRE scholars, educators and activists "recognise the mechanisms that privilege European/Western epistemologies and 'forget', silence, repress or 'damn' 'other' epistemologies" (Andreotti, 2011, p. 392). The most important question here for HRE scholars, educators and activists is how to conceptualise human rights as well as HRE epistemologies and pedagogies that enable the retrieval of concepts that pluralise the HRE field such as plasticity, counter-conduct, decoloniality, agonism and many others that have been discussed in previous chapters. These ideas can assist HRE scholars, educators and activists in transforming their orientation toward human rights so that they seek "to unsettle its coloniality, attend to its multiplicity, and maintain space for its strategic use" (Khoja-Moolji, 2017, p. 393). Questions that could guide further explorations in relation to re-writing the history of human rights and their teaching/learning could include (Andreotti, 2011, p. 392): How is modernity/coloniality recognised in HRE work? "How is the relationship between modernity and colonialism defined? [...] What analyses of power relations are at work? How are abyssal lined established? How are they contested? What counts as knowledge and whose knowledge counts?" These questions can inspire HRE scholars, educators and activists prompt their students to develop critical and pluriversal engagement with human rights across different contexts.

A critical and pluriversal HRE, therefore, is conceived as a process of advancing social-justice-oriented educational praxes by delinking human rights teaching and learning from Eurocentrism, capitalism and coloniality, while widening the lens of human rights by recognising and including the forms of knowledge that have been subjugated by modernity and coloniality. Needless to say, suggesting a critical and pluriversal HRE as an alternative to the current Eurocentric educational system of assimilation and marginalisation of epistemologies of the South is a huge and complex challenge that requires multiple strategies and interventions (Andreotti et al. 2011). The ideas discussed in this book create three important openings for HRE scholars, educators and activists to push critical engagement with the dominant discourses of human rights and HRE:

1. First, theoretical ideas in this book enable us to trace and confront the chasm between human rights knowledges and experiences coming from the North and from the South; this implies a pedagogical emphasis on critical and pluriversal strategies that recognise complexity, multiperspectivity and uncertainty in order to support learners develop their abilities for critical approaches towards human rights idea(l)s;
2. Second, these theoretical ideas promote the ecology of knowledges founded on the notion that there is no absolute and universal epistemology of human rights but rather plural epistemologies of human rights practices that are interdependent; this emphasises that the struggle for social justice will be advanced if learners are encouraged in HRE policies and practices to work for the unmaking of various forms of injustice;
3. Finally, the theoretical ideas discussed in this book require the invention of curriculum and pedagogical strategies that actively support 'translation' among different epistemologies and experiences concerning human rights; these experiences are not treated either as totalities or as insignificant parts, but rather as realities of human rights failures or successes that do not exhaust themselves in those totalities or parts.

The critical and pluriversal structure at the core of a reconceptualised HRE theory and practice allows for, and gives impetus to, a truly decolonial conception of human rights and HRE. Undoubtedly, this effort points to the need for more intellectual and pedagogical work towards a critical and pluriversal HRE, yet it signals an important step for dismantling the colonial conceptions of human rights embedded in many HRE curricula and practices and helps create the conditions for decolonial conceptions of rights and HRE, namely: to recognise the human rights epistemologies and practices that have been subjugated; to instil a solidarity-oriented transformation of HRE curricula and practices; and, to embrace an orientation of participating not only in the critical interpretation but also in the creation of new rights.

The labour of struggling for social justice is supported intellectually by disparate sources of wisdom such as the ones discussed in this book and many others that are eager to find their space in future explorations. This agonistic struggle forges new understandings of CHRE and generates a reparative relation to modernist, capitalist and Eurocentric discourses of human rights and HRE. What we learn from attending to these struggles and reparative efforts is that the project of renewal of HRE is incomplete, unfinished and always disruptive of our own ignorance in the face of the various complexities that emerge. Therefore, formulating a CHRE has no ending; our responses to the harsh realities of social injustice around the world obligate us—scholars, educators, activists in HRE—in a continual agonistics to build upon the transformative possibilities that emerge from our everyday struggles to advance social-justice-oriented educational praxes.

References

Andreotti, V. (2011). (Towards) decoloniality and diversality in global citizenship education. *Globalisation, Societies and Education, 9*(3–4), 381–397.

Andreotti, V., Ahenakew, C., & Cooper, G. (2011). Epistemological pluralism: Ethical and pedagogical challenges in higher education. *AlterNative: An International Journal of Indigenous Peoples, 7*(1), 40–50.

Apata, G. (2017). Review: Achille Mbembe, trans. Lauren Dubois, *Critique of Black Reason*. *Theory, Culture & Society, 34*, 7–8.

Barreto, J.-M. (2012). Decolonial strategies and dialogue in the human rights field: A manifesto. *Transnational Legal Theory, 3*(1), 1–29.

Barreto, J.-M. (2013). Introduction: Decolonial strategies and dialogue in the human rights field. In J.-M. Barreto (Ed.), *Human rights from a third world perspective: Critique, history and international law* (pp. 1–43). Newcastle upon Tyne, UK: Cambridge Scholars Publishing.

Barreto, J.-M. (2014). Epistemologies of the south and human rights: Santos and the quest for global and cognitive justice. *Indiana Journal of Global Legal Studies, 21*(2), 395–422.

Bassey, M. O. (2007). What is Africana critical theory or black existential philosophy? *Journal of Black Studies, 37*(6), 914–935.

Connell, R. (2007). *Southern theory: The global dynamics of knowledge in social science*. Crows Nest, NSW: Allen & Unwin.

DeCristo, J. (2017). Black critical and cultural theory. *The Year's Work in Critical and Cultural Theory, 25*(1), 316–333.

Khoja-Moolji, S. (2017). The making of humans and their others in and through transnational human rights advocacy: Exploring the cases of Mukhtar Mai and Malala Yousafzai. *Signs: Journal of Women in Culture and Society, 42*(2), 377–402.

Mbembe, A. (2017). *Critique of black reason*. Durham, NC: Duke University Press.

Mignolo, W. (2006). Citizenship, knowledges, and the limits of humanity. *American Literary History, 18*(2), 312–331.

Mignolo, W. (2009). Who speaks for the 'human' in human rights? Human rights in Latin American and Iberian cultures. *Hispanic Issues, 5*(1), 7–24.

Mignolo, W. (2011). *The darker side of Western modernity: Global futures, decolonial options*. Durham, NC: Duke University Press.

Rabaka, R. (2009). *Africana critical theory: Reconstructing the black radical tradition, from W.E.B. Du Bois and C.L.R. James to Frantz Fanon and Amilcar Cabral*. Lanham, MD: Lexington Books.

Santos, B. S. (2014). *Epistemologies of the south: Justice against epistemicide*. Boulder, CO: Paradigm Publishers.

Santos, B. S. (2015). *If God were a human rights activist*. Stanford, CA: Stanford University Press.

Woessner, M. (2013). Provincialising human rights? The Heideggerian legacy from Charles Malik to Dipesh Chakrabarty. In J.-M. Barreto (Ed.), *Human rights from a third world perspective: Critique, history and international law* (pp. 65–101). Newcastle upon Tyne, UK: Cambridge Scholars Publishing.

The manufacturer's authorised representative in the EU is Springer Nature Customer Service Centre GmbH, Europaplatz 3, 69115 Heidelberg, Germany. If you have any concerns regarding our products, please contact ProductSafety@springernature.com

Printed and bound by CPI Group (UK) Ltd, Croydon, CR0 4YY
25/09/2026
02222869-0017